THE CO-CAPTAIN'S LOG

KATHERINE GONZÁLEZ

WITH LOGS BY ANDRÉS GONZÁLEZ

POSADA
PUBLISHING

A Posada Publishing LLC Book, Doral, Florida
ISBN paperback: 979-8-9911668-0-5
ISBN hardcover: 979-8-9911668-1-2
ISBN eBook: 979-8-9911668-2-9

The Co-Captain's Log
©2024 by Katherine González and Andrés González
All Rights Reserved

Design by Tony Steck, DOXA/VANTAGE

Disclaimer: The publisher has verified the technical information including GPS coordinates found throughout the book, but these details are provided solely to support the narrative. This book should not be used as a guidebook, sailing instruction, or for navigation. Some names of people and boats have been changed for privacy.

Recipes from *The Boat Galley Cookbook* used with permission from the author. Text from *Sea of Cortez: A Cruiser's Guidebook* used with permission from the author. Text from *Every Moment Holy* used with permission from the publisher. Photos of crew (V1, I2) © Phyllis Woolwine. Photo of *Ana María* (Day 0) ©Kerri McHale. Photo of snorklers and manta (V2, I9) and whales (V3, I2) © Ann Montgomery. Photo of *Ana María* in Vava'u (V3, I1) © Parker Woo.

Library of Congress Control Number: 2024917049

www.cocaptainslog.com

Published in the United States of America.

To Mom, who taught me how to tell a story

To Daddy, who taught me how to write to make people laugh and to move them to tears

And to Andrés, who took me on the adventure of a lifetime

CONTENTS

Prologue 9

VOLUME 1

Issue 1: The Call to Adventure 15
Issue 2: If Adventure Is What We're Looking For 27
Issue 3: The Good. The Bad. The Uncertainty. 35
Issue 4: Foolish or Brave? 47
Issue 5: Facing Fears 55
Issue 6: What Dreams Are Made Of 63
Issue 7: Grudge or Grace? 75
Issue 8: On Your Mark. Get Set. Go! 87
Issue 9: One Day in the Life of a Cruising Couple 103
Issue 10: The Ominous Silence 117

VOLUME 2

Issue 1: The Incredible Mr. Fix-It 125
Issue 2: Transforming the Mundane into the Memorable 133
Issue 3: What a Difference a Year Makes 143
Issue 4: Are We Really Going to Do This? 155
Issue 5: Anchors Aweigh! 165

Special Edition: Pacific Crossing 173

Issue 6: Meet the Marquesans 233

The Captain's Log:
Passage from the Marquesas to the Tuamotu 245

Issue 7: The Dangerous Archipelago 251

The Captain's Log:
Passage from Makemo to Tahiti 261

Volume 2, Issue 8: Panic in Papeete 269
Volume 2, Issue 9: An Island (almost) to Oneself 277

The Captain's Log: Passage from Suwarrow to Pago Pago 285

VOLUME 3

Volume 3, Issue 1: Would You Rather …? 295
Volume 3, Issue 2: Swimming with Whales 305
Volume 3, Issue 3: The Tongan Feast 315

The Captain's Log: Passage from Tonga to New Zealand 329

Volume 3, Issue 4: 7 Truths About Your Adventure 343

Gratitude 359

Discussion Guide & Reader Resources 367

THE CAPTAIN'S CAMERA ROLL

Visit www.cocaptainslog.com/album or use your phone to scan the QR code below to see photos and videos of the people and places featured in *The Co-Captain's Log*.

53 nautical miles south of Cape Mendocino, California, USA
39° 31' 25" N 124° 21' 48" W

PROLOGUE

September 11, 2021
53 nautical miles south of Cape Mendocino, California, USA
39° 31' 25" N 124° 21' 48" W
Winds: NNW 30-40 knots
Seas: Bi-directional 10-foot swell every 6 seconds or less

We've rounded Cape Mendocino and are now only 95 nautical miles from Bodega Bay, north of San Francisco. All four of our weather forecast models agree: we should have 15- to 25-knot winds with 6-foot waves every nine seconds. These are conditions *Ana María* can handle easily with her current sail plan, even on the south side of the infamous cape. I try to focus on the celebration waiting for us when we arrive in California after seven days at sea, rather than the worsening sea state and wind speeds climbing higher and higher on the anemometer.

"Do you think we should take the mainsail down and sail only under the staysail?" Andrés asks as we make dinner and prepare to start the watch schedule for the last night of the sail.

He's right to ask. We have sustained 40-knot winds with 8-foot waves coming less than six seconds apart, with some waves coming from a different direction than the main swell. *Ana María* is overpowered even with a second reef in the mainsail, so while she is surfing down these waves, she is by no means a comfortable ride. The force of each wave thrashes her hull. The waves are so steep that, during many of the rides down the waves, her boom touches the water. We know this poses a serious risk to the structural integrity of the rigging.

I agree with my husband, thinking that if something goes wrong in the middle of the night, *Ana María* will be much more manageable with only the staysail up.

We put on our foul weather gear as we talk through the challenging procedure of the sail change, double-checking each other's tethers. We ensure they're connected to both our life jackets and the boat, thinking of the haunting words of the famous sailors Lin and Larry Pardey, "You fall over, you die."

We encounter problems just dousing the genoa, the winds making a mess of all the sheets and furling lines. Anxiety starts to build, as does the intensity. This is not going well.

In spite of that, we're able to turn down to a beam reach just long enough to douse part of the mainsail, turning back up into the wind quickly to avoid catching a wave broadside to our beam. Andrés roughly flakes the sail and gathers it into sail ties, a feat of gymnastics while tethered to the webbing stretched across the boat.

All we have left to do is attach the running backstay to keep the mast from pumping under the pressure of the staysail and then reset the Monitor windvane to steer for us.

Watching Andrés clip in the running backstay, I'm sure we've made it through the worst part of the process. I have both hands on the tiller, trying to steer steady across the onslaught of waves, when I turn my head to look over my shoulder.

It's like a freeze-frame in a movie. A slow-motion set of images I hope won't haunt me for the rest of my life.

Behind my right shoulder is a towering wall of water coming toward us faster than I can comprehend. Instinctively, I turn my back against the wave. When I next open my eyes, I see Andrés, horizontal and in mid-air, supported only by the lifelines on the boat and inches away from disaster.

Then ... black.

VOLUME 1

Mount Baker Highway,
Washington, USA
48° 53' 38" N 121° 58' 03" W

Landings boatyard,
Bellingham, Washington, USA
48° 45' 06" N 122° 29' 13" W

Inati Bay, Lummi Island,
Washington, USA
48° 40' 18" N 122° 37' 22" W

Green Lake,
Seattle, Washington, USA
47° 41' 32" N 122° 20' 30" W

VOLUME 1, ISSUE 1: THE CALL TO ADVENTURE

Five years earlier ...

January 30, 2016
Mount Baker Highway, Washington, USA
48° 53' 38" N 121° 58' 03" W
Weather: 45°F Rain/snow mixture

"I think it would be really cool to circumnavigate the world on a sailboat," said Andrés, the cute, dark-haired, funny guy from ski lessons as we barreled down Mount Baker Highway in a decades-old green school bus, while the mostly sober driver of the bus blasted Pink Floyd. Sailing the world was one in a series of crazy ideas this guy had shared since we met on the bus after skiing. The others, such as hiking 35 miles through the North Cascades and kayaking through the Everglades in Florida, seemed adventurous enough to me. By the second Saturday of ski lessons, I had fallen for my classmate and was smitten enough to think circumnavigating the world would be romantic, not kamikaze dangerous like any normal person would.

THE CAPTAIN & CO-CAPTAIN

"All sailing couples have an optimist and a pessimist. Without the optimist, they'd never leave the dock. Without the pessimist, they'd sink as soon as they left." —Beth Leonard, *The Voyager's Handbook*

Andrés is unquestionably our captain. Originally from Medellín, Colombia, he immigrated with his family to Miami, Florida while in middle school. During college, he honed his sailing skills on a small Laser dinghy and spent the hours between his computer science and economics courses sailing around the lake at the University of Florida, where capsizing meant the possibility of an up-close-and-personal encounter with an alligator. A job opportunity programming software for *Rhino 3D* in Washington state enticed him to trade his warm-but-gator-infested sailing grounds for the frigid waters of Lake Washington in Seattle.

His software engineering mindset and skill set transferred well to life aboard *Ana María*, where he is not only the captain but also the chief engineer. He's spent months of his life researching, planning, and designing the systems for *Ana María*. As our resident pessimist, he always thinks of how everything could go wrong and innovatively tries to prevent it.

As co-captain, I have the same level of sailing certification as Andrés (U.S. Sailing Basic Keelboat, Basic Cruising, Coastal Navigation, and Bareboat Cruising) but lack his extensive experience. Having grown up in landlocked Missouri, where many residents have never even seen the ocean let alone sailed on it, it was quite the shock to find myself in the sailing-obsessed Pacific Northwest thanks to a job transfer to Bellingham, Washington.

I brought to our new life transferable skills from my career in procurement at an energy company, using my professional expertise to buy the thousands of items we've installed on *Ana María*. My sailing skills will be refined on *Ana María* as will—my optimistic self hopes—my cooking-at-sea skills. Normally, a boat keeps a captain's log, but those tend to be dry and full of only technical details and events. As co-captain, however, I am free to tell you about the interesting characters we meet and places we see along the way.

April 30, 2017
Green Lake, Seattle, Washington, USA
47° 41' 32" N 122° 20' 30" W

We had survived our hike together through the North Cascades, the kayak trip through the Everglades, our first sail together on Lake Washington, and a summer of sailing on Puget Sound. To learn to sail on Puget Sound is one thing; learning to sail across the Pacific Ocean is another.

As Andrés progressed in his sailing curriculum, the conversation of "Should we sail the world, or shouldn't we?" felt imminent. In a rare reversal of our typical optimist/pessimist roles, I was sure the dream of quitting both of our lucrative jobs to move aboard a boat and sail to tropical destinations was just that: a dream. The dream felt far-fetched ... that is until we looked at the numbers.

We looked at what we had in our bank accounts, what we could sell, what it typically costs "budget cruisers" to sail full-time. We looked at reality. If we sold my condo, sold the cars, squirreled away every cent of our bonuses, found a boat at a good price, did all the boat work ourselves, and lived off a meager $3,000 per month, then, maybe, just maybe it would be possible. On our budget, we probably couldn't make it around the entire world, but we could make it to every cruiser's dream destination: the South Pacific.

To my shock, the farfetched dream appeared to be within our reach.

Yes, it would be a stretch. It would take dedication, commitment, and money. But once we answered the question "Could we or couldn't we?" the impossible dream suddenly felt like an actual possibility.

I could hear the whisper of The Call to Adventure. It was faint for now but growing more insistent.

So we started our search, found our diamond in the rough hidden in Poulsbo, Washington, and brought her up to Bellingham.

May 2, 2018
Landings boatyard, Bellingham, Washington, USA
48° 45' 06" N 122° 29' 13" W

Our newly beloved *Ana María* had just been lifted out of the water with a seaside crane, carried over our heads, and set down in the dusty boatyard. Like a new beauty queen moving into the neighborhood, *Ana María* was getting plenty of catcalls from the men loitering nearby. "Nice boat!" "Wow! She's a beauty!" The bolder men of the boatyard ambled up for an introduction. "Hey, gimme a call if you need electrical work done." "I could get her hull polished to a beautiful sheen." "Looks like she could use a fresh coat of bottom paint. I could have her lookin' pretty in no time."

Needing to return to my day job, I left Andrés to fend off the offers by himself.

Now, I've heard him tell this story so many times, it feels like I was standing next to him when it happened. A tall, lanky older man strolled up. Rumpled clothes, hair so messy it was clearly pulled out in recent frustration, forearms covered in remnants of a mixture of grease and sealant, and the scent of hand-rolled cigarettes: it was obvious he was a pillar of the boatyard community. Unlike the overly eager minions, his silent confidence, his appraising eyes that missed nothing, his strong hands that moved instinctively to grasp the rudder for a quick test of its strength, his unhurried and humble way of giving advice all gave this man the air of a baron.

After an uncomfortable minute of silent examination, he finally spoke in a thick South African accent. "This is a good boat."

"Thank you," answered Andrés, unsure how to respond to this stranger's discerning gaze and evaluation.

"Do you have a girlfriend?"

"Yes," answered Andrés, even more unsure where this line of questioning was going.

"Let me guess, the toilet's holding tank is under the port side v-berth bunk."

"Yes, you're right." Man, this man's knowledge was impressive.

"Imagine you take your girlfriend to sail here in the San Juan Islands," he started in his leisurely pace. "And when it's time to go to sleep in some beautiful anchorage ... she lays down in the v-berth ... and all she can hear is ... your sh*t ... sloshing ... beneath her head."

Andrés stared at him, eyes wide at this man's candor.

"If I were you," he started in what we would come to know as his preamble to all great advice he would impart, "I would tear out whatever fancy marine toilet you have in there and replace it with a composting head."

Ahhhh. Understanding seemed to settle on Andrés. What are the chances this man "happened to" have a van full of composting toilets sitting somewhere close, just waiting to be sold to a young naive new boat owner?

"Are you a marine toilet salesman?" Andrés asked.

The man took a long, relaxed drag on the cigarette pinched between his thumb and forefinger before flicking the butt on the gravel and pulling his wallet out of his back pocket. He thumbed through the aged wallet for a card to hand Andrés.

"Nope. The name's Hal. I'm a rigger."

And with that, Hal Thesen, of Hal Thesen Yacht & Rigging Services, gave *Ana María*'s hull a satisfied pat goodbye, grinned at Andrés, turned on his heels, and ambled back across the boatyard without another word.

It took me less than a week of boat work to realize we were in way over our heads. If we were going to be successful in this endeavor, we needed a guide. This mysterious man seemed to be our best option. So, I pulled out Hal's business card and punched in the number listed. My plea for help was no less panicky than the yelps of someone caught in a rip current at the beach, but it took some begging for him to agree to come aboard.

For the next year, we hired Hal to teach us what we didn't know. We trusted him to tell us when we didn't even know enough to know we didn't know. Enlisting the help of Hal Thesen, an expert sailboat rigger, experienced boat worker, and accomplished ocean sailor, turned out to be one of the wisest decisions we made during the entire refit.

There's a scene in *The Lion King* where Mufasa tells Simba, "Everything the light touches is our kingdom." I often say this to Andrés as we look around the boat. Everything we see on the boat has been renovated or refurbished with our own hands.

Ana María's like a dog you get from the pound. She has good breeding. She is on every list of best boats for cruising around the world, and she has good bones. The men who built her almost 30 years ago were careful craftsmen, but she suffered for years under the neglectful hands of previous owners.

It took over a year to break her in, to get her trained up and in good enough shape just to sail out of the marina. It took one more year to get her in cruising condition. It's taken yet another year to get her strong and comfortable enough to cross oceans.

We used epoxy and sealants to rebed over two hundred deck fittings because the most beautiful boat is a watertight boat. And we fixed rot. We replaced the standing and running rigging. We stripped, sanded, and varnished every piece of teak on the boat. We shoehorned our wedding between varnishing the interior and replacing the engine as well as 90 percent of the electrical infrastructure.

With our friend Joe, we rebuilt the compression post. We installed a propane oven and gimballed stove to ensure hot pans don't go flying with every swell of the sea. We rebuilt the fridge from scratch to triple its insulation. We installed new water hoses and repainted water tanks so we can safely enjoy water from the spigot. We installed a Wi-Fi radar in case we get caught in the fog. We rebuilt the anchor windlass and self-steering Monitor windvane. We made new cushions and created sea berths. We carefully repaired the hull damage inflicted by previous owners.

Ana María has demanded so many hours of our life, so many resources from our bank accounts, so much blood, sweat, and tears. Oh, but boy, does she sail like a dream: smooth, comfortable, and well-balanced.

July 14, 2018
Bellingham, Washington, USA
48° 44' 36" N 122° 28' 40" W

We were in the middle of the refit when Andrés' parents came to town from Florida to help us with the worst of the boat work. While Andrés and his dad put eight coats of varnish on the exterior teak, Jackie and I knelt on my garage floor and scrubbed mildew off the headsails. The work was awful but the conversation delightful. She told me about growing up in El Salvador, moving to North Carolina where she met Andrés Sr, and following him to Colombia. Together they raised Andrés and his sister Paula in the peaceful hamlet of Guatapé, nestled in tranquility on the side of a lake set against the striking Colombian Andes, far enough away from the rampant bombings and kidnappings of Medellín.

"Those were the best days of my life." Her words sounded familiar, though I'd never before heard them come out of her mouth. The warmth in her voice as she spoke of those years matched the warmth I'd sensed when Andrés described the combination of peace and adventure of his childhood in Guatapé. In her words, I could hear the Call to Adventure as clear as a bell. I knew that years spent sailing in the peace and adventure of the open ocean could be the best years of my husband's life. I knew we would cruise the world in a sailboat.

If you had the opportunity to give someone you love the best years of his life, wouldn't you too jump at the chance?

June 1, 2021
Inati Bay, Lummi Island, Washington, USA
48° 40' 18" N 122° 37' 22" W
Winds: NW 10-15 knots
Weather: 75°F Sunny and clear

Thirty-seven months after buying *Ana María* and two days after completing her refit, we've quit our jobs, sold our home, and loaded *Ana María* with tools, food, diesel, and propane. We've traded comfort and stability for the unknown.

What awaits us just over the horizon? Failure? Pirates? Poverty?

Will we make it to the South Pacific?

Will we survive the adventure? Will our marriage survive the adventure?

This morning, despite our uncertainty, we cast off from the familiar Squalicum Harbor dock, sailed across Bellingham Bay while we enjoyed the view of Mount Baker as she regally surveyed her kingdom, and anchored in a secluded bay tucked into one side of Lummi Island.

We left safe harbor and set sail for what we hope will be the best years of our lives.

Fair winds and following seas,

Katherine

⛵

IF YOU HAD THE OPPORTUNITY TO GIVE SOMEONE YOU LOVE THE BEST YEARS OF HIS LIFE, WOULDN'T YOU TOO JUMP AT THE CHANCE?

MEET THE HERO

Name: *Ana María*, named after my sister

Make: 1994 Pacific Seacraft

Purchased: March 2018 in Poulsbo, Washington

Designer: W. I. B. Crealock

Size: 34' long, 10' beam, 4'1" draft. In other words, she feels huge when I'm varnishing her but small enough that I feel as if I'm perpetually navigating the economy class aisle of an airplane.

Hull: Monohull with a modified fin-keel, skeg-hung rudder, and canoe stern

Steering: Varnished laminated tiller (no wheel) bolted directly to the rudder stock

Sail configuration: Cutter rig with one mainsail, one furling genoa headsail, one furling staysail, and one spinnaker in a sock to hoist in light winds

Ground tackle: 15kg Rocna anchor, 160' of 5/16" chain, and 140' of rope rode, all maneuvered with a SeaTiger 555 manual windlass

THE SYSTEMS

"Iron Wind": Yanmar 3YM30AE 3-cylinder 29 hp diesel tractor engine

Fuel tank capacity: 27 gallons plus 20 gallons in jerry cans strapped to the floor of the cockpit

Power: 12V with 3 AGM batteries charged by 340-watt SunPower flexible solar panels and an alternator bolted to the engine

Freshwater storage: 2 independent fiberglass tanks with 75 gallons total which lasts about 10 days of use by 2 people who shower daily, but could last 30 days if used only for drinking and cooking

The head: Airhead composting toilet which lasts about 24 days between changes with 2 people aboard

Radar: Furuno wireless radar

Communication: Vesper Cortex VHF radio, AIS transponder and receiver

THE SIDEKICKS

Our third helmsman: Monitor windvane attached to the stern, nicknamed "Paulita," after my sister-in-law

Paulita is our best helmsman aboard. She is a self-steering device connected through lines to the tiller. She has an airvane sticking up from the top, which gets shoved to and fro by the wind, and a water paddle, which hangs down into the water and responds to the movement of the airvane. These two components connected by a mechanical pendulum system allow her to steer the boat for us (in fact, better than us!) at a certain wind angle without the need for any electricity. Though we will always have someone awake and on watch in the cockpit, she allows us to take all our hands off the tiller.

Our transport to and from shore: Sea Eagle 380x inflatable kayak
Length: 12' 6"

Powered by: 2 paddles, i.e. no outboard, and occasionally the QuikSail for downwind jaunts

Carrying capacity: 750 pounds or about 3 full jerry cans, 1 captain, 1 co-captain, 30 pounds of propane, and 200 pounds of provisions

THE ROUTE

A 2-year whirlwind voyage down the USA's West Coast to Mexico's Baja Peninsula then across the Pacific Ocean to French Polynesia

Pelican Beach, Cypress Island, Washington, USA
48° 35' 33" N 122° 41' 39" W

VOLUME 1, ISSUE 2: IF ADVENTURE IS WHAT WE'RE LOOKING FOR

July 5, 2021
Pelican Beach, Cypress Island, Washington, USA
48° 35' 33" N 122° 41' 39" W
Winds: SSW 5-10 knots
Weather: 70°F Sunny and clear

The plan right out of the gate was to satisfy the U.S. Sailing's Coastal Passage Making certification requirement of a night sail longer than 45 miles. We would sail from Anacortes to the southern end of the San Juan Islands at Iceberg Point, then on a beam reach across the Strait of Juan de Fuca, crossing the congested shipping lanes three times in the dark, and landing at John Wayne Marina in Sequim at 2:00 a.m. It was going to be a long night, an important night. Luckily, we had our instructor, Captain Phyllis Woolwine of Shearwater University, aboard *Ana María* to coach us through the exercise.

This wasn't just hoop jumping for a certificate. Night operations skills are a practical necessity. On *Ana María*, any journey longer than 50 miles will include a night sail. Night passages are a routine part of cruising. There aren't any motels or rest stops on the side of the road where we can pull in to get some shut-eye. Instead, we must sail non-stop, always with one of us on watch in the cockpit and the other sleeping below until it's time to switch.

In addition to being routine, night passages are terrifying. We can't see anything right in front of us, like logs that could puncture our hull, crab traps that could wrap around our propeller, or other boats that could ram into us. We can't see anything far away from us, like the Olympic Mountains or Mount Rainier to tell us which way we're headed.

We started strong, practicing single-handed tacking and jibing, heaving-to, and reefing the mainsail. Sailing was smooth, smooth enough for me to go down below and cook soup for us. What a mistake! While I was below, we rounded Watmough Bay to come head-to-head with the notorious winds and waves of the Strait of Juan de Fuca. I climbed out of the galley into the cockpit to fight the nausea beginning to gurgle in my stomach. The best way to quell seasickness is to steer, so I took over the helm and sent Andrés down below to fetch motion sickness medicine. Sending him below deck and forward of the mast to look through hundreds of tiny pill packets turned out to be our second big mistake. Now we had two seasick crew members.

The winds continued to build, but the waves built bigger. Time to check the weather. NOAA says, "West wind 10-20 knots, 5- to 8-foot wind waves." Yes, that feels about right. Let's beat upwind to Iceberg. The more we beat upwind, though, the more the waves beat back. 8-foot waves then 9-foot. The winds from the Pacific Ocean were weakening, but the waves had spent all day and 80 miles building in the strait. That's a 10-foot wave! Steer into the wave, bear away. Push the tiller into the wave, pull it away. Push, *pull*. Push, *pull*. Push, push, push, *pull*. 10-foot wave, 11-foot wave. PUSH, PUSH, PUSH, PULL, PULL, PULL! 12-foot wave.

For an hour we pushed and we pulled. The winds weren't favorable, and our old flaccid sails scheduled for replacement next month weren't powerful enough to enable *Ana María* to make forward progress. Finally, a U.S. Coast Guard warning crackled over the VHF radio: a gale warning issued for the Strait of Juan de Fuca. Facing five more hours of forecasted winds of 25 to 35 knots, 12-foot waves, and two crew members struggling to keep dinner down, we remembered the wise words of our South African rigger Hal, "Never go out in a gale because then you're the idiot who went out in a gale."

We abandoned our best laid plans and tucked into Hughes Harbor on Lopez Island. Sometimes good seamanship is less about reaching your destination port and more about finding safe harbor for your crew and your boat. We'll have to make a second attempt on the night passage requirement for our course.

Our Coastal Passage Making course is the culmination of over four years of learning to sail with Captain Phyllis. It's quite rare for adults to pick up new skills from scratch. We forget what it's like to climb the learning curve.

"NEVER GO OUT IN A GALE BECAUSE THEN YOU'RE THE IDIOT WHO WENT OUT IN A GALE."

Learning as an adult is plagued with impatience and frustration. I've made million-dollar deals for my employer, and Andrés has designed software programs used by hundreds of thousands of people, so why in the world can we not figure out how to drop a hunk of metal into the seabed so it holds a little boat in place? Luckily, a newfound passion fuels our learning, and we are eager to build our skills and grow as sailors.

We try to be patient with ourselves and each other for the rest of the week as we build skill after skill: deploying the LifeSling and retrieving a man overboard under sail, navigating by radar alone, setting a bow and stern anchor, perfecting knots and line handling, jibing with the preventer in place. Each day we know a little more. Each day we've grown a bit more confident.

Finally, it was the last day of our class and time again to attempt the night sail. We spent all day piddling around, trying to distract ourselves by practicing sailor's knots. Knowing we wouldn't arrive at the marina until 2:00 a.m., we tried to rest, but inevitably our attempts to relax were thwarted by our anxiety. "What if our spotlight runs out of batteries? What if we hit a log? Should we have practiced using our autopilot?"

We completed all our To Do items and finished our pre-departure checklist a full hour before sunset. The hour of waiting gave the butterflies in my stomach plenty of time to flutter as I watched the sun dip below the hills.

"Is it dark enough yet?" I asked Captain Phyllis.

"No," she replied.

Five minutes later, "What about now?"

At last, it was time for the grand finale. We bundled up in our foul weather gear, turned all the lights red to preserve our night vision, and it was anchors aweigh.

The first challenge right out of the gate was to "thread the needle" of Lopez Pass, navigating the small, reefy thoroughfare in the dark under radar alone. Thanks to the previous day's exercises, we could identify the blotches of red and yellow on our radar screen as Rim and Ram Islands and were able to carefully navigate without a visual and without a map.

Once through the pass, we faced a new challenge, crossing Rosario Strait at midnight, trying to dodge cargo ships barreling through the Salish Sea to Seattle and beyond. If you hit a cargo ship, you don't live to tell about it. If a cargo ship hits you, they don't even feel it. Thanks to the AIS transceiver Andrés installed, we can see cargo ships on our iPad long before we can see them with our eyes. As we prepared to cross the strait, "WSF Ferry" suddenly appeared on the iPad, likely the vessel taking the last round of passengers from the San Juan Islands to Anacortes.

Then a boat named "Warship" appeared on the screen. "Wow, someone is a little cocky about their boat!" Curious to know what kind of sailor would name their boat *Warship*, I tapped the iPad to get more information and realized they weren't being boastful: "Military vessel engaged in military exercises. No length of vessel available. Speed over ground: 35 knots." *Uh oh.*

My heart began to race as I saw that the vessel was headed toward our destination. I quickly showed the other crew members its position and heading, and we changed course to stay far away from it. With the moving hazards identified, we got our binoculars and looked for navigation lights on Belle Rock, Burrows Island, Shannon Point Reef, and Cypress Island's Reef Point.

Slowly but surely, we crossed the peaceful seas of Rosario Strait, our path illuminated by the light of the moon and guided by the flashing patterns of the buoys and navigation lights. Just as we could see the blinking red and green lights indicating the entrance to Guemes Channel, the warship beacon

IF YOU HIT A CARGO SHIP, YOU DON'T LIVE TO TELL ABOUT IT. IF A CARGO SHIP HITS YOU, THEY DON'T EVEN FEEL IT.

appeared again on the screen. I went to the bow to look for the vessel—nothing. Five minutes later, still nothing. Maybe it's a submarine? I listened carefully for the drone of a diesel engine moving at 35 knots. Still nothing.

We moved slightly out of the channel to give whatever it was extra clearance. And then it suddenly appeared ... next to us. The most frightening thing I have ever seen. An imposing and silent gray behemoth charging rapidly toward us. Its movements were smooth, and its noise did not betray its speed.

With the weaponry mounted on its decks, it looked like the silent killer it probably is. We've crossed a lot of wakes in our travels so far, and whether it comes from a fast power boat, a tiny fishing skiff, or a huge cargo ship, it all leaves the same pattern: streamers of waves coming off the back of the vessel. Not the warship though. Instead of streamers, the ship left a wake woven like a basket, a pattern that would thrill any textile artist. Then we realized what it was, a stealth electric warship.

My heart still pounding, I watched it disappear into the darkness. Terror. Excitement. Pride. Here we are, dodging warships under the light of the moon, navigating through dark waters using the navigation lights as our guides. If adventure is what we're looking for, by George, I think we've found it!

THE HIGHLIGHT

The highlight of the month was finally seeing our parents after the 2020 COVID-19 shutdowns and travel restrictions separated us for the last year and a half of *Ana María's* refit. First, my parents met us at Rosario Resort on Orcas Island, where we ate seafood, explored the art and ceramics scene, and swam every day in the beautiful pool looking out over the islands. Then Andrés Sr. and Jackie met us in Friday Harbor on San Juan Island, where we ate seafood, rode Cannondale electric bikes for the first time, and tried to keep cool in the July heatwave by swimming in local lakes.

Both parents said the highlight of their trips was sailing with us on *Ana María*. For three years they have patiently listened to us complain about boat work and celebrated with us successes, both big and small. Andrés Sr. and Jackie have helped us for weeks at a time and been with us as we tackled the hardest jobs. When we finished the sail with my parents on East Sound, my mom remarked, "It's like the ultimate recital: all the years of work to get the boat ready and all the training and practice to use her, and we get to see all that work on display."

Andrés reflected after we waved goodbye to his folks, "We both have really great parents." Indeed, we do. What a pleasure to feast with them and savor every moment of togetherness!

THE LINGO

A gale warning sent us searching for safe harbor on the first night of our Coastal Passage Making course because it indicates strong wind and big waves. For context, we need to use the motor in anything less than 10 knots of wind in order to go anywhere. *Ana María* sails well in 10 to 30 knots. However, conditions get rough during a gale, with 34- to 47-knot winds (force 8 to 9 on the Beaufort scale). Anything stronger elicits a storm warning, and once 64 knots hit, it's a hurricane. We can deploy our sails in a variety of configurations to keep us comfortable in all but the most extreme conditions, but we are comforted by the fact that most long-term cruisers experience gale force winds only 1 to 2 percent of the time.

THE WILDLIFE

During our month in the San Juan Islands, we've seen bald eagles daily, blue herons, seals, ducks, loons, pigeon guillemots, cormorants, seagulls, porpoises, and even whales at Iceberg Point on my birthday.

THE CHALLENGE

Preparing to live full-time aboard a boat is like using an Etch-a-Sketch to meticulously write down all the routines you have in a day, a week, and a month and then shaking it until all your life's rhythms are completely erased. We've spent the past month shaking our life's Etch-a-Sketch. In fact, in all my years of moving about, I haven't felt this kind of dizzying adaptation since living with host families in France.

We have new routines, new rhythms, new rules for every aspect of our life. We're learning to live life in our floating home—drinking instant coffee, storing produce according to ethylene production and sensitivity, closing seacocks at night and before leaving the boat, efficiently inflating and deflating the kayak whenever we need to run errands, conserving water by washing dishes with foot pumps. The list goes on ... forever.

THE GALLEY

This month we ate a smorgasbord of Pacific Northwest seafood: Fresh crab cakes from Bucks Bay in Olga on Orcas Island. Grilled halibut cheeks. Fresh wild-caught king salmon from Alaska. Seafood pasta. Clams from Westcott Bay Shellfish Co on San Juan Island.

If you've never made a trip to the San Juan Islands, come for the food!

THE ENTERTAINMENT

While in port in Friday Harbor, we browsed through Griffin Bay Bookstore and picked up a copy of *What It's Like to Be a Bird: From Flying to Nesting, Eating to Singing* by David Allen Sibley. We've enjoyed reading a chapter each night and then seeing some of the birds flying, nesting, eating, and singing in their natural habitat here in the San Juan Islands.

THE HORIZON

We're taking *Ana María* out of the water to complete some annual maintenance, replace our old sails, and hopefully install a Spectra Ventura 150 reverse osmosis watermaker before we head out of the Strait of Juan de Fuca for good.

Fair winds and following seas,

Katherine

● 53 miles west of Coos Bay, Oregon, USA
43° 42' 56" N 125° 24' 53" W

● 53 nautical miles south of Cape Mendocino, California, USA
39° 31' 25" N 124° 21' 48" W

VOLUME 1, ISSUE 3: THE GOOD. THE BAD. THE UNCERTAINTY.

September 8, 2021
53 miles west of Coos Bay, Oregon, USA
43° 42' 56" N 125° 24' 53" W
Winds: N 10 knots
Weather: Thick fog

THE GOOD

We finished our boat maintenance and upgrades, left the Strait of Juan de Fuca, and made the Big Left Turn into the Pacific Ocean. Now we are on day three of our anticipated seven-day journey from Neah Bay, Washington, to San Francisco, California, and the past day has been nasty. Our GPS tells us we've sailed down most of the Oregon coast now, but the fog has been so thick, we haven't seen it at all. I'm still chilled to the bone from last night's 1:00 a.m. to 4:00 a.m. shift outside in the wet cockpit. The fog must have bullied the wind into leaving, resulting in 12 hours of engine use.

But there's a glimmer of hope and what feels like a good omen as we approach Coos Bay, Oregon. Forecasts predict enough wind to sail a couple hours with our spinnaker (our light wind sail), and we spot a whale 100 yards off our starboard side.

We eat our first truly fresh meal of the passage, Mille's One-Pot Chicken Lo Mein, and hurry to get the spinnaker ready to raise. Even if it's still foggy, it'll be nice to trade the noise of the engine for the soft flaps of the sail.

Andrés is at the bow, hoisting the spinnaker, while I am at the tiller back in the cockpit, pointing the boat 130° downwind to blanket the spinnaker with the mainsail. The spinnaker is hoisted and sheeted into position when I hear the first whale spout close to me. It must be within 50 yards, but we can't see anything in the fog.

"Did you hear that? It sounds super close!" I shout.

"Yeah, and did you hear the one up here? There are two, and I think they're singing to each other."

As we pick up speed under the spinnaker, the fog starts to clear and we see them, two whales to our port side ... no, three whales ... no, there's three more on our starboard side. Oh my gosh! There are four right over there and three more spouting up ahead a hundred yards!

The more the fog lifts, the more we see. Whales surround us in every direction. We can see their blows for miles, like a field full of Old Faithfuls. They swim close, these creatures twice the size of our boat, just 20 yards away. We know we're supposed to stay away from them, but with whales on every side, the best we can do is continue to sail quietly south through the pod migrating north and enjoy the sight.

For an hour, we find ourselves in the middle of a spectacular ballet performed by more than a hundred whales. The whales dance gracefully, sometimes alone, sometimes as a couple, sometimes as a trio. A great spout, the broad back gliding up through the surface of the water, the flukes elegantly raised straight into the air before sliding steeply into the deeper waters.

The whales lollygagging at the end of the migrating pod are a bit more playful, swimming closer and closer to *Ana María*. Near the end of the hour, while I continue to watch, mesmerized, Andrés rests below in the cabin. Twenty feet away from our port side, I suddenly see two spouts. Panic begins to rise.

"They're coming closer!" I yell downstairs. "There's nothing we can do. We're trespassing in their territory. Just make sure you're wearing your life jacket!"

I hold my breath as I watch the two sets of flukes disappear under the water, visions of the whales using our *Ana María* as a volleyball floating in my head. Sure enough, they pass right underneath our keel, and I let out a breath as they blow water 20 feet on our starboard side, stick their tails up, and swim away.

It was both a terrifying and awe-inspiring experience. We are but tiny guests of the ocean environment, lucky enough to get a small taste of the expansive and larger-than-life activities of this ecosystem.

MILLE'S ONE-POT CHICKEN LO MEIN

INGREDIENTS

1 pound boneless skinless chicken breast or thighs, cut into bite-sized chunks

1 box (13.25 to 16 oz) of fettuccine pasta

4 medium carrots, cut into thin 3-inch strips

1 medium red bell pepper, cut into thin 3-inch strips

1 bunch of green onions, white parts thinly sliced and green parts cut into 3-inch strips

¼ cup soy sauce

1 teaspoon garlic powder

1 teaspoon cornstarch

1 tablespoon sugar

½ teaspoon red pepper flakes

4 cups chicken broth

2 teaspoons extra virgin olive oil

Lime wedges, chopped cilantro, and more soy sauce, for garnish

DIRECTIONS

1. Add the cubed chicken to the bottom of a large stockpot. Break the pasta in half and place on top of the chicken. Add the rest of the ingredients to the pot and cover.
2. Bring to a vigorous boil over high heat, which takes about 15 minutes on *Ana María's* gimballed stove.
3. Uncover and stir, making sure to gently lift the chicken from the bottom of the pot.
4. Reduce the heat to medium-low.
5. Cook covered, stirring occasionally, for 15 minutes or until most of the liquid has evaporated and the chicken is cooked through.
6. Remove the lid and let the dish rest for 5 minutes so it can thicken before serving.
7. Serve with chopped cilantro, soy sauce, and lime wedges.

THE BAD

September 11, 2021
53 nautical miles south of Cape Mendocino, California, USA
39° 31' 25" N 124° 21' 48" W
Winds: 30-40 knots NNW
Seas: Bi-directional 10-foot swell every 6 seconds or less

We've rounded Cape Mendocino and are now only 95 nautical miles from Bodega Bay, north of San Francisco. All four of our weather forecast models agree: we will have 15- to 25-knot winds with 6-foot waves every nine seconds. These are conditions *Ana María* can handle easily with her current sail plan, even on the south side of the infamous cape. I try to focus on the celebration waiting for us when we arrive in California after seven days at sea, rather than the worsening sea state and wind speeds climbing higher and higher on the anemometer.

"Do you think we should take the mainsail down and sail only under the staysail?" Andrés asks as we make dinner and prepare to start the watch schedule for the last night of the sail.

He's right to ask: night is fast approaching and we have sustained 40-knot winds with 8-foot waves coming less than six seconds apart, with some waves coming from a different direction than the main swell. *Ana María* is overpowered even with a second reef in the mainsail, so while she is surfing down these waves, she is by no means a comfortable ride. The force of each wave thrashes her hull. The waves are so steep that, during many of the rides down the waves, her boom touches the water. We know this poses a serious risk to the structural integrity of the rigging.

I agree with my husband, thinking that if something goes wrong in the middle of the night, *Ana María* will be much more manageable with only the staysail up.

We put on our foul weather gear as we talk through the challenging procedure of the sail change, double-checking each other's tethers. We ensure they're connected to both our life jackets and the boat, thinking of the haunting words of the famous sailors Lin and Larry Pardey, "You fall over, you die."

We encounter problems just dousing the genoa, the winds making a mess of all the sheets and furling lines. Anxiety starts to build, as does the intensity. This is not going well.

In spite of that, we're able to turn down to a beam reach just long enough to douse part of the mainsail, turning back up into the wind quickly to avoid catching a wave broadside to our beam. Andrés roughly flakes the sail and gathers it into sail ties, a feat of gymnastics while tethered to the webbing stretched across the boat.

All we have left to do is attach the running backstay to keep the mast from pumping under the pressure of the staysail and then reset the Monitor windvane to steer for us.

Watching Andrés clip in the running backstay, I'm sure we've made it through the worst part of the process. I have both hands on the tiller, trying to steer steady across the onslaught of waves, when I turn my head to look over my shoulder.

It's like a freeze-frame in a movie. A slow-motion set of images I hope won't haunt me for the rest of my life:

Behind my right shoulder is a wall of water coming toward us faster than I can comprehend. Instinctively, I turn my back against the wave. When I next open my eyes, I see Andrés, horizontal and in mid-air, supported only by the lifelines on the boat and inches away from disaster.

Then ... black.

The first sensation is the burning feel of salt water filling my sinuses. I open my eyes to find myself slammed against the other side of the boat, Andrés crawling back onto the side deck.

We recover as quickly as we can. The wave that filled our cockpit must have shoved something into the draining scupper hoses. We start to bail the foot of water we're standing in. I shove my hand down into the scupper and yank out the cloth that is clogging the hose, allowing the water to gush down into the sea. We set the Monitor windvane to steer for us so we can take stock of the damage. Tons of water everywhere, including some inside the boat. The deck is a mess.

But the tethers holding us to the boat did their jobs. We are still attached to the boat, and, most importantly, we are still alive.

As the adrenaline begins to wear off, a glaring problem makes itself known: my left knee is throbbing and about three times its normal size. The wave must have slammed my joint straight into the cockpit's sidewall.

Andrés continues to put the boat back in order, keeping a close eye on the Monitor windvane's performance against the assault of the waves, while I head down below to fish an ice pack and ibuprofen out of our offshore first aid kit. He stays out there as long as he can, but the combined shock of the incident, mild hypothermia, and stress of the waves crashing over the stern again and again drives him inside. He huddles inside a thermal survival blanket for 30 minutes at a time throughout the night.

Ana María, our wonderful sailboat, and Paulita, our self-steering Monitor windvane, sail us safely and mostly independently the rest of the night. As daybreak approaches and even worse weather is forecasted for the afternoon, we have a decision to make: do we sail or try to turn on the engine? Thanks to the wave, our engine is covered in salt water, and we know the electronic control panel was completely submerged.

After quick desperate prayers—*wonder of wonders, miracle of miracles!*—the engine control panel turns on and our diesel engine starts to crank. We listen carefully for it to stall, knowing the fuel lines could be full of salt water, but instead, she runs well for several minutes.

Our best chance at beating the approaching gale is to motor to the next harbor. Since Andrés has been up most of the night and will also be the one to steer us in close quarters, I will steer for the next four hours while he sleeps, with my leg—now the size of a cantaloupe—propped up in the cockpit.

In the morning light, I eagerly look for the coastline and process our predicament in the context of the many stories in our cruising guides of couples calling the Coast Guard for help. Right now, *Ana María* is stable, sailing reliably. Her crew, though a bit worse for the wear, don't seem to be in immediate danger. But ... still ... maybe they can contact the marina for us? Let them know to hold a spot for *Ana María* so we can dock and get to a hospital right away?

I use the VHF radio to call into the local Coast Guard station. They ask all the questions I have anticipated, so I am ready with the answers. "This is sailing vessel *Ana María*. We are at 38°39N and 123°33W. We caught a wave in the cockpit off the coast of Cape Mendocino and we suspect one of our crew has a broken leg. We need assistance coordinating with a marina for our arrival and possibly help docking. There are two adult crew members aboard, both wearing life jackets. Our estimated arrival time is 16:00."

The Coast Guard responds with professionalism and care. To our relief, they make arrangements for us at the marina and patch me through to the flight surgeon, who confirms we are correctly triaging my knee. When we politely turn down the offer for rescue at sea, the station tracks our progress and asks each hour, "Are you still comfortable navigating in the current conditions?" We are mighty glad and surprised to see the Coast Guard ship at the harbor entrance buoy, waiting to escort us into the marina. We dock with the help of two Coasties who kindly carry me off the boat and straight into a taxi.

Instead of a night drinking champagne, we celebrate our arrival in California at the emergency room with a cocktail of painkillers and an x-ray in hand, showing a broken kneecap and a questionable quad tendon.

THE UNCERTAINTY

September 20, 2021
Miami, Florida, USA
25° 48' 59" N 80° 22' 58" W
Winds: ESE 5 knots
Weather: 90°F Thunderstorms

It's been a week since the E.R. doc in California wrapped my broken leg in a brace, issued strict instructions to not bend or put any weight on it, and referred me to an orthopedic surgeon. We knew I couldn't hobble around *Ana María* for the six weeks to six months it could take my knee to recover, so we decided to fly across the country, my leg once again awkwardly propped up in transport, to stay with my in-laws while I'm out of commission. We are now in Miami waiting on the results of an MRI of my left knee.

We are uncertain if the quad tendon has torn completely and if the kneecap is still in place.

Yet we are certainly thankful for a seaworthy boat and self-steering that got us into safe harbor.

We are uncertain if my leg will require surgery.

Yet we are certainly thankful for the care and support we received from the Coast Guard.

We are uncertain when my knee will be recovered enough to continue to sail.

Yet we are certainly thankful for the outstanding medical care I received in California—zero waiting in the emergency room and top-notch doctors who reviewed my case late on a Sunday night and fit me in for tests first thing Monday morning.

We are uncertain when we will be able to return to *Ana María*.

Yet we are certainly thankful for the exceptional hospitality shown to us by my mother-in-law's best friend who happens to live 15 minutes from the California hospital and hosted us for a week with great food to fuel my recovery, in a house and bed designed to accommodate limited mobility until the doctor cleared me to fly to Miami.

We are uncertain if we will have a weather window after my rehabilitation to continue to sail down the coast of California.

Yet we are certainly thankful for a tether system that worked exactly as Andrés designed it, keeping us attached to the boat, keeping us alive and together.

We are uncertain if we will be able to work through the trauma of the wave to ever sail confidently again.

Yet we are certainly thankful to be staying now in my in-laws' home in Florida, where I can recover and recuperate in peace and comfort.

We are uncertain if this event is simply a delay for our dreams, a redirection, or an unfortunate end.

Yet we are certainly thankful that we are making arrangements for flights and MRIs and physical therapy this week instead of much more painful and permanent arrangements.

We are uncertain what's ahead of us and *Ana María*.

Yet we are certainly thankful for a faith unshakable even by the force of mighty waves.

Indeed, we are uncertain, sad, and discouraged, *yet we are certainly thankful* it is not as bad as it easily could have been and certainly grateful for all the ways we have been cared for already.

Fair winds and following seas,

Katherine

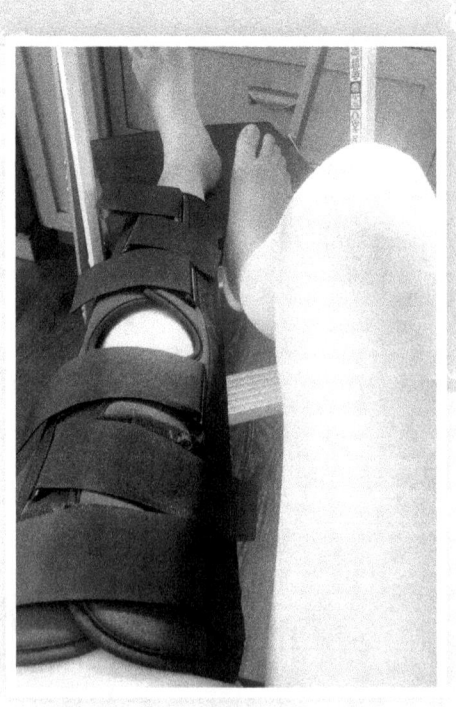

Miami, Florida, USA
25° 48' 59" N 80° 22' 58" W

AN UPDATE ON THE KNEE

September 23, 2021
Miami, Florida, USA
25° 48' 59" N 80° 22' 58" W
Winds: SE 3 knots
Weather: 82°F Hot and humid

Encouraging news from yesterday's appointment with the orthopedic surgeon: no surgery is required! The tendon is intact and the fracture is still "non-displaced," so my leg will be in a hinge brace for four to six weeks with lots of physical therapy scheduled in Miami. But after that, the surgeon said, "I don't see any reason why you can't go right back to the life you were living: sailing and hiking and whatever else you want to do."

We thank God for the great news!

We thank YOU for all the prayers, good thoughts, positive vibes, encouragement, and kind words you sent our way this week.

No firm plans yet, but we have hope that our adventure has not come to an end.

Thanks for being on this journey with us!

Fair winds and following seas,

Katherine

Spud Point Marina, Bodega Bay,
California, USA
38° 19' 45" N 123° 03' 30" W

Drakes Bay, California, USA
38° 00' 26" N 122° 55' 05" W

35 nautical miles northwest of
Monterey, California, USA
37° 03' 53" N 122° 23' 41" W

7 nautical miles west of Big Sur,
California, USA
36° 09' 31" N 121° 56' 37" W

San Luis Obispo Bay,
California, USA
35° 10' 23" N 120° 44' 15" W

Little Scorpion Bay,
Santa Cruz Island,
California, USA
34° 02' 47" N 119° 32' 44" W

VOLUME 1, ISSUE 4: FOOLISH OR BRAVE?

November 4, 2021
Spud Point Marina, Bodega Bay, California, USA
38° 19' 45" N 123° 03' 30" W
Winds: NNW 7 knots
Weather: 65°F Partly cloudy

Two months have passed since my accident, and where the little bits of uncertainty have receded, mounds of pressure have replaced it. We now find ourselves in between a rock and a hard place.

You know, the place where neither decision, neither course of action, seems easy, appealing, or hopeful.

Our rock: the immovable, uncontrollable weather. Our weather window to get down to the safety of Southern California is quickly closing. We are already seeing the gale winds push south from the Canadian Coast into the Oregon Coast. The coming winds and seas will pummel Northern California until next spring. If we want to continue sailing, we have no choice but to go now. If we don't go now, it's time to look for a broker, sell our three years of hard work, and figure out what to do with our lives.

Our hard place: my leg is not back to full strength. My surgeon and physical therapist have both released me to life back on the boat, but they don't really have a clue what sailing on the open ocean is truly like. To arrive in Southern California, we still have another 450 nautical miles to sail before we round Point Conception, 120 miles north of Los Angeles, dubbed the "Cape Horn of the West Coast" in the U.S. Coast Pilot.

We've discussed this decision, pondered the decision, fought over the decision, made the decision, changed our minds about the decision. As we waffle back and forth the night before we need to cast off, I remember watching the movie *Coco* with my in-laws on November 1 to celebrate the Day of the Dead. It's a cute movie, good music, simple.

At the climax of the movie, however, when the hero has his back against the wall, with little hope left of a happy ending, there we were, four adults watching a perfectly predictable Disney movie on the edge of our seats, cheering him on to push forward when all seemed lost—get up and fight one more time! So tonight, we chose the difficult path. We will leave the safety of Bodega Bay to sail south tomorrow, just in time to escape forecasted 50-knot winds.

If we leave and something happens to my knee or us or the boat, we will look back and know it was the most foolish decision we've ever made. If we leave and make it safely past Point Conception, we will look back at this moment where we, without an ounce of naïveté left, bravely faced the ocean once again to follow our dream.

Are we foolish or are we brave?

November 5, 2021
Drakes Bay, California, USA
38° 00' 26" N 122° 55' 05" W
Winds: NW 15 knots
Weather: 58°F Partly cloudy

What on Earth were we so worried about? So much drama, so much deliberation. Today the ocean greeted us warmly with 15 knots of wind and seas from behind for the 35-nautical-mile sail. We're alone in our anchorage and settled in for a peaceful night.

November 7, 2021
35 nautical miles northwest of Monterey, California, USA
37° 03' 53" N 122° 23' 41" W
Winds: NNW 20 knots
Weather: 60°F Mostly cloudy

This. This is what we were worried about. All day we have been surfing waves at speeds greater than our theoretical hull speed. The wind is stable, but the seas are rough. "This feels less like sailing and more like skiing moguls," remarks Andrés.

Thankfully we're not sailing against the wind and bashing against these waves, but our downwind course requires us to jibe *Ana María* several times to avoid running into land or sailing too far out to sea. Jibing is a stressful sailing maneuver because, if not done safely, the force of the wind can break *Ana María's* boom, rip her sails, and hurt the crew.

We start with the wind coming across one side of *Ana María's* tail end. Andrés handles the mainsail while I turn the boat directly downwind so that the back of the boat is facing the direction of the wind. Then I continue to turn until the wind catches the sails from the opposite side of the boat. We successfully jibe a couple of times in daylight before I go down to sleep while he stays in the cockpit for the first night watch.

"Katherine, it's time to jibe." His voice cuts through my dreams. I pull on my foul weather gear and tether. By the time I've climbed into the cockpit, the anxiety that has been simmering all day has come to full boil. We are about to jibe, at night, in rough seas. It isn't exactly the maneuver we were performing when I broke my knee, but it involves the same activities. Mainly, I would need to hand steer without being able to see the angle of the waves crashing behind me.

As I disengage the Monitor windvane, I can feel my mouth, dry as a dessert. Andrés brings the boom to center, and I head downwind to bring the stern through the wind. BOOM! We hear and feel the weight of the sails slam to the opposite side of the boat. He lets out the mainsheet as quickly as possible as I find the new rhythm of the seas on this tack. He jibes the genoa sail and re-engages the Monitor windvane. With the preventer re-rigged, the most stressful part of the night, the activity I have been dreading for weeks is finished. We had done it safely.

The worst may be over, but the night sure isn't. Andrés sleeps for the next shift, and as he sleeps, the wind dies briefly before clocking around from NW to E. In an effort to give him a full four hours of sleep, I put off waking him until it is 25 minutes too late. The wind has shifted our course, and we miss our cut before Point Pinos. He is rightly frustrated when he wakes up as he will spend the next two hours tacking upwind to get us back into Monterey Bay.

Thankfully, we survive our first night passage post-incident! We arrive just in time to put the sails down as the sun rises in the mountains behind Monterey, California.

November 12, 2021
7 nautical miles west of Big Sur, California, USA
36° 09' 31" N 121° 56' 37" W
Winds: NW 25 knots
Weather: 60°F Sunny

After resting and exploring a couple of days in Monterey, we embark on what is hopefully our last overnight sail in the United States. Forecasts show we can sail most of the day, and sail we do ... or surf! We sail under a second reef at 7 knots and surf down the 8-foot waves at 9 knots for most of the day. It's sunny, even if not warm, and the visibility is great, so the sail is more fun than stressful.

We sit together on the windward side of the cockpit, holding hands for a couple of hours as we sail past Big Sur. It occurs to me that this is the absolute opposite of scrolling on my phone. Truth be told, I am addicted to scrolling, quickly scanning my eyes over slews of stimulation looking for the next "hit" of something interesting. Today, however, we sit in quiet, watching the same mountains for hours, our vantage point changing at the slow crawl of 10 miles per hour. It quiets my brain and hopefully reprograms it.

November 14, 2021
San Luis Obispo Bay, California, USA
35° 10' 23" N 120° 44' 15" W
Winds: Dead calm
Weather: 87°F Sunny

We pull up our anchor hours before sunrise so we can round Point Conception and anchor again before the sun sets. We're tired from the previous night's passage, but today is forecasted to be dead calm at the point, so we will attempt to round it. Dead calm means motoring all day, which we hate, but it also means little chance of a Cape Mendocino repeat, which we would hate considerably more.

I take over the helm after rounding Point Arguello and head straight for Point Conception while listening to a podcast. The host of the episode asks,

"What story do you want to live?" As he talks, my eyes sweep over the mirror seas and up the sheer cliffs surrounding Point Conception. We made our decision a week ago to try for it, and here we are, finishing the final challenge of the West Coast. The cliffs remind me that the story could have turned out differently, with us in the kind of seas that created those cliffs. I am beyond grateful for the safe crossing. I think, though, even if our decision had shown us to be fools, I would still be proud of our choice to at least try to live the brave story.

THE HIGHLIGHT

November 22, 2021
Little Scorpion Anchorage, Santa Cruz Island, California, USA
34° 02' 47" N 119° 32' 44" W
Winds: WNW 5-10 knots
Weather: 62°F Partly cloudy

The Channel Islands National Park off the coast of Santa Barbara was the ideal place to recover from the string of stressful passages from Bodega Bay to Point Conception. At night, we had anchorages all to ourselves. We spent the days hiking—my knee did great!—and kayaking in Santa Cruz's many sea caves.

THE WILDLIFE

We saw wildlife up close on Santa Cruz Island. The island scrub jay and island fox species are unique to this island, and their adaptations are evident. The island scrub jay is the only bird in the continental U.S. that has evolved to be unique to one island. Its bright blue feathers make it easy to spot on our hikes, and it is a third bigger and sports a heavier bill than its mainland counterpart, the California scrub jay.

The island fox, found nowhere else in the world, is almost half the size you'd expect. The species' population decreased by 95 percent when the bald eagle's population declined, and the golden eagle invaded the island. The National Park and Conservancy took aggressive action to restore the bald eagle population to push out the golden eagles, which successfully brought back the island fox from the verge of extinction. We had several foxes the size of house cats scamper up to us on the trails.

THE GALLEY

Normally we eat well when we cruise, but we knew it was going to take all our energy and focus to sail down California's coast. To ensure we had a warm and filling meal each evening, we bought Mountain House dehydrated dinners to eat just like we do when we backpack in the backcountry. Not going to lie, the chicken and dumplings tasted pretty good in the cold evenings with rough seas.

THE LINGO

Jibing is the risky sailing maneuver we had to complete repeatedly as we sailed down the coast of California. The action puts considerable stress on the rigging so, before we leave the United States, we will install a whisker pole on *Ana María's* mast, which, when deployed, will minimize the need to jibe.

THE CHALLENGE

Our passage this month wasn't only psychologically challenging but physically challenging as well, given my leg. Generally, docking *Ana María* is a physical activity for me. Andrés stays at the helm in the cockpit, but I climb out of the lifelines, hold onto the shrouds, and step down, basically jumping backward onto the dock to tie us off. Docking in Monterey was especially trying. As we approached the harbor, we questioned whether my leg could handle it. Should we call the harbormaster to request assistance?

We deliberated and concluded that as much as docking represents a physical challenge, it represents a greater teamwork, coordination, and communication challenge. We have a well-refined routine, with communication protocols and well-defined roles. It seemed a greater risk to abandon those strengths than it was to make a slower approach to the dock.

So, with my leg in a brace, I stepped back onto the dock in Monterey as Andrés guided *Ana María* smoothly into her slip.

THE ENTERTAINMENT

We celebrated our safe arrival in Monterey by exploring the local farmers market, walking through the seaside village of Carmel-by-the-Sea, and wine tasting in Carmel Valley, California. If this is cruising, I could get used to this!

THE HORIZON

We are now staying temporarily in Marina Del Rey in Los Angeles, California, doing some prep on the boat before our sail to Mexico. We hope to ring in the New Year in Mexican style.

Fair winds, following seas, and a very Merry Christmas to you and yours!

18 nautical miles west
of San Quintín,
Baja California, México
30° 33' 05" N 116° 15' 01" W

VOLUME 1, ISSUE 5: FACING FEARS

January 12, 2022
18 nautical miles west of San Quintín, Baja California, México
30° 33' 05" N 116° 15' 01" W
Winds: N 10 knots
Weather: 68°F Sunny

Fear is ever present in our cruising life. Some fears, like my fear of sailing by myself during night passages, start strong and subside as we gain experience, competence, and confidence. Others, like running into a surprise storm, are persistent but not likely to occur if we stay vigilant. Yet other fears are birthed from hearing fellow sailors encountering trouble.

The fear is stoked when hearing of another sailing couple encountering the same thing and then another couple and then another. We hope we never have to face it, but deep down, we know it is probably just a matter of time. On our first passage down the Pacific coast of Baja, our time had come.

I climbed into the cockpit at 5:15 a.m. for my second watch of the night. We had been motoring since the sun went down, making decent speed of 4.4 knots. At least that's what we were making during my first night watch. Andrés hadn't been asleep long when I noticed our speed dropping.

We have two instruments that record our speed. We have a paddle wheel at the bottom of our hull that transmits the speed of the boat moving through the water, or "boat speed," while our speed over ground is calculated based on GPS position and tells us how fast we are traveling over the earth. The difference between these two speeds can be attributed to current.

If we have the current with us, Andrés likens it to being on a magic carpet ride: we enjoy more speed over ground than what our boat is actually earning. Current runs both ways, though, so we know we are running against the current when our boat speed is higher than our speed over ground.

On my first watch, with our engine running at 2000 rpm, we were making 4.4 knots boat speed and speed over ground, but now our boat speed had dropped to 3.4 knots and our speed over ground at the same rpm was a dismal 2.4 knots. What in the world was happening?! We were burning fuel but getting nowhere.

My first thought was current, a strong one dead against us. Sure enough, looking at tide charts for a bay close by, I saw we should have current of at least 1 knot against us, so that explained why the speed over ground was lower than the boat speed. But why was the boat speed so low?

Two reasons came to mind: a strong headwind against us ... or ... that which I feared. Kelp wrapped around our propeller. I raised the sails to harness some of the energy of the headwind, but they caused drag, decreasing our speed even more. I took them down again. As I watched our speed over ground dip to 1.8 knots, I knew that I would have to take a swim to try to clean off the propeller when we got to the anchorage in the afternoon.

Andrés woke up for the shift change to find me faunching, frustrated at our lack of progress and dreading my afternoon task. I gave him an update and shared my theory about the prop. We put the transmission into neutral and he leaned his head and torso out of the boat, over the stern, and down toward the propeller. "Oh yeah," he said, confirming our suspicion. "There's something huge on the propeller and a giant piece of kelp hanging off the rudder." Mystery solved! But we wondered what we should do about it.

"When we get into San Quintín, I will dive on the prop and clean it off," I offered. "At this speed, with that kelp acting as an anchor, it'll take us 10 hours to get there instead of three. If we leave it there, we risk damaging the prop, the shaft, the cutlass bearing, and the transmission." We both remember the Sunday afternoon in Elliot Bay Marina in Seattle when we heard a POP! come from a boat entering the fairway. A line had gotten stuck in their propeller, snapping the shaft in two and tearing a hole in the bottom of the hull. There is no way we want to risk that happening out here.

So here it was, the event that comes up in every cruiser's life. In the middle of the Pacific, one of us would have to jump out of the safety of our boat into ocean water that is as deep as three NFL football fields and dive to the propeller to furiously try to free it of the tangled mess.

Andrés is more athletic than I am. As in, he is athletic, and I am not. We have, however, discovered two exceptions to the rule: biking in sand, which we found out while racing to catch the last ferry off Cumberland Island, and swimming. Mom and Dad started me in swim lessons before I started kindergarten. Growing up, we spent our summer days entertaining ourselves for hours at our neighborhood pool. While he may be stronger, I am actually the stronger swimmer.

"I'll go in."

"I can go in," he counteroffers.

Neither of us wants to; both are willing. He does so many of the hard tasks on the boat. This is a hard task I can actually do for us.

"No, I am going in," I say resolutely. We turn off the engine completely, and *Ana María* bobs with the swell as we prepare everything. Luckily, my mother-in-law saw how much I enjoyed snorkeling in Key West at Thanksgiving and gave us warm wetsuits, masks, snorkels, and flippers for Christmas.

The preparation is excruciating. I am not one to delay the inevitable. Once I've decided to take a risk, I don't like to dillydally. I have an old video of myself at summer camp, jumping off a dive tower into freezing Lake Taneycomo in Branson, Missouri. You can hear the girl with the camera shout to me, "Okay, jump at the count of three! One ... two ... Oh, she already jumped." So, it's torture for me to pull on the wetsuit an inch at a time.

If my husband had been putting on the wetsuit, he would have taken the moments to strategize his plan of attack against the kelp. Me, I let the fears percolate in my belly. What if the current is so strong I get separated from *Ana María*? What if the swell causes me to knock my head on the bottom of the boat? What if I see a shark? A whale? A sea lion? Even a dolphin?

We mitigate the risks we can, tying a dock line tightly around my waist and securing it to the boat's stern cleat. We study the swell patterns, relieved to see they are quite slow and predictable.

Having donned my gear, given a final tug at the knot at my waist, and waited for a swell to pass, into the deep blue ocean I jump.

The Pacific is freezing, and I feel my muscles seize up. Last week when we snorkeled to clean and inspect the boat below the waterline, we learned that our bodies panic for a minute after we've jumped into the cold water, so holding onto the boat and the rope, I take deep breaths in an attempt to relax my body and mind. Once acclimated, I dive down to the prop and see the mess Andrés had seen from above. I try twice to untangle it with my hands to no avail. Rising to the surface, I yell for Andrés to give me a knife. He hands me one, and I dive once again.

Two swipes of the knife and six dives later, I've cleared the shaft and propeller of all kelp. The rope is doing a great job of keeping me close to the boat, but every time I look down, I worry that I'll meet the eyes of a wild sea creature. I gather courage and look down once more. There's still a huge piece of kelp stuck at the very bottom of the rudder, causing drag for the boat. I dive once but don't make it. I dive again. Still can't get it. It's wrapped around the deepest part of the skeg, and I am buoyant in this salt water.

Fighting panic, I imagine myself diving for quarters as a kid in the deep end of the neighborhood pool. I kick and kick my feet, grab hold of the kelp, push the rudder to the side and YANK! Relieved, I watch it float away from the boat, already caught in the current.

I can tell Andrés saw it float away too when I rise to the surface and see his beaming face. "You did it! I'm so proud of you!" I climb back aboard, peel off my wetsuit, and take a hot shower on the bow to rinse off all the cold salt water. Andrés turns the engine back on and points *Ana María* toward San Quintín. "We still have current against us, but our boat speed is back up from 3.2 to 4.4 knots." I hear his report from the cockpit. I had fixed it! I dove on the propeller in the middle of an ocean passage. I had faced yet another fear, a fear I hope I never have to face again.

THE LINGO

A current is what caused us to lose a knot of speed over ground close to San Quintín. There are different types of current, but as we stay relatively close to land, we most often encounter tidal currents. Tides, of course, are the vertical movements of water (high tide, low tide) caused by changes in the lunar cycle. Tidal current is the horizontal movement of water that ushers water between high tide and low tide. In one way, the relationship is simple: flood currents precede high tide; ebb currents precede low tide.

But land masses and the ocean topography can make the patterns quite complex. The currents were stronger and more complex around the San Juan Islands in Washington than what we see here in the open ocean. When sailing in Washington, we had the benefit of current stations, which told us when currents would be with us or against us. Here off the coast of Baja California, there are few stations, but we were able to deduce the currents based on tide calendars.

THE HIGHLIGHT

Between Los Angeles and Mexico, we made a pit stop at Catalina Island. Catalina Island is part of the Channel Islands but is privately owned and considerably more developed than the national park islands. The island is popular with Californians, and now we understand why. We spent several days in the remote anchorage of Cat Harbor, so we could kayak, explore the little town of Two Harbors, and hike a portion of the Trans-Catalina Trail to see Shark Harbor.

THE WILDLIFE

A Trans-Catalina thru-hiker warned us on the trail, "There is bison up ahead, just off the trail." Bison? Here? Sure enough, we reached the ridge, and about 150 feet off the trail there he was. Apparently, someone brought bison to the island sometime in the twentieth century. Maybe that person turned his back to the roaring sea, looked across the island's landscape, was reminded of Montana, and brought in the bison.

THE CHALLENGE

In *Ana María*, we crossed the international border between the United States and Mexico without incident. It was quite the bureaucratic ordeal, though. Andrés started the mountain of paperwork back in November. After arriving in Ensenada, we hoisted the yellow quarantine or "Q" flag signaling, per international maritime law, our request to clear into a foreign port.

The marina there facilitated the process for us, which included a health screening, stacks of yet more paperwork, a visit to immigration, a visit to the port captain, and a visit to customs. Crossing borders is serious business. We did not want to make a mistake and wind up in jail in Mexico or have our boat confiscated. It seemed to go smoothly, except for when the port captain's office closed without notice. With our official clearance in hand, we were proud to lower the quarantine flag on *Ana María* and raise the Mexican courtesy flag in its place.

THE GALLEY

We asked a fellow American cruiser where we should eat in Ensenada, and she sent us to La Birrieria La Guadalajara. We feasted on braised beef and lamb with chili sauce and freshly made corn tortillas. A two-man mariachi band provided entertainment during the meal, serving dual roles as musicians and comedians. What an experience to welcome us to Mexico!

THE ENTERTAINMENT

Thanks to the Christmas generosity of friends and family, we had plenty of audiobooks to keep us entertained on watch: for me, *Four Winds* by Kristin Hannah and *Learn Spanish* with Paul Noble, and for Andrés, *El Amante Japonés* by Isabel Allende.

THE HORIZON

We have 600 miles of sailing down the rugged coast of the Baja Peninsula in front of us. All our forecasts predict four days of 15-knot winds coming from behind us, so we will sail as fast as we can toward Cabo San Lucas.

Fair winds and following seas with kelp-free props,

Katherine

Bahía Los Frailes,
Baja California Sur, México
23° 22' 47" N 109° 25' 24" W

VOLUME 1, ISSUE 6: WHAT DREAMS ARE MADE OF

January 23, 2022
Bahía Los Frailes, Baja California Sur, México
23° 22' 47" N 109° 25' 24" W
Winds: N 12 knots
Weather: 73°F Cloudy

I lived by two rules when I was a Rotary youth exchange student and later Ambassadorial Scholar:

1. Accept every invitation extended to me.
2. Try not to embarrass myself or my hosts.

I mastered the first rule. I've been to French operas about Mississippi brothels, cricket matches, Afrikaans karaoke bars, heavy metal concerts, boxing fight nights, East German-style parking garage dance parties, horse races, road trips across the African wild, and more birthday parties for strangers than I can count. Disciplined following of this rule has led me to some incredible life experiences I would never have sought out on my own.

The second rule … well as you'll see, I'm still learning.

We escaped the pandemonium of Cabo San Lucas and found quiet refuge 45 miles north, in Bahía Los Frailes. We'd hoped to snorkel upon arrival, but the wind and seas forced us to hike instead. We hiked the mile scramble up Cerro Los Frailes, crawling over cacti and following the cairns placed every 20 or so feet. From the top, we could see *Ana María* safely anchored near three boats of similar size, as well as one superyacht. On the other side, we could see Cabo Pulmo reef quite clearly. We scrambled back down the hill, planning tomorrow's snorkel excursion.

We had put the kayak in the water to paddle to *Ana María* when a man on a paddleboard landed on the beach and two goldendoodles jumped off and ran toward me. These pups clearly hadn't been on land for a couple of days. They were energetic and friendly, so we exchanged pleasantries with their owner Joe. We found out that we're both from Seattle, as are his friends, Tom and Kathy, who arrived on the second paddleboard.

"Do you guys have plans for dinner?" asked Joe.

We looked at each other, both thinking of the strict meal plan carefully arranged to avoid food expiration dates. We also think of Lin and Larry Pardey's rule: "There are a lot of weird people out there. We never accept an invitation first off. We always plan for the next day. That usually weeds out the flakes."

But in the end, Andrés responded, "Not firm ones, no."

"Why don't you come have dinner on our boat? Three of the other cruisers are already coming."

"Uh, okay. Um. What can we bring?"

"Oh, nothing. I'll just tell my chef we're having five extra for dinner. That plus the eight of us, that's only thirteen."

(The next day we would joke that Andrés' response should have been, "Oh, okay. I'll just tell my chef there will be two fewer for dinner. Katherine, there will be two fewer for dinner onboard tonight." Haha!)

Instead, Andrés asked, "Ok, what time?"

"How about 5?"

"Sure. Which boat are you?"

"The blue one."

The blue one. He could have easily said, "The only superyacht here, you doofus." Instead, he described the color rather than its audacious size.

We paddled back, my mind racing to come up with a hostess gift. What exactly do you bring to a host on a superyacht when you yourself live on a tiny boat with bare minimum provisions, no bottles of wine, six miles from the closest remote village, with only a three-hour notice?

By the time we made it back to *Ana María*, I had an idea for a hostess gift. We had the ingredients to make some gingerbread muffins I'd been wanting to try. They have little sugar and lots of ginger, so they alleviate seasickness and make good passage-making snacks. Joe had told us they would leave after dinner for Puerto Vallarta, so the muffins would be a nice homemade treat during their passage.

I baked the muffins, hurting a bit at the sacrifice of the precious muffin tin liners, then tasted a muffin to ensure they were edible—not too bad! We showered and thanked our lucky stars that we had acceptable clothes to wear. A navy dress with a quick-dry skort for me, so I don't flash anyone while getting out of the kayak, and the only collared shirt Andrés owns, the aquamarine fishing shirt Dad found on a $10 rack at Ace Hardware. Dad bought it because, though he had never seen his son-in-law wear anything like it, he couldn't pass up the deal. Andrés hadn't worn it yet, so it was still nicely creased. I deemed us presentable, and we loaded into the kayak for the quick jaunt over to the superyacht.

We stepped aboard *Naoki* and into the middle of white-haired yachties, as Hal calls them, all wearing khakis and various versions of navy Helly Hansen sweaters. There was Joe and his wife Linda, *Naoki's* owners; Tom and Kathy, whom we'd met at the beach; Dean and Barbara, from the other Pacific Seacraft in the anchorage; and finally, mild-mannered, even-keeled, recently retired plumber Fred on *Kaylee*. I hand Joe the still-warm-from-the-oven gingerbread muffins, which he kindly accepts. Our hosts offer us drinks, and with two precious LaCroix in hand, we tour the 125-foot *Naoki*, which is as long as a 12-story building if it were lying on its side.

We start the tour on what Joe calls the flybridge, where he prefers to control all the sails. He recounts the hassle of getting the hydraulic controls worked on as they were protected by some crazy intellectual property rights. Next, we head down to the main dining room, peek at the helm seat with enough controls to fly a 737, visit the library that'd make Gatsby jealous, and walk past the galley, where three crew members were working to prepare a meal for five extra people. We then tour three staterooms and an office, walk through the crew's quarters and past the fridge, deep freezer, pantry, two sets of washers and dryers, and into the engine room.

The engine room is three times as large as our entire boat. Looking at the room with all its systems, we recognize almost everything, having installed similar hardware ourselves, except our systems look like toy models compared to the Goliaths here. Joe is in the maritime industry, which we learn, is in an entirely different league from the marine industry we know. He proudly shows us all the cool features he installed, like the stabilizers, which he claims are the only installation of stabilizers on a boat of this size.

It felt like we were all back touring the megayachts at the Seattle Boat Show, except we don't have to feign any ability to purchase the boat, and our captain doesn't have to pretend to dutifully explain all the available features to a bunch of ruffians with holes in their socks. We had a simple arrangement—he boasts and we marvel. We marvel at the complexity, marvel at the meter showing 3,200 gallons left in one of his diesel tanks (for comparison, *Ana María's* tank fits 27 gallons), marvel at the varnished teak throughout, and marvel at how meticulously the boat is kept.

On our way back to the hors d'oeuvres, we meet Captain Tim and the other three crew members. Captain Tim tells us of his start on a 75-foot schooner without engines back in Boston. He prefers sailing the closely knit bays on the East Coast to the wide expanse of dangerous remote coasts of Washington, Oregon, and Northern California.

Our tour complete, our mouths started to water when Joe offered us hors d'oeuvres. We'd all had an active day, so we dove right into the salmon mushroom canapés and cheese puffs. We picked up enough to stave off the deep rumbling of our stomachs but not so much as to be rude. Sarah, the young woman with a slightly exotic accent offered to take my empty plate, to which I obnoxiously responded, "Oh no! We hiked that hill right over there. I'm still starving!" *Did I just say what I think I said?* Mortified, I feel a wave of bright red embarrassment wash over me.

Still feeling a bit flushed by my verbal faux pas, I refocus my attention on the beauty of the outdoor dining area, where heaters and blankets were keeping us comfortable. A few minutes later, Sarah brings out beautiful plates embellished with a cursive *Naoki* and full of roasted pork tenderloin, steamed green beans, and sautéed cauliflower, garnished with fresh rosemary sprigs. The food is delicious, the conversation between the mariners even more delightful.

I once read an essay by Nora Ephron on how to be a good guest at a dinner party. "A good guest always brings a good story to share, an interesting topic for the table to discuss, and a good question for each person to answer." We regale them with the Cape Mendocino tale of the rogue wave and my broken leg. We trade accounts of freeing fouled props. We swap stories of how each couple met. We describe our interactions with the humpback whales the day before. We talk of fast boats with nice lines, sail configurations, lessons we'd learned so far. We each share a location still on our cruising bucket list.

The chef comes out of the kitchen to receive our compliments and shares her own stories of working as a food editor for Martha Stewart in the early years of her fame. She brings her dessert, homemade blueberry pie with freshly whipped cream. Sublime!

She explains that she is not giving our hostess a piece of pie because, due to medical conditions, she must closely watch her sugar intake.

And it is here where I once again show my true uncouth colors.

"Oh!" I exclaim, remembering the recipe for my hostess gift. "The gingerbread muffins I brought have very little sugar!"

As the words leave my mouth, another wave of embarrassment immediately washes over me. I finally understand what everyone else already knew: We are on a yacht with a full-time Martha-Stewart-surviving chef. My muffins would most likely be eaten by the goldendoodle puppies currently lounging in the laps of their owners rather than the owners themselves.

I nearly slap my own mouth shut.

Luckily, everyone at the table is kind, and the awkward moment doesn't last long. We get up from the table, exchange contact information, and promise to keep in touch. We shake hands, share hugs, and wish everyone fair winds and following seas. Our hosts hold our line as we climb back into our dinghy. As we wave goodnight, I hear one woman exclaim to the others, "How cute is it they came in their KAYAK?!"

We paddle toward *Ana María's* illuminated anchor light. We've only been back at the boat 10 or so minutes when we see Captain Tim turn on *Naoki's* running lights, pull up her anchor, and sail toward Puerto Vallarta.

The next morning, our cruising neighbors, Dean and Fred, pull their dinghy up alongside our boat to ask about the trailhead to the top of Cerro Los Frailes. I give them directions and wish them a good hike when Fred turns to me. "Last night was ..." He started, searching for adequate words. "Last night ... that was really something, wasn't it?"

"Really something indeed, Fred."

THE CHALLENGE

Keeping us fed for a 12-day then 19-day stint without access to a grocery store was an overwhelming challenge. We all learned during the 2020 pandemic shutdown what a luxury it is to swing by a grocery store to pick up a jug of milk or ground beef if we had a sudden hankerin' for grilled burgers. It takes careful planning to fully provision ourselves for the 12-day sail from Ensenada to Cabo San Lucas, then do a second round of provisioning for the 19-day stay in remote anchorages between Cabo San Lucas and La Paz.

Complicating this challenge is that we have no freezer, and our refrigerator has only 3 cubic feet of space. It is likely smaller than the YETI cooler you have in your garage for those weekend camping trips.

Furthermore, it is always a challenge to grocery shop in a foreign country where I don't speak the local language. Labels take three minutes to decipher. Plus, brands are different. Products are different. Store layouts are different. Customs are different.

The first time I went grocery shopping in Hamburg, Germany, I spent an hour trying to find the 10 basic items I needed to survive the first week in my new apartment. My Rosetta Stone courses had taught me "coffee" but not "ground" or "whole bean." Finally satisfied with the items in my basket, I put all of them on the conveyor belt and started to re-bag them in my reusable shopping bag as I watched the cashier ring them up.

I handed him my credit card and received a very stern "Keine Kreditkarte!" in return. No credit cards? My mind reeled. I didn't have enough cash to cover it. I had opened my Deutsche Bank account the day before, so it would be a couple of days before I received my debit card in the mail. There was nothing else to do but shrug my shoulders, whisper "Sorry," and sheepishly leave all of those carefully selected items at the bagging station.

I cried as I walked back to my new home. About halfway back to the apartment on Dillstraße, I realized my bag was heavier than it should be. I looked inside and was aghast to see a box of laundry detergent. Somehow in the cultural chaos back at the store, I had accidentally walked out with the laundry detergent in hand. I had never stolen anything in my life. Five days in a new country and I was already a thief.

Confident Rosetta Stone had not armed me with the phrases to explain to the cashier why I was back, I could imagine the thought bubbles over his head: *This idiot American thinks you bring items TO the grocery store.* I carried the box home, bawling the rest of the way. As overwhelming as provisioning was, at least this time in Mexico, I didn't steal anything, and I didn't cry.

THE GALLEY

If provisioning was 3/4 challenging, it was also 1/4 fascinating. For years, Mom has taught the course Consumer Behavior to university students. When it came time to take her three children (ages 11, 13, and 15) overseas for the first time, she taught us others' customs and behaviors are not weird or strange but interesting. Our first foray into the Mexican *supermercado* yielded some interesting observations:

1. Everyone's temperature is taken as we enter the store.
2. A gigantic barrel of bulk pinto beans stands guard at the corner of each produce aisle.
3. There isn't a frozen food aisle, only some small coolers for ice cream like those in a convenience store. We had read refrigeration and freezers are not as common on the Baja peninsula.
4. The eggs are not refrigerated.
5. For whatever reason, the only beer for sale is Bud Light.
6. The large jars of Nutella are locked away in the hard liquor cabinets.
7. There are aisles and aisles of pan dulce that look and smell delicious.
8. We didn't see anything organic, but packages have labels indicating "Excess Sodium." "Excess calories." "Excess saturated fat." Turns out, when you're provisioning for several weeks, you end up buying items with all three labels.
9. We looked and looked but couldn't find a can of diced tomatoes anywhere.
10. The meat counter is still manned by a butcher.
11. No date of any kind is stamped on the chicken packages.
12. We gave the customary tip to the bagging lady at the till.

THE ENTERTAINMENT

We've enjoyed world-class snorkeling since we rounded Cabo San Lucas. Los Frailes is only 3 miles from the 5,000-year-old Pulmo Reef, which is the only hard coral reef in the Sea of Cortez. An estimated 200 species of fish, marine invertebrates, and mammals live off the reef. We saw fields of coral. Every few feet we saw schools of fish, loner fish hiding in the rocks, neon fish, polka-dotted fish, tiny fish, Moorish idol, king angelfish, damselfish, and parrotfish. It felt like we were swimming through a real-life Dr. Suess book: 1 fish, 200 fish, red striped fish, blue spotted fish. Andrés was lucky enough to swim with a *Tortuga golfina*. Pretty incredible!

THE HIGHLIGHT

Jimmy Cornell describes the sail south from the Pacific Northwest to Mexico and beyond in his book *World Cruising Routes*: "It may also help to know that, however hard the start, the rest of the passage will be quite pleasant."

"... however hard the start ..."

Really, Jimmy? "However hard," like break-your-kneecap hard?

Sailing through the "Roaring Forties" of Washington, Oregon, and Northern California, we felt like someone took us to the top peaks to teach us how to ski on double black diamonds. We've come down the mountain, looked around us, and realized everyone else is skiing the blue runs.

"... the rest of the passage will be quite pleasant."

The sail from San Quintín to Cabo was quite pleasant indeed. No, "pleasant" doesn't capture it.

Idyllic.

Paradise.

Perfect.

We sailed 600 miles down the Baja Coast with 15 knots of wind and 3-foot seas behind us. On night watches, instead of enduring hour after hour, instead of distracting ourselves with audiobooks and music, we relished the glorious sight of the stars, the sound of the wind gently filling the sails, the water lapping against the side of the boat, and the rocking of the hull as *Ana María* rode smoothly over the waves.

It is the first time I've understood the phrase, "A powerboat will get you to your destination. On a sailboat, you're already there."

This is the kind of sail that acts as a siren call, beckoning sailors to leave safe harbor and sail out to the open ocean.

This is the sail dreams are made of.

THE WILDLIFE

It's humpback whale season in the Sea of Cortez, and we see the migratory whales nearly every day. If sailing through the pod of whales off the coast of Oregon was like sailing through a natural ballet, sailing through pods of humpback whales is like sailing through a monster truck rally. The whales burst without warning from the surface and crash back, creating a massive water crater. They want us to see the full force of their might.

In Bahía Los Frailes, they are more docile, surfacing quietly 10 feet from *Ana María*. They frolic in the bay all night long. We are awoken throughout the night by the sound of their forlorn calls coming through the hull.

THE LINGO

Sailing Wing-on-wing: Using a whisker pole to pull the headsail (normally the genoa or spinnaker) to the windward side of the boat, leaving the mainsail on the leeward side. This sail configuration is aptly named because it truly looks like we have two wings, one on either side of the mast, as we sail smoothly downwind.

Hal, our South African rigger, recommended we refit the whisker pole already installed on the boat. We finally followed his advice while in Los Angeles, replacing the hoisting line and topping lift, adding a foreguy and afterguy. With this setup, the aluminum pole can be hoisted up and down the mast, becoming a second boom. When deployed, the whisker pole securely holds the foresail out to the side of the boat.

Wing-on-wing has been a game changer! When the whisker pole holds the headsail out on the windward side, the mainsail no longer blankets it from the wind, so we sail faster with more power. Wing-on-wing allows us to sail at a deeper angle when sailing downwind: 150° off the wind, instead of only 110°. This means we sail more directly to our destination, making fewer jibes and fewer sail changes. From San Quintin to Cabo, we averaged two sail changes per day instead of five or six.

THE HORIZON

We will enjoy civilization for a week in La Paz before leaving to spend three-ish weeks anchored off the grid in the Isla Espíritu Santo National Marine Park.

Fair winds and following seas,

Katherine

● Agua Verde,
  Baja California Sur, México
  25° 31' 23" N 111° 04' 25" W

● Isla San José,
  Baja California Sur, México
  24° 52' 17" N 110° 35' 03" W

VOLUME 1, ISSUE 7: GRUDGE OR GRACE?

April 10, 2022
Isla San José, Baja California Sur, México
24° 52' 17" N 110° 35' 03" W
Winds: N 15 knots
Weather: 80°F Sunny—haven't seen a drop of rain in over two months

"A dinghy or kayak trip through the mangroves to the main lagoon is the highlight at Amortajada on Isla San José and should not be missed."

Coming across a sentence like this in our copy of *Sea of Cortez: A Cruiser's Guidebook* automatically guarantees the activity a place on our Bucket List.

We read the description of the seven-mile loop and laughed at the memories of our first kayak trip through the Everglades National Park when we left three hours late and battled the current the entire trip. We misread the nautical charts and paddled for hours toward the horizon before we realized we were crossing the Gulf of Mexico and headed for the Texas Coast. The armies of mosquitos weren't threatened in the least by our armory of DEET products. The raccoons spent all night trying to steal our food supply from the cooler. We went to sleep gazing up at the stars through the open ceiling of our tent and woke up at 3:00 a.m. to a thunderstorm flooding our tent. Thank goodness we've gotten better since then!

Still, the reviews posted on ActiveCaptain, the Yelp of marine anchorages, gave us pause: "The mangroves are good but there are no-see-um bugs everywhere. It doesn't matter if you're covered in DEET, diesel, or kerosene. They're gonna eat you alive. I spent the next three days covered in cortisone cream!" And just like when we ignored the Everglades Park Ranger's advice about currents, navigating the mangroves, the mosquitos, and wild animals, we know now we should have heeded these warnings as well.

Sure enough, Mr. Redneck Cruiser was right. We swat away swarms of bloodthirsty no-see-ums as we set up our inflatable 3-chamber, 12-foot kayak with the skeg.

If *Ana María* is our home, our kayak is our car. We pack it with seats, paddles, water, lunch, and Andrés' iPhone with the maps of the mangroves.

Stepping off *Ana María* we hopped into our tandem kayak. Captain Phyllis, our sailing instructor, calls it a "divorce kayak" and now, after using it for nearly a year, I understand how it got that nickname. Making progress in the kayak requires two strong-willed individuals, each with his or her own idea of how best to get to the destination, to work in perfect unison in a tiny space. We're each impacted by the other's slightest mistake, both quick to judge the other's actions, both slow to appreciate the other's best efforts.

We eventually find our paddling rhythm, cruising along at 3 knots. A couple of weeks ago, we spent an hour improving my paddle stroke while exploring the sea caves on Isla Espíritu Santo; the 50 percent improvement in our speed today is a great return on our investment of time.

Andrés whips out his iPhone to check our position against the entrance to the mangroves shown on the charts (a nautical map). "We're coming up on shallow water," he sees in the chart. And just like that—oof! —we run aground. I hadn't paid enough attention to the shoaling in front of us.

Tempers immediately flare. If we run aground and pop our kayak, there goes our car, our means of transportation. We'll have to swim back to the boat and stay on the boat full-time until we can buy a replacement dinghy. We both hop out to carry the kayak across the 60-foot sandbar, bickering and sniping at each other the whole way. We're still peeved when we hop back in and paddle toward deeper water.

Another sandbar. Another carry across. Another discussion punctuated by frustration. On this crossing, we have a decision: we can either fight and ruin the day, or we can reset and try to enjoy this once-in-a-lifetime experience. We learned the art of the reset during the hard days of the boat renovation. After a couple more bouts of bickering, we realize we're going to need a hard reset, the special kind of reset we had to master when we fought while fiberglassing the hull, under pressure to finish in time to put the boat back in the water on schedule.

We pass a Mexican charter catamaran with a guide on a paddleboard prepping his kayaking customers on how to enter the passage against the current. We then see the entrance and know that it's no-holds-barred if we want to get through the ebbing current.

We paddle, paddle, paddle against the strong current to enter the mangroves. In my head I sing the march cadence Dad taught me as a little girl: "I LEFT my wife on the verge of starvation with 22 children and only one hamburger LEFT, LEFT, LEFT …" We paddle as hard as we can, and I glance furtively to the side to see if we're still moving forward. We're making progress, but it's painfully slow. My never-before-heard-from oblique muscles are crying to go back into hibernation.

Paddle! Paddle! Paddle! Paddle!

Finally, we pass a "Y" in the mangroves where two currents converge, and we sigh with relief that we're through the hardest part of the day. We look back and see the other explorers with their guide trailing farther and farther behind us.

We've entered the sanctuary of the inner mangroves—so far so good! I hear Andrés rustling through things behind me. He must be looking for his phone to take a picture. The tempo of the rustling changes to a more panicky beat. Obviously, he's having trouble finding it. I'm not worried, though, as he isn't known for his search skills.

He checks the bag behind my seat. He checks the bag behind his seat. He checks the bag on the back of the kayak. He rummages through our waterproof backpack. Still, I'm not worried.

I offer to look and check the bag behind my seat, the bag behind his seat, the bag on the back of the kayak, and the waterproof backpack.

Nothing.

Now the tempo of my rustling reaches a fever pitch as I dig into crevices in the kayak and seats, checking all the bags once again. Nothing.

We lost his phone.

We lost the phone we use to get forecasts. We lost the only phone with the tide charts. We lost the phone we use to set an anchor alarm to notify us if we drag toward rocks in the night. We lost the phone we use to take all our pictures. We lost the phone we use to check in with our families.

A knot starts to form in my stomach. How are we going to find it? Unfortunately, "Find My Phone" doesn't work without a signal, so we have no idea where it might be. Surely, it's at one of the places where we walked the kayak across a shallow sandbar.

The iPhone is rated IP67, which means we have 30 minutes to find it from the time it dropped in the water. It's been at least 15 minutes since we entered the mangroves, so we've gotta act fast.

We go back to the last place we got out, the sandbank guarded by the blue heron. We comb the bottom with our eyes and feet as the Mexican tour group curiously observes us.

We kayak back to the entrance of the mangroves and are pushed out with the tide to the next sandbar.

We walk right and left, eyes sweeping the sand as we move forward. Another five minutes of searching and still no dice.

There's only one sandbar left—the sandbar where we initially ran aground. We paddle over and climb out, our legs laden with discouragement.

I look for the phone knowing it's a fruitless search. "I promise to help you look for the phone you dropped on the bottom of the ocean" wasn't explicitly stated in our marriage vows, but I'm pretty sure it was implied.

I know it's futile to even pray we find it, but Andrés has a bit more faith.

I'm half-heartedly continuing the search when I hear him yell.

"I FOUND IT!"

I turn around and see him holding his iPhone high into the air.

"I looked down and there was something shiny, halfway covered in sand, and here it is! It was still on when I picked it up. What are the chances?!"

It's pretty amazing when you think about it: We had no idea exactly where we stopped, and we were in the middle of the open sea with shifting sands. Imagine how many iPhones could fit along the path we've kayaked. It's a miracle he found it.

I rush over so we can quickly rinse it with fresh water from our water bottle and try to beat the 30-minute clock. We jump back into the kayak and paddle like hell the mile back to *Ana María*.

I. Am. Pissed.

I can't believe after all this effort, after all the bickering of the morning, after our battle with the currents, he dropped his phone in the ocean! I take my anger out through my paddles, crashing them forcefully into the water with each stroke. I've never paddled more furiously or faster in my life.

With my demon paddling, we're back to *Ana María* in no time. Andrés jumps onto the boat and throws the iPhone into a bag of desiccants and rice.

AM I GOING TO HOLD THIS AGAINST HIM AND LORD IT OVER HIM? OR AM I GOING TO LET IT GO, THANKFUL THAT WE FOUND IT, REMEMBERING THAT TIME I DROPPED MY KEYS INTO THE WATER AT THE MARINA AND WE SPENT AN HOUR FISHING THEM OUT?

The physical exertion has released some of my anger. As he triages the phone, my melting heart begins to weigh the decision: grudge or grace?

Am I going to hold this against him and lord it over him? Or am I going to let it go, thankful that we found it, remembering that time I dropped my keys into the water at the marina and we spent an hour fishing them out?

My heart melts completely and grace wins over grudge.

So, forgiveness, yes, but do we try again? Even if there is forgiveness, there are still consequences.

This is the second time today we have to make the decision.

Should we go? Should we give up? The current that was bad before is going to be worse now as the water gushes from the lagoons through the tiny entrance.

He feels guilty. "Whatever you want to do, I'll do it, and I'll have a good attitude."

I go back and forth and back and forth before finally leaning into the adventure once again. "We're here. Let's give it one more try."

As we kayak back to the entrance to the mangroves, we strategize on how to avoid the current that has definitely gotten worse. The Mexican guided tour is leaving as we pull up. "Leaving" may not be the right word. The guided tour is being ejected from the mangroves like a toboggan gets spit out of Splash Mountain.

They turn around and watch us try to paddle back into the mangroves. You can see the thought bubbles over their heads: "What in the heck are these crazy gringos doing?" Andrés catches their stares and exclaims, *"¡Sí se puede!"* Yes, we can! They laugh as we hop out to walk the kayak on the beach to avoid the worst of the current.

Our strategy works, and for the second time that day, we kayak easily through the main channel of the mangrove. Without Andrés' iPhone, we're kayaking blind, relying on our memory of the chart. We find the main lagoon we remember seeing on the chart and slow our paddling so we can eat a sandwich alongside the pelicans fishing for their own lunch.

We too quickly find ourselves at the exit of the mangroves and decide to explore a little further. We're suddenly in a labyrinth of rarely visited mangroves, thankful for the extremely shallow draft on our kayak. The protection offered by the hard-to-get-to coves allows the diversity of the mangroves to thrive. Blue herons sit on top of the mangroves. Long skinny cornetfish squirm beneath us. Neon orange crab scamper to and fro. We catch glimpses of brown speckled fish so camouflaged that we wouldn't have believed they were fish if we hadn't seen them move with our own eyes. The bright green rubbery leaves of the surrounding mangroves stretch toward the sun, helped by their roots and trunks acting as stilts lifting them out of the water and toward the sky.

"Ooooo do you see that bird?" we whisper back and forth, our voices slipping into hushed tones so we don't disturb the sacred silence. It's so quiet we can hear the air disturbance created with each flap of the birds' wings as they fly from one perch to the next. We watch and listen as a bird takes flight, calling like a toddler with the croup. We paddle forward slowly and listen as another bird, hiding somewhere just out of sight, calls like a traffic cop who's just been given a shiny new whistle.

The next passage looks particularly dicey. Should we keep going or is it time to turn back? We take one more offshoot, round a corner, and gasp. The tight narrow mangrove opens into a shallow lagoon with a hundred snowy white egrets peacefully fishing. They turn in unison to see us arrive on our blue kayak, clearly as surprised to see us as we are to see them. The path to get here was so shallow, we can't imagine many dinghies ever make it here.

We're overwhelmed by the peace of the place. So far on this paddle, we've been mystified by the sights as if seeing a gold brick placed in front of us. Now we've entered Fort Knox with unimaginable beauty and splendor surrounding us in every direction. We sit in the magic, sharing the moment of surprise delight, the moment made sweeter by the trials and adventures it took to get here. We soak it in for a while before realizing, without a phone, we have no idea what time it is. The tide could be turning, and we could find ourselves fighting the current in the entrance to the mangroves for the third time today.

Thankfully, we finish the 9-mile kayak trip and make good time getting back to the boat. The no-see-em bugs are going to finish us off tonight if we don't get out of here, so we deflate the kayak and store her. We raise the mainsail, pull up our anchor, and sail away from Isla San José, trailed by dolphins dancing in our wake, our skin covered in bug bites and our souls basking in the grace of the day.

THE LINGO

Agua Verde, Baja California Sur, México
25° 31' 23" N 111° 04' 25" W

A cruising guide is a cruiser's Bible out here in the remote areas. We read it. We study it. We apply its truth to our lives.

We're on our third guide, *Sea of Cortez: A Cruiser's Guidebook*, having used *Exploring the San Juan and Gulf Islands* last summer and *Exploring the Pacific Coast: San Diego to Seattle* for our passage down the West Coast. Each guide differs slightly, but all of them tell us where we can safely anchor, where we can find wind and swell protection, where to avoid reefs and submerged rocks, where we can find hikes and snorkel sites, and where we can find restaurants and places to re-provision.

Here's what we read in our cruising guide that drew us to spend a week in Bahía Agua Verde:

> *The beautiful, protected waters of Bahía Agua Verde, together with the dramatic backdrop of the Sierra de la Giganta range, have long been a popular destination for boaters. The bay has good snorkeling and diving as well as excellent hiking along the various goat trails and dirt roads leading to the highway. This small fishing village is connected to Mexico Highway 1 by a 25-mile dirt road. The village supports two small* tiendas, *a school, a couple of restaurants, and a goat dairy. When approaching Agua Verde from the south, use caution near Punta San Marte and Punta San Marcial as dangerous reefs*

are found off the points. San Marcial Reef lies 1 mile northeast from Punta San Marcial and is marked with a framework light tower. The reef extends northwest to southeast with a large portion of it submerged. ... For northerly wind protection, anchorage can be taken in the northwestmost portion of the bay, tucked up near the low sand spit which connects Punta San Paquel to mainland Baja. Depths range from 18 to 48 feet over mostly sand.

THE HIGHLIGHT

We lingered in Bahía Agua Verde, México over a week because it truly lives up to the expectation set by the cruising guide. We hiked to see cave paintings. We chatted with the locals. We snorkeled. And best of all, friends whom we first met in Cabo, then again in Los Frailes, Los Muertos, and La Paz, caught up again with us here. It was nice to spend a couple days with them, venting about failed boat projects, exploring the village, and watching baby dolphins learn to fish.

THE ENTERTAINMENT

"I've run out of reading material, so I've been reading the Apple User Agreement," Andrés mentioned to our buddy boat friends, Sam and Jesica on *Hariya*. They must have recognized the desperation in his voice and graciously showed up to *Ana María* the next day bearing John Kretschmer's *Sailing a Serious Ocean*. John Kretschmer is a crazy yacht-delivery captain whom people pay to take them sailing in hurricanes, gales, and ocean crossings. We read aloud his stories and trembled at his accounts of sinking boats, grounded boats, and holding onto boats for dear life. Once finished, we moved on to the short stories of Kipling's *The Jungle Book* with its similarly riveting adventures that, thankfully, feel a little less close to home for us.

THE WILDLIFE

This is manta ray country. Watching the rays spring from the surface and do a triple backflip before quickly disappearing below reminds me of watching the Olympic gymnasts compete on the vault, their movements at once powerful yet seemingly effortless. Unlike whales or dolphins, they don't tend to surface more than once in the same place, so it's always a treat to catch a glimpse of their marine gymnastics.

THE GALLEY

"*¿Tiene queso de cabra?*" I mustered the courage to ask the smiling lady at the *tienda* counter. We had spent the morning hiking the goat trails in Agua Verde. If the fresh scat on the trails was any indication, I thought we might be able to score some fresh goat cheese for today's afternoon snack.

"*Sí! Sí! Claro!*" She turned to a cooler, pulled out a hunk of white semi-soft cheese, cut us a slab, and handed it to us, double-bagged and unlabeled.

We learned of the "excellent" goat cheese from our cruising guide, but every time we asked fellow cruisers, the reviews were not as favorable. "Um ... well ... I'd say the cheese is an acquired taste." "Eating that unpasteurized cheese gave me the worst bout of food poisoning I've ever had."

Naturally, we were both hesitant and excited to try the cheese when back on *Ana María*. We spread fruit jam on a cornmeal cracker and topped it with a piece. We tasted it, wondering just how many bites it would take before we acquired the taste. Turns out, one bite was enough. It tasted like a sharp queso fresco. *¡Delicioso!*

We were back inside the boat, monitoring our tummies for early signs of food poisoning (thankfully none ever came!) and cooking dinner when we heard a woman on a neighboring boat call to her husband and dog on the beach nearby. "Ted! Ted! There's a herd of goats coming your way. Watch the dog!"

We scrambled out of the companionway and looked for the herd. Sure enough, we heard the tinkling bells around their necks before we saw 30 of them come out of a tunnel in the hill, climb along the cliffs in a single-file line, and navigate the big boulders and patches of scree with ease. We watched them forage in the desert bushes as they climbed the hill for their nightly meanderings in the mountains.

THE CHALLENGE

We use a satellite phone to check in once daily with our parents via 80-character text messages. Unfortunately, these are the texts we received this past month from my parents:

"Dad in hospital. Emergency surgery. Blood clot in leg."

"No surgery for Dad. Blood clot not moving. Dr not sure why."

"Blood clot stuck due to inflamed lymph nodes. Will do lymph node biopsy."

"LYMPHOMA. PET scan and bone marrow biopsy to see how far it's spread."

"Lymphoma stage 2 maybe 4. Chemo starts Wednesday."

These are terrible texts to receive when you're 1,338 miles away from your family.

While it is spectacular here, it is hard to be here when they are there.

But my husband is here. Our dream is here. The fruit of our long, arduous labor is here.

But … my parents are there. Their fear is there. Their suffering is there.

I spent the month torn. Should I be here? Should I be there?

I spent the month with half of my heart in the Sea of Cortez and half of my heart in Springfield, Missouri.

THE HORIZON

In the end, I decided to split my time between here and there. I plan to fly back to Springfield to be with my parents for my dad's second round of chemo. When I get back, we'll continue to sail north to spend the summer in the remote northern tip of the Sea of Cortez.

Wishing you fair winds, following seas, and a renewed sense of hope this Easter season,

Katherine

P.S. We turned on the iPhone the morning after it went for a swim and it works better than ever. Can you believe it?!

Caleta Ramada, Baja California Sur, México
26° 22' 52" N 111° 25' 51" W

San Juanico, Baja California Sur, México
26° 22' 08" N 111° 25' 50" W

Bahía la Salina, Baja California Sur, México
25° 59' 24" N 111° 06' 15" W

Puerto Escondido, Baja California Sur, México
25º 49' 40" N 111° 18' 41" W

VOLUME 1, ISSUE 8: ON YOUR MARK. GET SET. GO!

May 12, 2022
San Juanico, Baja California Sur, México
26° 22' 08" N 111° 25' 50" W
Winds: N 22 knots
Weather: 86°F Sunny, getting hotter by the minute

It's 4:45 a.m., dark enough still to see all the stars in the night sky. No one is stirring in the six other sailboats with us in the anchorage. Not even the bay's resident pelicans have awakened to start the frantic fishing they'll do all day.

Yet we crawl out of bed and begin to prep for battle.

We have a 50-nautical-mile sail ahead of us, the longest sail we've done since January. A 50-mile sail is particularly tough because, with our average speed of 4 knots, we'll have to sail for at least 12 hours. We only have 13 hours of good daylight, so if we dillydally our way north, we'll be anchoring in a poorly charted area in the dark, definitely not fun and potentially dangerous.

Andrés has studied every weather forecast model, and we've decided that today is the day to make the jump. We're up early so we can sail with the last bit of the Coromuels, the nightly westerly winds. We'll motor a bit while the wind clocks around to the south, then we'll fly the spinnaker as the wind builds. Once the winds get strong, we'll pull down the spinnaker and sail wing-on-wing (mainsail to leeward and genoa pulled out with the whisker pole to windward). All the forecasts say we'll have 22 knots behind us for the entire afternoon, so we should practically fly all the way to Bahía Concepción.

Like any good sailor, however, we don't trust the wind to behave as the forecast predicts. In our sail a few days ago, the wind bucked against the puny forecasts and showed up 25 knots strong with 5-foot steep waves. With our complicated lunch planned, our reliable but weak autopilot in place, and our wing-on-wing equipment buried deep in a locker, we felt like we showed up with a knife to a gunfight. "Oh, so you thought you were just out for an afternoon cruise?" The wind taunted us with each dousing of salt water across the side of the boat.

Today we brought out the big guns: Dramamine to head off seasickness, our hefty offshore autopilot, a quick sandwich lunch, and all sailing equipment at the ready. We will not let the wind beat us today just because we've underestimated it. *Ana María* is prepped for 30-knot winds. We're determined to make the most of the strong winds and sail the vast majority of the 50 miles.

Unfortunately, we're off to a disappointing start. The Coromuel winds we planned to ride out of here are a no-show. Oh well. Not a big deal. We'll just motor one more hour than we planned.

We've been motoring for almost an hour when I catch a glimpse of a mast behind us. Must have been one of the other sailboats in our anchorage. I keep an eye on it for the next hour as it quickly gains on us. We're making a steady 4.3-knot progress at our fuel-optimizing 2000 rpm. An hour later, the sailboat passes us, and I see its name, *Tutui*, and its husband-and-wife crew. It's at least a 36-footer and burning more fuel than we are. I itch to rev the engine up a bit so we're not left trailing them. Then I remember the "fun" of performing engine oil changes and hand-carrying jugs of diesel to the boat. I sit back and try to let it go as I watch them pass us.

It's not long before we begin to close the distance, so we pull out our binoculars to see what they're up to. We see white sails going up! They've found the beginning of the wind and have started to sail.

The wind hasn't quite filled in for us yet, but we decide to start the long process of raising the spinnaker. By the time we get her flying, we'll have reached the wind. We methodically work our way through the steps, and, thanks to good coordination, we are flying the huge red, white, and blue sail in no time.

The conditions are great: a steady 7 knots of wind to fill the sail and no waves forming speed bumps yet. We're cruising along at 4.5 knots, faster than we normally motor, and we're catching up to *Tutui*.

As we pass them, we can almost hear the wife ask, "Honey, why is that small boat going faster than us with only one sail?" We imagine him muttering in response, "I thought this was a gentleman's white-sail-only race. But there they go, flying that colorful spinnaker, the cheaters."

We study our opponents. They're in the same battle with the wind, but they have slightly different weapons at their disposal. Winds are light enough that, if they had a spinnaker, they'd probably be flying it. Our spinnaker gives us an advantage in light wind races.

Life is not a race. We're not racers. We strictly cruise. Today's sail is not a race ... or at least it wasn't.

Suddenly today is no longer just about sailing. Today is about sailing faster!

Now we're racing and we can feel the adrenaline start to course through our veins as we adjust our sails and look to our starboard side to monitor *Tutui*'s progress. We're pretty much neck and neck, like horses at the Kentucky Derby, as the wind starts to build and our keels gain traction in the ocean's motion. As *Tutui* sails 200 feet from our beam, we watch confused as she starts to slow down. The man hops out of the cockpit and up to the foredeck. Are they trying to fix a problem? Only moments later we see a whisker pole pop out windward. He heads back to the cockpit, and they unfurl the genoa to windward. They get a burst of speed as the wind fills both their genoa and their mainsail in a wing-on-wing configuration.

Both boats settle into a course, and we watch each other carefully. With our lighter-material spinnaker sail up in these lighter winds, we estimate we're going 0.1 knot faster than *Tutui*. It seems like every 15 minutes we gain about a foot on them.

We're sailing with the rocky coast of the Baja Peninsula only a couple miles off our port side. It's obvious we're both trying to clear Punta Concepción before rounding the point and taking refuge in Bahía Concepción. With the point as our goal, the treacherous shoreline that is a formidable obstacle to our left, and the wind coming directly from behind us both, this race is all about wind angle.

The wind is almost exactly 180° off the point. Neither of us can sail at 180°. *Tutui*'s wing-on-wing setup can get them probably to 150°, but it also means they have a mainsail and boom out. If they get too close to 180°, the wind could clock around the stern to back the mainsail, slamming the boom to the other side of the boat, jibing the boat, and causing damage to their rig and crew.

We're flying under the spinnaker alone with our boom sheeted tightly in the center of the boat. We know from experimentation that we can reliably sail at 175° with close monitoring. A jibe for us could mean damaging the spinnaker, but in this wind, if we watch carefully, we will see the spinnaker collapse before *Ana María* jibes. Every couple of minutes we recite our plan: "If she starts to jibe, go fast 30° to starboard." For now, though, even if our speeds are nearly the same, Tutui's angle to Punta Concepción is probably 20° worse than ours.

We spend the next hour watching the sails and the wind angle like hawks. Forecasts predict the wind will shift to the east throughout the day. We're both fast on the trigger with any degree of wind shift. "Go 2° downwind please." "Aye, aye, Cap'n" becomes our refrain, repeated every couple of minutes. Each degree of shift in the wind is matched with a shift in our tiller. We get a little aggressive from time to time and watch the sail collapse, so we head back upwind until the spinnaker fills again.

They're being aggressive as well. We keep looking back, studying their course against the wind angle. They must be sailing at 170°! "Look how far downwind they're sailing. So close! There's no way they aren't on the cusp of a jibe." The woman must be pleading in vain, "Come on, Honey. Let's head upwind. Our rig is not worth losing just to win this race." We watch as their mainsail starts to flutter, a sign they're dangerously close to an accidental jibe. They must have seen it too because they resign to a controlled safety jibe, heading offshore, losing their great angle toward Punta Concepción. They may have speed now, but they're not heading in the right direction.

Confident in our lead, we give our tiller a break from our micromanagement and relax a bit. That is until the wind starts to pick up just as forecasted. The spinnaker gives us a great course to Punta Concepción, but it has its limits. If we leave it up too long, it gets dangerous to take down and we risk ripping the sail into shreds. We start to see 20 knots of true wind and concede that we don't want to lose the spinnaker just to win this unofficial race. It's time for a sail change.

We dread the sail change because it's gonna take forever. We have to douse the spinnaker, bring down the spinnaker, coil all the lines so they don't catch in the prop, turn on the engine, turn around to motor directly into the wind, raise the mainsail, turn back downwind, trim the main, set up the whisker pole for wing-on-wing, and unfurl the genoa to windward. *Tutui* just jibed again, so while we do all of that, we're going to be eating their dust. They're headed straight for the point, making 4.5 knots while we putter around with the sails.

The sail change goes off without a hitch and soon we are trailing them toward the point. They're on a better course, but we're still crossing our fingers for the wind to shift to the east. An easterly wind would force them to jibe again and put us on the inside track.

Instead of shifting, the wind ... dies. It just dies. Instead of the 22 knots on our beam forecasted for 3:00 p.m., we have a dismal 4 knots behind us. We're headed away from the point at a leisurely 1.7 knots. Maybe it's a fluke. Sometimes the wind dies right before the wind shifts. Maybe that's what's happening. Unfortunately, though the wind has disappeared, the seas have shown up in full force. Every time we gain a bit of speed, a set of three 4-foot-high waves crash into our stern, sending us spinning and drastically slowing us down.

The wind we prepared to battle all day, the wind that was supposed to propel us easily into Bahía Concepción, is nowhere to be seen. All that hype and nothing to show for it. I go down into the galley to make the teriyaki sauce for dinner and try to take my mind off the frustrating situation.

"Hey!" Andrés calls from the cockpit. "They're speeding up!" I climb up with the binoculars so we can see more clearly. Did we make a tactical mistake? Is there some kind of bizarre wind close to shore where they are?

Nope! We watch in the binoculars as they take down their sails. They've turned on their engine and are motoring straight for the point. Cheaters, cheaters, pumpkin-eaters! So much for racing for pink slips. We didn't want their stupid boat anyway.

With the motion of the boat getting worse, no wind on the horizon, and our competitors forfeiting the race, do we continue our disappointing battle with the wind, or do we, too, throw in the towel?

We seem to have reached a stalemate with the wind. What's the wind scheming? Has it given up? Or is it just waiting for us to let our guard down?

We look at the forecasts we downloaded this morning. None of them predicted this. We look behind us. Thankfully, we see fewer whitecaps, which means the waves and swells are beginning to subside. Unfortunately, this also indicates there's not much wind behind us.

Can we make it to the anchorage in the daylight if we keep sailing? We do the calculations. With the smoother seas, we're averaging 2.5 knots. If we can keep this speed, we'll crawl into the anchorage at 7:50 p.m. and still have 20 minutes of light to anchor. It's close, but it's not the closest we've ever cut it.

"What if I make dinner while we're still sailing? We can eat the chicken teriyaki in big bowls in the cockpit then sail into the anchorage." Andrés likes my suggestion but wonders if we should take down the wing-on-wing and fly the spinnaker again.

More calculations. We'd gain a half knot of speed, but we'd lose around 20 minutes in the sail change. The spinnaker would save us 20 minutes total, not a convincing argument for the energy-zapping spinnaker, especially at the end of a long day.

"Yeah, and we are about to go around Punta Concepción," Andrés notes. "The wind always does weird things around a point. Wing-on-wing gives us more flexibility to respond to whatever the wind throws at us."

I head back down into the galley to finish dinner as we sail wing-on-wing toward the point. The wind picks up a bit, so *Ana María*'s motion improves as I dice the chicken below. "We're picking up speed. 3 knots ... 3.1 ... 3.5 ..." Andrés calls from the cockpit. "I'll need your help to jibe the boat in probably 20 minutes ... well 15. Maybe 10?" I quicken the pace of my chopping so I can have the chicken in a place where I can safely abandon it to jibe.

Within five minutes, we pass Punta Concepción, and I chuck the chicken into the pan on the gimballed stove.

We quickly furl the genoa from the cockpit then go forward to lower the whisker pole and set it up on the other side. We can feel *Ana María*'s speed increase even under the power of the mainsail alone. The wind must be picking up. We raise the whisker pole on the other side, securing the fore- and after-guy to keep it stable while we jibe the main.

It's hard to center the main under the increased wind, but we manage to jibe the mainsail safely and without much pull on the rig. We unfurl the genoa to windward, and I skedaddle down below to finish dinner.

"With this wind, we have an hour before we need to take down the mainsail to anchor," Andrés says. That gives me plenty of time to sauté the chicken and veggies and steam the rice. We'll have dinner and be ready to anchor. Perfect timing.

I've just put the rice to simmer when I feel the boat heel before I even hear Andrés' report from above. "The wind's picked up. I'm seeing 20 knots of wind. We're flying at 6 knots now. We may only have half an hour until we anch...woah! Just saw 7.1 knots. Maybe only 20 minutes."

We've rounded the point and whoosh! The wind fills in behind us at the perfect angle. We're averaging 7.5 knots with an occasional 8 knots popping up on the knot meter.

I rush to throw the rice into bowls and top it with the teriyaki chicken and vegetables. With only 10 minutes left before we have to anchor, I hand a bowl to Andrés and tell him to go ahead and start eating while I crawl up into the cockpit.

We scarf down our food while we scope out the anchorage. Five boats have already settled in for the night, and we have a boat on our starboard side coming in from the north. We're galloping toward the anchorage at 8 knots, and if we don't take down the sails RIGHT NOW, we will beach this boat.

We throw our half-eaten dinners into the sink and rush to furl the genoa. We don't have time to take down the whisker pole. Andrés winches the mainsail into the center of the boat as he heads upwind. I climb up to the mast to set up the lazy jacks. As soon as they're secure, I yell back to the cockpit, "I'm ready!" "Okay! Going to loosen the mainsheet then drop the main halyard. Watch the boom!" I hold onto our granny bars at the mast and wait to see the sail drop and lose power. "Boom is secure!" He gives me the signal that it's okay to move aft. I hold fast to the boom and pull the mainsail all the way down, so it flakes inside the lazy jacks while he turns the boat back downwind.

It's only 6:00 p.m., so we have plenty of light to see the sandy bottom. Content with our chosen spot, we drop the anchor, set it well, and take a deep breath.

We did it! We sailed 42 of the 50 miles! AND we're here safe AND with two hours of daylight to spare AND probably only 30 minutes behind that cheater boat.

It wasn't the battle we'd been expecting. The day was much more about patience and tactics than hand-to-hand combat with the wind and seas, but we won. We finish our lukewarm dinner, immensely satisfied with our day, our teamwork, and our performance.

THE LINGO

The "no-go zone" is probably unfamiliar if you've spent most of your days on the water in a powerboat. In a powerboat, you turn on the engine and point the boat in the direction you want to go. You throttle up, you throttle down, turn right, and turn left at your whim.

On a sailboat, however, the wind is king. The wind does not bend to one's will. It does whatever it wants. It shifts. It dies. It builds. And we just have to deal with whatever it throws at us.

The sails can only use the wind at certain angles to propel the boat forward. If the wind is coming from directly in front of the boat, the sails can't catch the wind and they flap violently, leaving us dead in the water or "stuck in irons." The front or bow of the boat has to be pointed at least 30° to either side of the source of the wind before the sails fill and the boat moves. If, heaven forbid, the wind is coming from our desired destination, then we have to point 30° left or right of our destination. We sail awhile and then turn the front of the boat to cross the wind and go 30° to the other side. These 30° on either side of the wind source become the "no-go zone" because while in it, we no-go anywhere.

Our boat loves to sail when the wind comes from the side or beam of our boat at 90°. She also sails well when the wind comes from behind the boat (90° to 150°). If the wind starts to come more directly from behind (close to 180°), then we get into a smaller no-go zone. Wind from behind still fills the sails, but at any moment, the wind could shift and backwind the mainsail. If the wind catches the mainsail from the other side, it'll push the mainsail and boom across the boat with huge force. This is called an accidental jibe. It's terrible for the rigging that holds the mast on the boat, and it's incredibly dangerous for any crew member's head who happens to be in its way.

THE HIGHLIGHT

Puerto Escondido, Baja California Sur, México
25° 49' 40" N 111° 18' 41" W

I spend a lot of my life trying to keep up with my husband. I didn't realize exactly how true that is until I wrote it just now. It hasn't always worked out for me: I have a broken elbow and leg to show for two failed attempts. But 99 percent of the time, by following him, I wind up in astonishingly beautiful places I would never have explored on my own.

I was nervous when he mentioned wanting to climb Steinbeck Canyon while in Puerto Escondido. Known as Tabor Canyon by the locals, gringos know it as the canyon where John Steinbeck and biologist Ed Ricketts were taken by locals to hunt bighorn sheep during their 1940 expedition detailed in Steinbeck's *Log from the Sea of Cortez*. The hike is classified as a Class 3 Scramble, and I hesitated after hearing the trip report from our friend Rob. "There are ropes you have to climb, and they're sketch! But you have to use the rope. I made it to the third rope." Third of how many? I wondered.

"Yeah, AllTrails says the ropes are kind of sketch, but I only want to make it up to the pools after the third rope. It's only four miles. We don't have to go the full six," Andrés tries to reassure me.

He really wants to do it, and I don't want to hold him back, so we set out early one morning for the pools after the third rope. We walk on dusty burro trails for two miles before arriving at the canyon. For 3 miles, we follow the cairns set every 50 feet or so. We're accustomed to the groomed trails in the Cascade Mountains, which are quite different from bouldering up canyons. Here we have to use our whole bodies to climb, pulling up to the tops of the boulders, exercising our triceps to push up to the next level of rock.

We arrive at a spot where we see no way to continue. We look around, trying on the left side, then the right. Dead ends. Then we see a rope hanging from one of the boulders. We found the first rope!

The first one isn't bad, not much longer or more difficult to scale than a rope on a children's playground.

We haven't climbed far when we come across the second rope. This one is way more challenging, involving a U-shaped climb across logs propped up to give footholds. It takes me five minutes full of coaching from Andrés and some pauses and deep breaths to grab hold of the rock at the top. I glance down 20 feet below to the bottom and feel nauseous. "Even my heart was racing on that one," Andrés admits. A quarter mile later, we reach the third rope, which is thankfully not as daunting as the second.

We hike half a mile before we start hearing frogs. Frogs! We've been hiking for four miles in a dry dusty canyon. Frogs must mean fresh water! Sure enough, we can see palm trees up ahead.

Pushing ourselves up on boulder after boulder, we finally see them: pools of fresh water! The cool water looks so inviting after our sweaty climb up. We haven't seen anyone else on the trail, but we listen for voices behind us anyway. Not a peep. We're all alone up here, so we strip off our clothes and slide into the rock pool. The bottom of the pool is slippery, but the cold water feels divine. We soak up all the refreshment we can get before we start our climb back down.

THE CHALLENGE

Food poisoning from the nachos we ate after we finished the Steinbeck Canyon hike knocked us both off our feet for several days.

THE GALLEY

Caleta Ramada, Baja California Sur, México
26° 22' 52" N 111° 25' 51"W

"G'morning! You want some fish for lunch?" Andrés is making us French toast for breakfast in our deserted anchorage. We're the only boat in Caleta Ramada, and we're alone save the VW van camping on the beach. Andrés is quite surprised to look out the galley portlight to see the man in a kayak making the offer.

We scramble out to the cockpit to see what we're in for and are delighted to meet Roger, the VW camper, fishing from his green Hobie kayak. While we were sleeping in, Roger was up and peddling the kayak around the bay, catching the five colorful fish now sitting under his legs. One of the fish hasn't quite given up yet and is thrashing around the bottom of the kayak. "This one here gave me quite the fight. It towed me around the bay for a good while before I could bring him up. So, which one do you want?"

I stare at the fish, unfamiliar with all of them. His offer is generous, but I have no idea what I'm going to do once we accept his gift. My copy of *The Boat Galley Cookbook* explains how to filet a fish, so I guess I'll start with that. Surely we can figure it out from the instructions. But the blood, all that bright red sticky blood running all over the pristine white gelcoat Andrés just washed. This is not going to be pretty.

"Any of them are fine, thanks! But, I just, um ... I've never made a whole fish before," I admit. "How do I, you know, do it?" Some people would have rolled their eyes and regretted their offer, knowing this girl surely can't appreciate what a special gift this is, but not Roger.

Roger whips out his knife and teaches us how to prep the fish and cook it. "First you gut it," he starts. As he shows us, he explains he's from a "holler in West Virginia." No wonder I like him; we're both just two hillbillies who've somehow found their way to the sea. He pulls out things from the fish that we don't recognize, douses the fish in the salt water, and continues with his story of his enlistment in the Navy. It was while he was stationed in Long Beach that he fell in love with a little Catalina sailboat. "So, I call up my cousin in West Virginia and say, 'Man you gotta come out here so we can learn to sail,'" he goes on as he flips the knife and starts to scale the bright orange fish. He recounts his adventures of breaking moorings during a sea trial on Catalina Island and of sailing in the Baja Haha Rally down the Baja Coast.

He takes a break from his stories to paddle toward his Mexican street dog Pico, who is attempting to swim the half mile from the beach to meet Roger. Roger comes back with our fish still in hand. Pico sits patiently at the bow of the kayak while Roger teaches me how to make diagonal slits on the belly of the fish. "Now what you really want to do is go to the beach, build a bonfire, let the fire burn down a bit, and put the fish on the coals. Put some salt and pepper on it and cook it 10 minutes on each side." With those directions, we extend a bucket into which Roger plops our prepared lunch. In exchange for the fish, we send Roger on his way with a bar of Theo dark chocolate from Seattle. We wave as he peddles away, promising to keep in touch.

By the time lunch rolls around, we're too impatient and hungry to build a fire on the beach so we settle for the grill. We're setting up the propane grill when we see the problem: this huge fish may not fit on our tiny 12" x 9" grill. We position the fish on the diagonal and laugh as we see the fish tail stick out of the back of the grill. Twenty minutes later, we're feasting on deliciously tender fresh fish. What a treat, both the man and the fish!

THE WILDLIFE

Bahía la Salina, Baja California Sur, México
25° 59' 24" N 111° 06' 15" W

We pick a calm day to snorkel the wreck of a 200-foot fishing boat that sank on the shoals of Salinas on Isla Carmen. We're astounded by the sheer number of fish filling and surrounding the wreck. There are literally tens of thousands of fish swimming all around us. I look down at the brown rusting hull, which looks like a giant sardine can, packed to the brim with little brown fish constantly wiggling and rearranging themselves in the tight compartment.

The snorkeling is so good that, though Andrés has finished, I decide to make one more pass along the wreck before we leave. I'm so enthralled with the sights below that I am oblivious to the action going on at the surface. I arrive back at the kayak and see Andrés sitting stiffly and looking behind me. I twist in the water and see a small powerboat only 30 feet away from us. I didn't feel or hear it come up, but I can still see the wake settling behind it so it must have arrived fast.

I listen to Andrés speak in Spanish to the three men, but I only pick out the word *pistola*. Pistol? Gun? Did they drop a gun and want me to dive for it? I'm not that good of a swimmer. Then I see their hands are all resting on the holsters of their own big handguns. My heart starts to beat a little faster. The exchange continues, brief questions from the men, brief responses from Andrés. Apparently, whatever it was has been resolved. They wave and speed away.

"What was that all about?" I ask when they're out of earshot.

"They're federal fishing game wardens. They saw us here at the wreck from far away and came to see if we were spearfishing. Spearfishing is illegal for gringos. I told them over and over we don't have any spearguns and that we're just snorkeling. I think they thought the kayak paddles were spearguns."

Phew! Glad that encounter didn't involve their guns, but I am grateful this beautiful wildlife is actively protected.

THE ENTERTAINMENT

San Juanico, Baja California Sur, México
26° 22' 08" N 111° 25' 50" W

Most boat manufacturers try to sell you a boat using images of an expansive cockpit table, covered in delicate appetizers, platters of fresh seafood, and glasses of fine wine. "Buy this boat," they say, "and you can have the ultimate al fresco dining experience. Buy this boat and you can throw the most amazing parties in the marina. Buy this boat and you can host your friends in the most spectacular anchorages."

Not Pacific Seacraft. "Buy this boat and you can safely cross the most treacherous oceans," they promise. Pacific Seacraft manufactured *Ana María* to care for her crew during rough ocean passages, so she has a small, protected cockpit, with no room for a cockpit table installed for the frivolous purpose of impressing your friends. Still, during her refit, I held onto the dream of eating fancy meals outside in the cockpit while anchored in picturesque bays. When Andrés decided to replace the wooden hatchboards that serve as the companionway door between the cockpit and the cabin, I was thrilled to hear him announce, "I can redesign the hatchboards so they convert into a cockpit table."

Andrés used 3D design software he knows, *Rhino 3D*, to design custom hatchboards that fit precisely into the oddly shaped doorframe, feature a Lexan polycarbonate resin thermoplastic window to allow natural light into the cabin, and, yes, convert into a cockpit table. He used a CNC machine and laser cutter to fabricate the design from the *Rhino 3D* model. A couple days after his announcement, *Ana María* had a custom-built door and my dreams of al fresco dining had become a reality.

This cockpit table has provided front-row seats to some spectacular sights, often delivering both dinner and a show. Last Fourth of July, we ate grilled hamburgers and watched a young bald eagle learn to hunt in a bay in Washington's San Juan Islands. This morning, I sat for hours at the cockpit table, sipping coffee, nibbling on cinnamon toast, and watching thousands of blue-footed boobies as they fished for their own breakfast. These birds dive from great heights, their beaks aimed like an arrow directly at the water. *SPLASH!* They disappear from view for only a second before they return to the surface with fish in their beaks, furiously flap their wings to take off again, circle the school of fish from above, and dive once more. *SPLASH! SPLASH, SPLASH, SPLASH!* This bay must be their equivalent of an all-you-can-eat buffet. It's hard to turn away from the spectacle.

THE HORIZON

Hurricane season starts May 15, so we need to hustle north to the top of the Sea of Cortez to get out of the way of tropical storms. We'll pass through Santa Rosalía before moving up to Bahía de Los Angeles, where we hope to find cooler water and weather.

Fair winds and following seas,

Katherine

P.S. Thank you for all your kind words, texts, and prayers for my dad after the last log. I'm thankful I could be with my parents for round two of his six chemotherapy sessions. They're hanging in there, having just finished round three. We're hopeful for a full recovery.

El Quemado,
Baja California, México
28° 55' 44" N 113° 24' 30" W

Isla Estanque,
Sea of Cortez, México
29° 03' 50" N 113° 05' 45" W

Santa Rosalía,
Baja California Sur, México
27° 20' 13" N 112° 15' 48" W

Posada Concepción,
Baja California Sur, México
26° 45' 29" N 111° 53' 40" W

VOLUME 1, ISSUE 9: ONE DAY IN THE LIFE OF A CRUISING COUPLE

June 19, 2022
Posada Concepción, Baja California Sur, México
26° 45' 29" N 111° 53' 40" W
Winds: N 13 knots
Weather: 103°F Strong sun

"What will you do all day every day?" This question occupied our thoughts before we set off a year ago. When people asked us this, we would look at each other, bewildered. What *would* we do all day, every day, on a sailboat?

We had no idea what to expect, but we figured we'd be sailing every day, tacking and jibing through channels the way we spent our days sailing in the San Juan Islands.

A year later, we know better.

In reality, we only spend one to two days a week sailing. On average, we spend another two days each week doing boat maintenance and cleaning the boat (the inside, the outside, and the underbelly below the water).

The other three or so days, well, today I will give you a peek into a day in the life of a cruising couple.

What follows is an account of an actual day, not necessarily a typical day as we now go several weeks between hints of civilization, though it is not atypical either. It's a day full of working around the constraints of boat life, exploring, suffering the effects of stupid decisions, and soaking in magical delight. It's our life, and so far, we love it.

⚓

IT'S A DAY FULL OF WORKING AROUND THE CONSTRAINTS OF BOAT LIFE, EXPLORING, SUFFERING THE EFFECTS OF STUPID DECISIONS, AND SOAKING IN MAGICAL DELIGHT. IT'S OUR LIFE, AND SO FAR, WE LOVE IT.

7:00   Reveille! It's up and at 'em. Last night, since we were at anchor, we didn't sleep in the spacious bed in the bouncy front of the boat (the v-berth). Instead, we slept in the dining-room-turned-bedroom. Like one does in an RV, we convert our bed back to the dining table. Andrés climbs out of the boat to check the anchor, the wind, and the position of the other boats in the anchorage.

7:30   For breakfast I eat instant oatmeal while he eats cereal with almond milk. "I don't even remember what a banana looks like," he bemoans. We haven't had fresh produce since our last grocery shop, 22 days ago.

8:00   I prep the black beans for lunch. On the boat, a lot of our meal planning and cooking methods are based on the constraints of boat life. Our tightest constraint is trash space. Our goal is to go 28 days between trash drop-offs, but so far, we've only made it to 21. The second constraint, which Andrés enforces with vigor, is boat weight. The heavier the boat, the slower we sail, so it's imperative to stay light. The last constraint is propane. We carry two 30-pound propane tanks, but they're quite difficult to refill. Plus, the more propane we use, the hotter the boat gets. Now that it's over 100°F, we loathe adding any more heat to the boat.

We eat beans almost every day, but canned beans are terrible for the trash and the boat's weight. Cooking dried beans on the stove for an hour would turn the boat into a sauna. Instead, following the instructions I found in *The Boat Galley Cookbook*, I soak the dried beans overnight, bring them to a boil on the stove, then put them into a thermos. Four hours later, we have deliciously cooked beans without adding anything to the trash or adding much heat to the boat.

8:30   Time to drop the kayak into the water and put together our paddles for the trip to shore later.

9:30   Andrés uses our IridiumGo! satellite phone to download weather forecasts. He downloads several different models, and we compare them to strategize for the days ahead. Looks like we can stay here in this anchorage tonight, but we'll need to leave tomorrow morning to get some protection from the southerly wind and waves coming. The twice-daily forecast check is something we didn't foresee would be a daily chore. Every day we must ask ourselves, "Where can we sleep safely and comfortably tonight?"

We also need to start thinking about the month ahead. We need to be in Puerto Peñasco, México, by the end of June. We back into the timeframes so we know when we need to leave Santa Rosalía, when we need to be in Bahía de Los Angeles, etc. We sketch out a rough calendar while keeping in mind the truism, "Cruisers write their plans in the sand at low tide."

10:30   Reading hour. I'm working my way through some meatier books since I have some mental space to ponder. I just finished *Hope in Times of Fear* and am about to start the *New Jim Crow*. Andrés re-reads the watermaker operating manual for the hundredth time, a seeming waste of time that somehow always manages to pay off in the most opportune moments.

11:30   Lunch is spicy black bean tuna salad with the black beans from the thermos and fresh cilantro from the farm in San Juanico.

12:00   Together we hand wash all the lunch dishes. We spend an inordinate amount of time washing dishes.

Andrés sets up the solar shower so we can take hot showers later. *Ana María* had a water heater when we bought her, but the water heater had corroded and was leaking water over the ENGINE BATTERIES! We yanked that sucker out of the boat and looked for another place to install one. We quickly learned why the factory installed the water heater over the batteries ... there is literally nowhere else to fit it on the boat. We decided to sacrifice hot water on the boat for reliable batteries. We use a kettle to heat water on demand, but we use a solar shower to heat water for our showers. It's a 5-gallon black bag that traps heat when we put it out in the sun. After only a couple of hours, the water is heated enough for a warm shower.

12:30 We plan to spend the rest of the day onshore doing a variety of excursions, so we start to pack up the kayak with seats, our hiking backpack, our water bottles, snorkeling gear, the sail for the kayak, money for dinner ashore, snacks, and lots of sunscreen.

13:00 Finally we have everything ready to go, so we hop into the kayak and set up the sail. We're in dangerous territory, not because of the sea but because of the task: One Person Steering the Kayak + One Person Wrestling with the Sail + 3-foot Waves + 18 knots of Wind = Instant Conflict. We wonder aloud if we fight more than the average couple because we have two strong personalities ("as iron sharpens iron") or if marriage wasn't designed to withstand daily tandem kayak trips. After briefly considering giving up and heading back to the boat, we apologize, make peace, and get the sail and kayak pointed in the right direction.

It turns out to be an exhilarating ride! We surf the 3-foot seas in the kayak, covering the 4 nautical miles to Burro Beach in no time with only a couple of strokes of the paddle to steer. We round the point flying at 5 knots, faster than we typical sail on the sailboat, and nearly crash land on the beach.

WE WONDER ALOUD IF WE FIGHT MORE THAN THE AVERAGE COUPLE BECAUSE WE HAVE TWO STRONG PERSONALITIES OR IF MARRIAGE WASN'T DESIGNED TO WITHSTAND DAILY TANDEM KAYAK TRIPS.

13:30 Up the "Zick-Zak" hike we go with Bell Rock as our destination. As we hike, we knock on the reddish-brown rocks that ring like bells due to the high concentration of iron. The hike is brutal, the heat unbearable. I struggle up the switchbacks but make it to the top slowly, with frequent water breaks and vows to never ever hike at this time of day again. The view is worth the climb. At the top of Bell Rock, we're treated to a panoramic view of the bay and *Ana María* tucked into one of the anchorages below.

14:30 On the hike down, we look for the Amerindian petroglyphs that supposedly line the trail but are disappointed not to spot any. We hike above Hwy 1 and are surprised by the lack of traffic. We count two cars per minute on the only paved road from Tijuana to Cabo San Lucas. We thought we were in a remote location, but now we really feel it.

15:00 In search of some bananas for Andrés' breakfast, we explore JC's, which turns out to be a combination restaurant, fire station, and library. No produce though. Andrés asks the owner if there's a *tienda* nearby.

15:10 We head toward the *tienda*, walking in the brush to avoid the highway traffic. It's a great time for a mini-Spanish lesson for me. Andrés' encounter with the owner of JC's just now included some very useful phrases, so I make him replay his conversation so I can learn. He recounts it, but all I hear is "blah blah blah." *"¿Puedes hablar más despacio?"* He slows down, and for the next 10 minutes, he breaks the phrases into pieces I can manage. I repeat, he corrects, until finally I can mimic his earlier conversation: *"¿Lo puedo hacer una pregunta? ¿Sabe si hay una tienda en esta autopista?"*

15:20 This *tienda* is a treasure! Coolers are filled with Cokes and vegetables. Shelves have bread (only half the loaves have already expired), lots of snacks and chips, and fresh tortillas from Santa Rosalía. We buy bottles of Pedialyte and Coca-Cola (both cold!), limes, bread, and syrup for French toast tomorrow. I mess up when I try to say, "Have a nice day!" to the cashier, but my botched Spanish is received with a smile. We sit outside the *tienda* to sip our drinks and recover from the hike.

15:40   We walk from the *tienda* to Playa el Burro, passing the luxury rental yurts and the many RVs from British Columbia. The houses on the other beach were made of stone, but the houses on this beach are ... well, they're interesting. A reviewer on ActiveCaptain describes the development as "a very friendly anchorage in a bay lined with houses which appear to be primarily made of materials which wouldn't be missed if a storm blew them away." Up close they're clearly well maintained, but they are made of a mishmash of plywood and mesh.

16:00   We had hoped to snorkel, but the wind hasn't died yet, so the surf is too rough for snorkeling to be any fun. Instead, we swim at the beach. Unlike other areas of Baja, this seems to be where Mexicans come to vacation. Except for the RV-ing Canadians, we share the beach with Mexican families. We swim in the waves next to dads teaching their kids to swim, delighted with the giggles as the children surf the waves themselves.

17:00   We get out of the water and let the hot sun dry us off so we can go to dinner.

17:20   Tonight we take a break from the galley and washing dishes to eat at the highly-recommended Bertha's restaurant. We settle into a corner table with a gorgeous view of the beach and our kayak. We watch the kayak like hawks, making sure no one decides they want it more than we do. We order guacamole and the waiter-recommended tacos. We're relaxing to the DJ-mixed Spanish guitar music and waiting for the food when a tiny car with three men pulls up and blocks our gorgeous view. The men sit at a table next to us and we start to talk. They are on a road trip from Tijuana to Cabo and back. Each way takes them about 20 hours, and they've decided to use the time to practice their English. They're friendly, outgoing guys.

   Shortly after we get our food, the waiter brings out a huge bottle of Pacifico beer we didn't order. One of the guys turns to us, "I always love it when I feel welcome in your country, so I want you to feel welcome in mine. Enjoy a beer on me! Cheers!" We clink our bottles with theirs and offer a *¡Salud!* of our own. How nice are they?!

The only downside to their generosity is we must drink the entire thing out of respect *and then* we must kayak four miles back to *Ana María*. We eat our shrimp tacos and gulp our beer.

18:40 It's time to leave Bertha's if we want to make it back to the boat in the daylight. We wave goodbye to our new friends and start to paddle. The paddle back is much harder since we are paddling against the wind that still hasn't died completely, not to mention the beer still gurgling in our tummies.

An older gringo pulls up beside us on his jet ski and asks, "Where are you going?" "We're headed to our boat in Playa Santispac." Our boat isn't really anchored there, but we have a policy to not tell others exactly where our boat is while we are away from it. It's the cruising version of leaving your lights on a timer switch when you go on vacation. The man seems skeptical that we'll make it, but we reassure him that we'll be fine. He offers to tow us back to our boat, a generous offer, but he is oblivious to the fact that his jet ski is spouting water directly into the kayak and swamping us. We politely decline, and he idles beside us as we paddle, kindly telling us where to find the hot springs nearby and letting us know there will be a lunar eclipse tomorrow. Finally, he takes off, and we paddle the rest of the way against the choppy seas.

19:40 We arrive with daylight to spare and notice six new boats in the anchorage, with one anchored uncomfortably close to us. We'll keep an eye on it to make sure it doesn't swing into *Ana María*. The sun was working while we were out playing and the water in the solar shower is now a piping 115°F. Andrés hangs the bag from the mast, leads the hose through the portlight into the head, and sets up the shower curtain. We take turns in the shower, sharing the five gallons of hot water, then dry the shower curtain and wipe down the head to minimize mildew.

20:30 Time to download new forecasts so we can confirm we're still in a safe anchorage. We use the satellite phone to send our parents the once-daily "we're safe" text then sit under the full moon in the cockpit, sipping chilled Abuelita (Mexican cinnamon-spiced hot chocolate), eating cookies, and reading aloud to each other from the *Bird Way* by Jennifer Ackerman.

21:30 To ensure a boat doesn't run into us in the night, we flip on the anchor light at the top of our mast before brushing our teeth and converting the dining table back into our bed for the night.

22:00 We pray the prayer Andrés has prayed since he was a little boy in Medellín: *"Ángel de mi guarda, mi dulce compañía, no nos desampares ni de noche, ni de día. Hasta que nos dejes en paz y alegría, con todos los angelitos, con Jesús, José, y María. En el nombre del Padre, del Hijo, y del Espíritu Santo. Amen."* We fall asleep with the light of the full moon streaming through the hatches.

THE HIGHLIGHT

Santa Rosalía, Baja California Sur, México
27° 20' 13" N 112° 15' 48" W

Imagine a town with narrow, winding streets, people on every block carefully sweeping their sidewalks shaded by flowering desert trees.

Imagine a town so safe that parents let their little kids walk home from school and play in the streets at dusk.

Imagine a town so amiable that even the marina security guards stop by your table to greet you while you eat your dinner on the patio at the local restaurant.

Imagine a town built by a French copper mining company, full of Mexicans, now run by Koreans.

Imagine a town where, at the turn of the twentieth century, huge sailboats from Hamburg, Germany arrived via Cape Horn to deliver provisions and equipment, before making the 200-day return journey full of copper.

Imagine a town where when you hear the scuffs of tennis shoes against a court floor, you cross the street to follow the sounds and find yourself at a competitive regional basketball tournament.

Imagine a town in rural Mexico where you can attend Mass in a church designed and submitted to the 1889 World's Fair by Eiffel (as in the Tower), then broken into pieces, shipped via sailboat, and reconstructed by the Boleo Mining Company.

Imagine a town that's turned into a television production set, complete with two hundred extras, high-tech production equipment, and a plaza-turned-county-fair scene all for the Netflix show *American Jesus*.

Imagine a town full of people so warm and helpful that when looking for a resistor for your broken voltmeter you head to the local hardware store. The cashier doesn't think they have any, but she brings over the manager to check. Though the store doesn't have the part, the manager says, "There's a customer in the store right now who fixes coffee makers. He might have one. I'll go find him." He quickly returns with the repairman who looks dubiously at the part needing to be replaced. "I don't know that I have one, but I'll look at my house and come by your boat later." Though you doubt you'll ever see him again, two hours later, the friendly marina security guard knocks on your boat: "I have an electrician here to see you." The repairman gives you 10 resistors that might work. You're blown away by the level of service and kindness of strangers.

You've just imagined Santa Rosalía, the best little town in Baja!

THE GALLEY

Have you ever seen the cases of sweet breads or pan dulce in a Latin American supermarket? Pan dulce is said to have become a staple of the Mexican diet when France invaded parts of Mexico under Napoleon. We've tried it once or twice, but we didn't love it until we arrived in Santa Rosalía. The Panadería Boleo Bakery was established in 1901 and has been serving fresh French baguettes and flaky pan dulce ever since. Their treats rival anything you can find in a boulangerie in Paris, and you can't beat the price!

THE ENTERTAINMENT

"Do you want to be on my kayak team on Sunday?" asks Pansho, the marina's front desk guy, when he finds out we're extending our stay in Santa Rosalía due to weather. "Uhhh?" Andrés looks at me, wondering if I've understood what Pansho just asked. "Is it competitive?" Andrés queries. "Oh very!" We're not sure if that's a good thing or a bad thing. I'm not even sure what it means for us to be on "his kayak team," but Andrés agrees for both of us.

It turns out, we're in Santa Rosalía during a weeklong celebration of the Navy, which includes a soccer tournament, a fishing derby, a volleyball game, and a kayak race in the harbor. The various harbor institutions (the marina, the Navy, the Port Authority, etc.) enter teams into the events with cash prizes, and we find ourselves representing the marina. The air buzzes with excitement as a crowd of about 100 people gathers, while the participants grow jittery about this "very competitive" kayak race.

The jovial emcee welcomes everyone to the event: "We've got a great turnout today from the port authority, the technical school, the mining company, and ..." he turns, gesturing toward Andrés and me, "we even have FOREIGNERS!" I've never been introduced quite like that before ... I'm not sure if he's setting high expectations for us or low, but all eyes turn to rest on us as we smile meekly in return.

The mile-long race is more challenging than expected with the wind and current fighting us. The other kayakers seem to have mistaken this for bumper boats, and we get knocked around a bit as our fellow racers get control of their kayaks. We stay balanced and manage to stay in our kayaks the whole time, successfully avoiding a water rescue from the Navy boats standing guard to pull kayakers-turned-swimmers to safety. I come in fifth in my heat, but Andrés finishes fifth overall! He says he didn't want to win and take the cash prizes away from the locals (Uh huh, sure ...).

A good time was had by all!

THE WILDLIFE

El Quemado, Baja California, México
28° 55' 44" N 113° 24' 30" W

"Aaaaa-wooooooooo! Aaa-WOOOOOOOOO!" These days we go to sleep to the sound of howling coyotes. We're in very remote areas, so the coyotes roam the beaches of the anchorages. It's fun to listen to at night, but it makes us a bit skittish on our trips to the beach. Thankfully, we found out on our hike from El Quemado to Ensenada El Pescador that the coyotes are as scared of meeting us on the beach as we are of them.

THE CHALLENGE

Isla Estanque, Sea of Cortez, México
29° 03' 50" N 113° 05' 45" W

The farther north we travel, the fewer well-charted anchorages there are with accurate depth soundings. This makes anchoring quite stressful. After one particularly rocking, sleepless night in San Francisquito, we gave into the temptation of an anchorage called Estanque or the Pond. It promised swell protection from all directions, which persuaded us despite the absence of any reliable charts for the rocky entrance.

We were quite pleased with our entrance into the Pond. We went in at high tide, giving us our best chance at avoiding any rocks. The sun was high and behind us, perfect conditions to practice our tropical navigation skills, so Andrés climbed up the mast to spot the shallow waters from above and direct me to safe areas. When we first started boat work, we weren't exactly stellar communicators, but we eventually learned some key lessons that we put into practice for this situation. We used walkie-talkies to communicate instead of the adrenaline-producing yelling. We worked out a communication protocol: "I'll always tell you the direction to go, not the direction to avoid."

We were feeling pretty snug in our smooth anchorage until we realized, "How are we going to get out of here?" The tides were weakening over the next couple of days, so we wouldn't have the safety of the extremely high tide we had coming in. We also couldn't leave at night the way we entered, otherwise we would sail in the dark to the next anchorage. To mitigate our risk of running aground, we decide to make our own depth-soundings and chart a way to exit.

It doesn't take us long to make a lead line by marking feet on a string and tying it to one of my diving belt weights. We jump in the kayak and trace the path we used to enter the Pond. It's quite scary to see at low tide all the rocks that had been right under our keel as we entered. I'm dropping the weight out of the boat to the bottom and marking the depths so we can find a better way out when "PLOP!" The line and weight slip out of my hands and down to the bottom of the sea. "Make a location mark on your phone!" I yell to Andrés. He marks it and we spend 10 minutes searching for the line in vain.

It's too hard to see the bottom without goggles, so we kayak back. I pull on my wetsuit and snorkel gear, and we head back for the mark showing where I had dropped it. Not a minute later, I spot it and have it back in hand. This view of the underwater topography turns out to be much clearer than the view from the kayak, so we spend an hour with me taking depths in the water and Andrés recording them.

The next day we're ready to leave, confident in the safe-water channel Andrés has created out of the depths we sounded. The channel is marked on our iPad chart plotter, and I get ready to steer through the channel while Andrés climbs the mast as a backup navigation method.

A problem becomes pretty clear pretty quickly: The GPS on the chart plotter doesn't update as fast as we're moving. I'm steering with a significant delay in the position reading. In such a tight channel, that means I am way off course. "PORT! PORT! GO TO PORT!" he screams in the walkie-talkie. "STARBOARD! NOW STARBOARD!" Despite our fancy work to chart an electronic channel, we end up leaving with old-fashioned eyeball navigation and screamed directions. My mouth goes dry when I see in our depth sounder: we only have 6'2" under the waterline and we have 4'1" of boat under us! Thankfully, we manage to slip through the exit without scraping the rocks at the bottom.

THE LINGO

Tropical Weather Outlook from the National Hurricane Center (NHC): The report that tells us whether we are in the path of a tropical storm or hurricane. The NHC publishes an update we can download on our satellite phone. It's a human-generated forecast, not just based on theoretical models, which provides probabilities of cyclone activity evolving into a storm or hurricane over the course of a week. We're already seeing named storms pop up in the outlook, but luckily Agatha, Blas, and Celia have all passed way south of us.

THE HORIZON

I never thought I'd say this, but we're sailing toward Arizona. We're avoiding the tropical storms by sailing as far north in the sea as we can, about 50 miles south of the Arizona border. We plan to haul out the boat and spend hurricane season out of the water, working on the boat, and spending some time with our families.

Fair winds and following seas,

Katherine

● Puerto Peñasco,
Sonora, México
31° 18' 30" N 113° 32' 40" W

● Puerto Refugio,
Isla Ángel de la Guarda,
Sea of Cortez, México
29° 32' 10" N 113° 33' 00" W

VOLUME 1, ISSUE 10: THE OMINOUS SILENCE

June 28, 2022
Puerto Refugio, Isla Ángel de la Guarda, Baja California, México
29° 32' 10" N 113° 33' 00" W
Winds: SE 10 knots
Weather: 105°F HELP! Please send an AC!

After six months of traveling north up the Sea of Cortez, tonight's our last night in the sea. We are in the most remote anchorage we've visited yet. No other boats in sight. We are a hundred miles from the coast in every direction, so we just have to trust that civilization exists out there somewhere.

Tomorrow we will sail the final 120 nautical miles to Puerto Peñasco, where we will put the boat on land during the worst of the hurricane season.

Just in time, too, as weather conditions are deteriorating. Hurricane season here is accompanied by a scary wind phenomenon, the dreaded chubascos. They aren't forecasted like other weather, but thankfully we subscribe to the daily "Chubasco Report," which is sent to our satellite phone each night from a helpful amateur meteorologist/fellow cruiser. Tonight is June 28, and the reports don't start until the risk of chubascos builds on July 1.

The timing of our escape from the sea isn't coincidental. We've heard stories from fellow cruisers who've encountered chubascos in the middle of the night. "We got hit by a chubasco one night. Woke up when the wind hit the boat so hard and fast that we thought another boat had rammed into us." This warning from Dirk and Silvie on *LisonLife* was motivation enough to avoid the Northern Sea of Cortez in late summer.

We sip bedtime tea and download new forecasts. Conditions look good for tomorrow's sail, but the Cape Index for tonight ... well, that's a different story: "The CAPE (Convective Available Potential Energy) Index is an indicator of atmospheric instability, which can lead to showers, thunderstorms, and squalls." Tonight's Cape Index is sky-high, the highest we've ever seen.

Apparently, we're not the only ones who've taken notice. Andrés downloads the emails from the satellite phone, and our hearts start to beat faster as we read "Chubasco Report for Tonight! Well, folks, looks like the chubascos are starting early this year." Groaning, we read the detailed report, a bit relieved that he is forecasting all the activity to roll across the sea to the south of us.

Out of an abundance of caution, we go outside to check on the anchor and make sure everything is shipshape. Outside the air feels strange ... eerie ... like how the air feels the evening before tornadoes strike in the Midwest. Some days in Missouri, you just know you're going to spend the night huddled in shelters and listening to tornado sirens wail. There are no sirens here, and we'll just have to trust we've anchored in safe shelter.

We take extra precautions to put things away, asking ourselves, "What could fall and hit us on the head or cause damage if the chubascos show up?"

I manage to fall asleep but awake at midnight when Andrés climbs out of bed for a drink of water. He stares out the companionway hatch. I watch him, his silhouette illuminated by flashes of lightning.

"What do you see?" I ask groggily.

He keeps his eyes trained on some unseen point.

"Lightning ... and it's coming our way."

He continues to watch the sky then climbs back in bed beside me.

We lie here stiff as boards as if waiting for the boogeyman. As a kid, you know the boogeyman is lurking in the shadows. But maybe, just maybe, if you lie still enough and try not to breathe, he won't detect you.

OUTSIDE THE AIR FEELS STRANGE ... EERIE ... LIKE HOW THE AIR FEELS THE EVENING BEFORE TORNADOES STRIKE IN THE MIDWEST.

But it's not the boogeyman stalking us. It's a force of nature.

Lightning lights up the sky above *Ana María*, yet we are struck by the stillness and the silence.

The ominous silence.

Our skin feels balmy, the static electricity seeps into our pores.

And then the silence is broken.

"Wind," I whisper. Sounds like it is stampeding across the sea. "I can hear it coming."

WHOOOOOOOOOOOOOOOOSH!

The chubasco is here to take us on a ride. Suddenly, *Ana María* transforms into a Tilt-a-Whirl at a carnival. The wind lays the boat down sideways until the chain and anchor are pulled taut.

We get out of bed to turn on the wind instruments and see readings of 35 knots. It must have hit us at 40. We brace ourselves in the boat. The anchor seems to be holding and everything else is staying in place. We whip out a trusty coping mechanism. We verbally rehearse the plan if the anchor starts to drag: "Jump in the cockpit. You do a line check, I'll turn on the engine, put the transmission in forward to take the strain off the anchor."

We wait, transported back to childhood as we estimate how close we are to the storm. Lightning strike. One Mississippi. Two Mississippi. Thunder. The lightning is making its way toward Baja, and the thunder isn't far behind.

As the clock ticks past 1:00 a.m., we watch the gusts slip from 30 knots to 20 knots and finally down to 15. We crawl back to bed, thankful to have survived our first encounter with the chubascos and hopeful we'll never meet again.

THE LINGO

A chubasco is a convection cell or thunderstorm that develops in the afternoons in the Sierra Madre Mountains then moves across the Sea of Cortez in the middle of the night. These cells bring wind gusts up to 60 knots, though 35 knots is average.

THE CHALLENGE

Puerto Peñasco, Sonora, México
31° 18' 30" N 113° 32' 40" W

We hauled *Ana María* out of the water in Puerto Peñasco (aka Arizona's beach) for annual maintenance: new varnish, new bottom paint, polished hull, fixes for everything that's broken. We've done this work before but not in such grueling conditions. The heat index has been 115°F and the UV Index stays stuck on "11." 11?! We didn't even know it went up to 11. We adapted by starting the work by 5:00 a.m. and taking a daily siesta. The work is done, and *Ana María* is now in great shape for another cruising season.

THE WILDLIFE

Stray dogs here. Stray dogs there. Stray dogs everywhere! Peñasco is full of 'em.

THE HIGHLIGHT

My in-laws graciously allowed us to escape the worst of the Mexican summer heat at their home in St. Augustine, Florida. We reveled in a month of quality time with both families, boogie boarding, walks on the beach, high-speed Internet, long showers, and a dishwasher.

THE GALLEY

During our months on land, we ate no Mexican food, beans, or canned tuna. We did eat lots of ice cream, Colombian arepas, and fresh produce.

THE HORIZON

We all made it to Volume 2! We are excited to continue to cruise this year. We plan to meander south along the Baja Peninsula before making bigger passages this winter.

Fair winds and following seas,

Katherine

VOLUME 2

● Puerto Peñasco,
Sonora, México
31° 18' 30" N 113° 32' 40" W

● Bahía Willard,
Baja California, México
29° 48' 55" N 114° 23' 49" W

VOLUME 2, ISSUE 1: THE INCREDIBLE MR. FIX-IT

October 7, 2022
Puerto Peñasco, Sonora, México
31° 18' 30" N 113° 32' 40" W
Winds: N 10 knots
Weather: 90°F Partly cloudy

I married the Incredible Mr. Fix-It.

"All sailing couples have an optimist and a pessimist. Without the optimist, they'd never leave the dock. Without the pessimist, they'd sink as soon as they leave." –Beth Leonard, *A Voyager's Handbook*

Today is the day we've been working toward since July. The day we've been eagerly anticipating. The day *Ana María* finally goes back in the water after being hauled onto land for maintenance.

Today is also the day we've been dreading for a week. The day we see if, when we splash *Ana María*, she still floats after spending the summer in the heat of the Sonoran Desert.

We've had plenty of material for our nightly nightmares this week. Cruisers have told us story after story of seals breaking, O-rings splitting, and

⛵

"ALL SAILING COUPLES HAVE AN OPTIMIST AND A PESSIMIST. WITHOUT THE OPTIMIST, THEY'D NEVER LEAVE THE DOCK. WITHOUT THE PESSIMIST, THEY'D SINK AS SOON AS THEY LEAVE."

–Beth Leonard, *A Voyager's Handbook*

thru-hull sealant melting in the 115°F heat. You don't discover these problems until the boat hits the water. If any of this happens to us, then we have to haul her out again to fix them.

Finally, the moment has arrived. The crane lowers the slings holding *Ana María* into the water. She stays in the slings supported by the crane while we check thru-hulls for leaks. We scamper from thru-hull to thru-hull checking for any sign of water ingress.

Andrés spots two leaks in the cockpit scupper drain thru-hulls, and I find our "dripless" shaft seal is dripping water. A leaking shaft seal could sink the boat or, at the very least, make a huge mess.

Last summer, Helen, our Swiss cruising friend on *Dada Tux*, imparted sound wisdom when I asked her what to do when things go wrong at sea: "Andrés is your captain. Give him the time and space and silence to think. Do what he tells you to do. He'll be able to fix it."

I soon put her guidance into practice when we splashed the boat in Bellingham and caught an air bubble in the engine's raw water intake. I tried to stay quiet. I tried to be patient. I tried to hand him every tool he requested. Sure enough, within the hour he had diagnosed and fixed the airlock.

Now, after analyzing the three leaks we found today, Andrés thinks we have all the tools necessary to fix them while still in the slings. It's worth a shot. We'd hate to put *Ana María* back in storage on land. If we take her out, she might be out another month, and who knows what else could break while she is back on land. Besides, on land without the seawater trying to make its way in, how can we be confident we've fixed the leaks?

We poke our heads out of the engine compartment to see 10 pairs of eyes staring expectantly at us. The crane operators are standing by to take the boat out of the slings. Our friends Tiemo on *Coconut*, Richard on *Leilani*, Stephanie on *Credence*, and Bob and Bonnie on *Scout* are holding our dock lines and standing by, graciously ready to lend us a hand or a tool. The boatyard owner, the always friendly but stoic Salvador Cabrales Sr., is waiting for us to say we're ready to leave.

Andrés calculates the repair time before yelling up to Salvador, "I need to fix some leaks. Can I have an hour in the slings?" Salvador contemplates the request before responding with a relaxed shrug, "Yeah, sure, you can have an hour." He nods to his crane operators to give them a break and casually wanders off.

Having negotiated only one extra hour, we switch from troubleshooting mode to operation mode. Andrés calls out for me to hand him the various scalpels of his trade: "Screwdriver with 9/16-inch hex." "Vice grips." "Rubbing alcohol." "Teflon tape." "Set screws." I scurry about the boat, fetching the items from various tool bags.

I watch him crammed into the back of the tiny engine compartment. It's so hot that sweat drips off his bare back, but it's hard to tell which drips are from the leaks and which are from his perspiration.

He carefully inspects the thru-hulls and valves. He loosens the hose clamps on the scupper hose. With brute strength, he removes the hose from the plastic elbow fitting. Then with vice grips, he twists the elbow off the thru-hull. Just as he expected, the sealant had melted and crumbled, allowing water to seep through.

Watching him work methodically reminds me of our old life on land when he worked as a software programmer. At 11:00 p.m. or 4:00 a.m., he'd get a call from international colleagues, "The servers are down." Frustrated architects in London or Tokyo would impatiently stand by as he worked to diagnose and fix the problem to bring the servers back online. Hunched on the floor, he would rub his chin and then type furiously for a while before tapping "return" to implement his fix. Soon enough, he'd get the servers back to working order and architects around the world would be back to designing their 3D models.

He works as efficiently and effectively today as he did back then. His fingers deftly wrap Teflon tape around the fittings and spread an even coat of sealant paste to seal them. All of his attention, thoughts, and energy concentrate on fixing the problem.

Thirty minutes later, Salvador returns to the crane, a little less casual than his departure. "How's it going? Are you finished? Can we set you loose?" I look at the time, confused. Surely an hour hasn't passed. Nope, only 30 minutes. "Going great. Just need a little more time," I assure him as he checks his watch.

"Hey, Chica!" Our friend Bonnie calls out. She leans a little closer to warn me, "They have another boat waiting to come in, so they are getting stressed waiting. You need to hurry."

I run interference between the onlookers and Andrés, trying to buffer him from the pressure so he can work with a clear mind. I wish I had a zipper so I could physically zip my own mouth shut to stop myself from asking him panicked questions every two minutes. "Are you done? ... what about now?" I muster enough self-control to keep quiet.

Ten minutes later, Salvador appears again. "We have another boat coming in that we need to haul out. Are you finished?"

"Very nearly! He's already fixed two of the three leaks. He's finishing up the last!" I try to portray confidence and ease to Salvador to buy Andrés precious minutes to fix the final leak on the shaft seal.

It is in situations like these that I am so thankful for the partner I have chosen. Right now, my heart is pumping adrenaline throughout my body. My adrenaline comes out in jitters, and I begin to drop things and make mistakes.

In situations like these, Andrés is cool as a cucumber as he carefully but swiftly switches out and tightens the set screws on the shaft seal, effectively ending the persistent drip ... drip ... drip of the seawater into the boat.

Two minutes later, Salvador, clearly close to panic himself, pleads, "There is another boat waiting. I am about to lose my crane operators for the evening. I need you to leave."

Andrés pops out of the engine compartment stressed but triumphant. He has fixed three leaks in 45 minutes, coming in 15 minutes under the hour grace period he was promised.

We close the engine hatch, and we pray the engine starts. Sure enough, she comes alive and purrs sweetly. Salvador gives the order, and the crane operators slip the slings from *Ana María*'s underbelly. Our friends untie the dock lines and hoist them into my waiting arms. We putter slowly and carefully out of the concrete slip and tie to a dock not far away so we can check once more for leaks and clean the salt water off the transmission.

Andrés' fixes look strong and reliable, so we feel confident leaving the Peñasco harbor. We hope to sail through the night back to Bahía Refugio, but we're not quite out of the woods yet. Before we make the 100-nautical-mile jump, we need to ensure the engine works, the sails work, and the watermaker works. Otherwise, it's back to a roach-infested marina and the "thrill" of the shrimp boat/bumper boat rally that is Puerto Peñasco.

We run the engine all the way out of the channel to exit Puerto Peñasco. Everything looks and sounds normal.

We purge the watermaker of its storage pickling compound then taste the water. Tastes delicious.

We hoist the sails and trim them for the close-hauled sail to Refugio. They're working beautifully.

I look to my Captain, the Incredible Mr. Fix-It, and smile.

Engine: check!

Watermaker: check!

Sails: check!

All systems go!

We can sail straight for Bahía Refugio. We don't have to turn back to Peñasco.

We're out of here baby!

I dish up some of the Mediterranean pasta salad I made last night for the passage dinner. We eat here together in the cockpit, our bodies and minds only now starting to relax as we recount the day.

"Man, what a stressful splash," he sighs.

"Yes, incredibly stressful. But I am so incredibly proud of you."

Together we watch the sun set over the Baja Peninsula with the warm wind in our faces as *Ana María* sails at 5 knots toward our destination and I think, *"Home*. After three months of boat work and travel, this ... this feels like home."

THE LINGO

Haul-out: the process of using a crane to pick the boat up out of the water.

Splash: the process of using a crane to put the boat back in the water.

"For a vessel made to be in the water, your boat spends a lot of time on land," remarked our friend Christine. She's right. *Ana María* spent much of her refit years on land.

Now she comes out of the water once a year so we can varnish the teak, repaint the bottom below the waterline, polish the hull, and check the thru-hulls. Thru-hulls are holes in the boat with hoses attached to either allow water to come into the boat, such as to cool the engine, or allow water to drain from the boat. *Ana María* has 19 thru-hulls. A leak in a thru-hull below the waterline can sink the boat.

THE WILDLIFE

Tropical storms bring fresh water to this arid land. Fresh water brings bugs, swarms of them: bobos, no-see-ums, flies, and mosquitoes.

THE GALLEY

We couldn't leave Puerto Peñasco without a working watermaker. When living off the water grid, boaters have three ways to get water: collecting rainwater, spending days lugging jerry cans with water of questionable quality from shore to the boat, or using a reverse osmosis watermaker to turn salt water into fresh potable water. Rain, of course, can be extremely undependable, and we prefer snorkeling to hauling water all day, so we elected to install a watermaker.

Our Spectra watermaker uses a high-pressure pump and a series of filters and membranes to filter the salt out of the seawater to produce six gallons of fresh water per hour. It fills our water tanks for the week in about 10 hours. It produces fewer gallons per hour than some other models available on the market, but ours can run off solar panel energy.

World health standards consider any water with less than 1000 ppm of contaminants to be safe for long-term consumption. The manufacturer says anything below 500 ppm is good. Our watermaker puts out water with less than 100 ppm, and it tastes delicious!

A watermaker is a luxury on a small boat like ours, yet it affords us other little luxuries that make this life a bit easier: daily showers for the crew, a weekly washdown for *Ana María*, and as much drinking water as our hearts and parched bodies desire.

THE ENTERTAINMENT

We're currently reading *The Sex Lives of Cannibals: Adrift in the Equatorial Pacific*. It's a catchy title for a book that notably doesn't say much about sex or cannibalism. Instead, it recounts the cultural assimilation of an American as he adapts to living on an atoll in the Kiribati Islands in the Pacific. A highly entertaining and informative read as we set our own sights westward.

THE HIGHLIGHT

Bahía Willard, Baja California, México
29° 48' 55" N 114° 23' 49" W

The highlight was making it out of the boatyard and Puerto Peñasco and arriving in Bahía Willard. We intended to land in Puerto Refugio, but the resident angels on Isla Angel de La Guarda must have been standing on the northern coast blowing *Ana María* toward Bahía Willard, and we are glad.

Bahía Willard has been our favorite anchorage in the Sea of Cortez: pleasant breezes yet flat calm at night, a restaurant and convenience store a short kayak ride away, hikes and sandy beaches where we can swim and cool off in the heat of the day, and Jacques. In the evenings, Jacques, our French boat neighbor on *Arpatas*, would swim over from his boat to ours for 15 minutes of human interaction and a mix of French/English/Spanish conversation after a long day of boat work. What a character!

THE HORIZON

We're hoping to celebrate All Saints' Day/*Día de Los Muertos* in a town or village somewhere. We will hunt for a traditional candy my mother-in-law recommends we taste.

Fair winds and following seas,

Katherine

P.S. A quick update on my dad: after months of chemo and radiation, the PET scans and labs this week show no sign of cancer.

Woohoo!

We are so relieved and grateful for this outcome.

Ensenada la Gringa,
Bahía de los Ángeles,
Baja California, México
29° 02' 19" N 113° 32' 39" W

VOLUME 2, ISSUE 2: TRANSFORMING THE MUNDANE INTO THE MEMORABLE

October 12, 2022
Ensenada la Gringa, Bahía de los Ángeles, Baja California, México
29° 02' 19" N 113° 32' 39" W
Winds: N 10 knots
Weather: 82°F Clouds forming over the peninsula

You know those people who have that special gift, that magic touch, the ability to transform the mundane into the memorable?

They seem to be half host and half Tinker Bell, both ensuring your comfort and ensuring your delight. They know how to give you an experience you'll never forget. It's quite a rare gift.

I once met one of these people in an Afrikaans karaoke bar in Cape Town, where I was studying as a Rotary Ambassadorial Scholar. Only a few songs had been sung before Elsje invited the group to spend a weekend at her family's beach house up the coast. I would never turn down a beach house invitation, but still, I had low expectations.

To my great surprise, Elsje gave us an unforgettable weekend: breakfast spreads full of juicy fruit from the Western Cape, a guided nature walk through the swirling tide pools teeming with wildlife, an expedition to pluck mussels off the rocks at low tide, a *braai* (barbecue) on an isolated sandy beach where we feasted on homemade barbecued bread and mussels steamed with white wine and butter.

Eleven years later, I can still taste the juicy papaya, feel the spikes of the sea urchins plucked from the tidal pools, smell the sweet aroma of the bread and mussels, and feel the heat of the fire as we listened to the waves crash on the beach behind us. Thanks to Elsje, the weekend and much of my year in Cape Town was magical.

Today we're back at a familiar anchorage. We stopped here at Ensenada La Gringa back in June. It's a fine anchorage: good holding for our anchor, no bugs, no noise. It'll do for a couple of nights before we head somewhere more fun.

Last night we were thrilled to meet back up with our friends Sam and Jesica on *Hariya*. It's a full moon, so they had spent the day before floating the lagoon with Max and Karen, anchored on *Lusty* next to us.

Today they've invited us to come along. "It's fun. Like a lazy river." A lazy river in the wild? Sounds like an okay way to spend the afternoon.

The only problem is that Max and Karen have four floats (two inflated cylinders connected by a mesh). What can Andrés and I use to float? We have some pool noodles, but we can't find a way to fashion them into a decent float. What else? Andrés and Sam see the buoyant fenders we use to dock the boats and an idea strikes. Two long fenders tied together look a lot like the inflatable chambers on their floats. There's no mesh, but, hey, we'll get a free ab workout today. They use two ropes and a sheet bend knot to tie pairs of fenders together and we're off.

Admittedly, we do not look cool. My redneck roots are on full display as I try to arrange myself in between the two fenders. The mesh of the real floats enables a graceful takeoff. Without the mesh, we resort to plopping – yes PLOPPING – into the water and wiggling around until we have one fender under our knees and one fender supporting our necks. A little adjusting and we're swept away into the hillbilly water park.

We're floating in the current formed by the high tidal water in the lagoon. Since it's a full moon, the water is deep and the current fast. It only takes a few minutes before we have huge smiles plastered on our faces.

The current twists and twirls us around like a teacup ride. In the deep sections, the current picks up and speeds us around the corners. In the shallow parts, whoever is in the lead shouts back to the rest, "Butt up!" to warn the rest of us of the low-lying rocks. We race through the lagoon, no one wanting to be the rotten *huevo*. We're transported back to childhood, laughing gleefully, delighting in the sensations, racing and spinning.

Max and Karen act as our tour guides: "Move to port unless you want the grass up ahead to clean your bottom." "Over there is a big, sharp, barnacle-covered rock." "See those cormorants nesting to your right?" They lead us to some small Chutes & Ladders shortcuts, where the current has cut a fast pass through the gravel.

Just like a man-made lazy river, the lagoon forms a circular route, and we are quickly shot back out of the lagoon to the beach next to our kayak.

"Let's do it again!" cry Max and Karen.

We eagerly follow their lead and take three more rides around the lagoon. The tide is going out, so the lagoon gets progressively shallower with each round.

With a wriggle of his eyebrows, Max dares us, "Anyone up for a danger round?"

Not wanting the fun to end, we go one more round, keeping our eyes open for those sharp rocks now sticking up and working our core to keep our butts lifted as we barely pass through the shallow channels.

High on happiness, Max and Karen invite us all over to their 57-foot sailboat for sundowners. Sam and Jesica offer up a mahi-mahi they caught near Mitlán, and the cocktail plan evolves into mahi fish tacos for dinner. Luckily, I picked up some fresh tomatoes in Bahía Willard, so I offer to bring homemade pico de gallo for the tacos. We disperse to shower before meeting up on *Lusty*.

Instead of the basic spaghetti Bolognese I had planned for dinner, we find ourselves experiencing the hospitality of Max and Karen. A fun country music playlist reaches our ears before we even reach their boat. A full charcuterie board greets us on arrival. We sip on cold drinks complete with ice, an unheard-of luxury on *Ana María*, while Karen deep fries the breaded mahi and grouper. She serves us fresh coleslaw, juicy limes, garlicky pico de gallo, warm tortillas, and piping hot fish tacos. Anyone else would have served them on simple plates. Not Karen. She serves them in the red plastic baskets with the red and white checked paper you would get in a beachside restaurant. It's her attention to the small details like the serving baskets that somehow make the tacos taste even better.

We bask in the joy of the day, feasting on the tacos, swapping stories, and laughing at each other's jokes.

The next day we are keen to repeat yesterday's fun and kayak back to the lagoon at high tide. We're disappointed to discover the waning moon has decreased the tidal strength. We'll be lucky if we get one danger round out of the lazy river today.

Still, if we hurry, we can get one ride in. We're floating along, walking like crabs through the shallowest parts, when we start to hear Max yell every few minutes "Got one! ... Got another one!"

I twirl around and see him holding up clams he's pulled from the bottom of the lagoon. By the end of the ride, he's collected about 10 of them. Motivated by the bounty ripe for pickin', Max and Karen exclaim, "Let's get clams for dinner tonight!" Max dinghies to his boat and comes back with a shovel and a huge bucket.

They lead us to a curve of the lagoon where the knee-high water is running fast over a pea-gravel bottom. "The clams in gravel are sweeter because they aren't buried in sand," they explain to us newbies. We've never clammed before because it's illegal for gringos. Karen, though, is a Mexican national, so we feel more comfortable, especially since she is the one holding the bucket of clams.

"Stick your hand straight down in the bottom about six inches and pick up whatever your hands can grab," she instructs. I try a couple of times, each time pulling out two handfuls of rocks. I plunge my hands a bit deeper and am thrilled to see two clams mixed in with the stones. Planting my feet to stabilize against the fast current, I plunge my hands over and over into the bottom. I get the hang of it, getting faster and pulling out more and more clams.

We move as a group as the pickings become slim, shifting a couple feet in search of fresh sources. We adjust our systems. Sam shoves both hands into the water, pulls up two large handfuls, and I sift through the stones in his hands to pull out the huge clams. Max uses his shovel to lift the sand, revealing lots of clams that we clamor to collect before the water washes the sand over them once again.

We're giddy from the instant gratification of such quick work and the promise of pasta with fresh clam sauce for dinner. In 30 minutes, we have a bucket so full of clams that Max has to carry it on his head back to the dinghy.

We meet back on their boat to watch them prepare tonight's dinner. Max and Karen show us how they wash, dry, and steam the clams in garlic, onion, butter, and white wine. Just after the clams pop open, Max shucks a clam for each of us to try.

Oh my goodness. Melt-in-your-mouth. Delectable. Divine.

Our appetite is sufficiently whet for the meal.

No plastic baskets in sight or "Chicken Fried" by Zac Brown on the stereo tonight, not for such a fancy feast! We listen to Pink Martini sing in Portuguese as Karen serves the pasta with clam sauce in fancy white seafood pasta bowls perfect for the occasion. A sprinkle of parmesan, a squeeze of lemon.

It's hard to remember a more memorable dinner. When's the last time I harvested my food from the earth? When's the last time I did it while laughing and thoroughly enjoying the "work" with friends?

We can't help but eat second portions of the pasta, chucking our clam shells overboard into Ensenada La Gringa.

It's hard to believe this bay is the same La Gringa we experienced back in June. Sometimes it takes friends to unlock the magic of the place.

We are reluctant to break the spell Max and Karen have cast over the place for us, but we have quite the kayak ride against the westerly winds back to *Ana María*.

Because I am Mark Rhoades' daughter, I serenade Max, Karen, Sam, and Jesica with a song he taught me as we paddle away:

This has been a real nice clambake
We're mighty glad we came
The vittles we et
were good you bet
The company was the same
Our hearts are full
Our bellies are warm
And we are feeling fiiiiiine
This has been a real nice clambake
And we've all had a real good time!

THE GALLEY

If you ever find yourself with a big bucket of fresh clams, you too can make Clam Pasta *á la Lusty*:

CLAM PASTA Á LA LUSTY

INGREDIENTS

Fresh Littleneck or pasta clams, about a pound per person
1 yellow onion, finely diced
4 garlic cloves, minced
3 tablespoons salted butter
2 cups dry white wine, such as Sauvignon Blanc
Linguine, about ¼ pound per person
¼ cup fresh parsley, chopped
Zest from 1 lemon
½ teaspoon red pepper flakes
½ cup cream
½ cup finely shredded parmesan cheese, for garnish
Juice of 2 lemons, for garnish

DIRECTIONS

1. Hang clams in a mesh bag over the bow of the boat as you sail to rinse the sand out of the clams. (If on land, let them soak in cold water for 30 minutes so they release any sand.) Wash the shells with fresh water and dry them with a beach towel.
2. In a large shallow pan (clams cook more evenly spread out than piled high in a pot), sauté onions and garlic in salted butter until the onions are translucent but not browned, about 5 minutes. Pour in white wine. Pour in the washed clams. Cover and steam until the shells pop open, about 5 minutes. Discard any shells that don't open.
3. Reserving the liquid in the pan, shuck most of the clams, leaving some in the shells for serving. Chop the clam meat and set aside.
4. Bring the liquid from the pan and enough water to fill a pot to boil, then boil linguine until al dente, about 10 minutes or according to the package. Drain. To serve, toss the pasta with the clam meat, chopped parsley, lemon zest, red pepper flakes, and cream. Top the pasta with the clams still in the shells. Sprinkle with parmesan and lemon juice.

THE LINGO

Spring Tides vs. Neap Tides: We're able to float the high water in the lagoon because we are experiencing spring tides as a result of the full moon. Both the full moon and the lack of the moon pull the world's water into extreme positions resulting in higher high tides and lower low tides. The Northern Sea of Cortez is famous for its tidal differences where there can be up to a 23-foot difference in the water level between low and high tide. The dramatic high tide flooded the lagoon, allowing for our afternoon's fun.

The mid-cycle moon phases bring neap tides, in which the deltas between low tide and high tide are much more mellow.

THE CHALLENGE

This month we struggled to make the appropriate paradigm shift and we got pummeled by currents thanks to our stubbornness.

In the boatyard mindset, our stubborn streaks provide a real advantage. Setbacks and challenges occur daily - nay, hourly - and we can only complete all our boatyard tasks by pushing for progress every single day. Did we forget to buy the 15 feet of triplex marine wire for the high-water alarm in the bilge? We gotta be scrappy to come up with some today and not wait for some to be delivered in a week. Do we have to put three coats of paint on the bottom of the boat before 2:00 p.m.? We have to start at 4:30 a.m., armed with snacks and water, and push through no matter how hot, how grueling.

When cruising, though, we are rewarded for our patience. We move at the permission and mercy of the weather. Sailing from Puerto Refugio down to Ensenada La Gringa, we were determined to leave Refugio, undeterred by the forecast showing the northerly winds weren't going to show up after all. Without the winds to counteract the spring tidal currents, we spent the entire morning motoring against a 3-knot current. With clenched teeth, we watched our speed over ground linger at 1 knot of progress toward our destination.

Wiser cruisers would have seen the updated forecast and stayed put until the wind filled in.

THE WILDLIFE

We listen to Channel 16, the "hailing and distress channel," on the VHF all day. Rarely do we hear distress calls, but up here, we often hear the chatter of the local fishermen. I was alarmed when I heard them talking about a *tiburón*. "Andrés! There is a shark somewhere close!" "No, listen to the second word. *Ballena*. It's a whale shark."

The marine biologist who named the whale shark took quite a bit of creative liberty as the animal is not a whale at all. It is the largest species of fish, weighing up to 15 tons and growing as long as 45 feet. This is significantly larger than our boat, so we are thankful they are mild-mannered and prefer to eat enormous amounts of plankton instead of snorkelers.

THE HIGHLIGHT

The lagoon float, mahi tacos, and fresh clam pasta were not only the highlights of the month but possibly some of the highlights of our year here.

THE ENTERTAINMENT

"We've spent a lot of money going to a lot of marriage counselors to discover: opposites attract." –Wade and Shari Farmer

Andrés and I are opposites in many ways, but the one temperament difference that causes the most friction in the ordering of our common everyday life is my extroversion to his introversion. We struggle to find fulfillment for both his need for quiet peaceful isolation and my need for the stimulation I get from interaction with people.

This month, I'm reading *Quiet: The Power of Introverts in a World that Can't Stop Talking* to better understand, appreciate, and love my Introvert. This intellectually challenging read contradicts much of what I thought was true and universal, but it has been insightful. I highly recommend reading it if you are an Introvert, are married to an Introvert, have a child who is an Introvert, or work with an Introvert.

THE HORIZON

We'll celebrate *el Día de los Muertos* then cruise slowly to La Paz, Mexico to catch the World Cup.

Fair winds and following seas,

Katherine

● Cala San Francisquito,
Baja California, México
28° 25' 41" N 112° 51' 55" W

● Santa Rosalía,
Baja California Sur, México
27° 20' 14" N 112° 15' 40" W

VOLUME 2, ISSUE 3: WHAT A DIFFERENCE A YEAR MAKES

November 4, 2022
Cala San Francisquito, Baja California, México
28° 25' 41" N 112° 51' 55" W
Winds: W 9 knots
Weather: 79°F Finally getting some relief from the heat!

"Are you leaving for Santa Rosalía on the 'sleigh ride' on Monday?" asks Ethan, our neighbor on *Eyoni,* when we meet him in Cala San Francisquito.

It's a question we've been asking ourselves as we've studied the forecasts and made plans for the 80-nautical-mile trek south. It's a tricky passage because we normally travel at 4 knots, so it should take us 20 hours.

A 20-hour passage means we need to plan carefully to avoid arriving at night. Our cruising guide warns, "During a nighttime approach, keep in mind that the bright lights of Santa Rosalía will be in the background, making it difficult to discern the navigational lights of the breakwater." We'll leave mid-afternoon to ensure we arrive in the morning light.

We loathe the idea of leaving Sunday and motoring the entire 80 nautical miles. Instead, we will wait until Monday and catch the "sleigh ride" with 22 knots of sustained wind from the north. We expect 30-knot gusts and know the winds have hundreds of miles to build fetch so the waves will be steep. The conditions could be reminiscent of those we faced a year ago at Cape Mendocino when I broke my leg.

This year for this sail we will be better prepared.

I wake up Monday morning, dreading today's journey, but almost immediately a quote from Brené Brown's *Atlas of the Heart* comes to mind: "[Dread] is terrible because even if it goes well, I'm so dread-exhausted that

I can't enjoy it." I share the quote with Andrés, and we promise each other that we won't dread this sail. Instead of using our energy to dread it, we will redirect our energy into preparing for it.

We pull out the After-Action Review we completed last year after Cape Mendocino to ensure we haven't forgotten what we learned. One thing Hal, our trusted South African rigger, mentioned we could try in the future is dropping the mainsail to remove the boom from the equation and sail under a genoa pulled out with the whisker pole. We haven't had the right conditions to try that yet, but we had put his recommendation in our back pocket for later.

We set out about our preparation tasks, with balls of anxiety quietly churning in the pit of our stomachs.

We run jack lines so we can attach our tethers as we move about the boat. We develop and practice a safer way to set up the whisker pole to run wing-on-wing. We charge headlamp batteries. We set up Paulita, our self-steering Monitor windvane. We take sea sickness medication. We take down solar panels, take out our foul weather gear, and set up the lee-cloths in the berths. We move snack bars to within reach of the cockpit and move cans around the food lockers to prevent "items shifting during flight."

We discuss tactics. Can we limit the necessary jibing, the dangerous act of bringing the stern through the wind, to only three times? We decide to jibe the first time by 6:00 p.m., while we have plenty of light for the sail change.

And then, finally, it's time to leave. We pull up the mainsail, pull up the anchor, and we're off.

We're off to a rough start. We're forced to motorsail upwind in order to clear Santa Teresa Point south of us. Every five seconds, *Ana María* crashes head-on into a wave, drenching us with buckets of salt water. Dave Gable's joke about sailing comes to mind: "Want the experience of sailing but don't own a boat? All you have to do is stand under an ice-cold shower in front of an industrial fan and rip up hundred-dollar bills." Yeah, that sounds about right.

Twenty minutes of bashing later, we clear the point, and we can turn downwind. We find ourselves being pushed by the waves instead of colliding with them. The ride is immediately smoother. Now that we're sailing downwind, we have a great wind angle to sail wing-on-wing.

Andrés, who has been hand-steering against the onslaught of waves, hands me the tiller so he can unfurl the genoa to windward. I struggle to steer with the 8-foot waves pushing our stern around. Just this morning, looking at our After-Action Review, we were reminded that I was supposed to practice hand-steering in heavy weather. We really need to follow through on that commitment. Still, we're able to pull the genoa out on the whisker pole and set the Monitor windvane to steer without incident.

We're sailing—no, flying—with a wing-on-wing configuration under a second-reefed mainsail. We have 2 knots of current and are surfing down these waves at 10 knots, even though our theoretical hull speed is only 7 knots.

"11.6 knots! I just saw 11.6 speed over ground!"

Andrés studies the conditions, the forecasts, the charts, adding, "My calculations show if we don't slow down, we're going to arrive in Santa Rosalía at midnight."

Once again, we find ourselves in heavier winds than forecasted. Just like last year, we have to make a decision: pull down the mainsail and risk getting stuck in the troughs of the waves or leave up the mainsail and risk a dangerous boom-breaking jibe. We decide now is the time to implement Hal's recommendation. The genoa is already out on the whisker pole, so all we have to do is take down the mainsail. We need to make the sail change **now** while we still have plenty of light to see.

I clip my tether into the jack lines and move forward to the mast. I raise the lazy jacks to help us flake the sail while Andrés steers upwind and brings the boom in. "Ready!" I call back. "Watch the boom! Dropping the sail!" He responds. I hold tightly to the granny bars at the mast while he releases the halyard. The sail bounces around violently until I can yank it all the way down the mast. He heads back downwind to avoid getting these waves on our beam, risking a repeat of last year's knockdown.

"Boom is secure!" he calls, giving me the cue to move aft to tie down the sail. I hug the boom and patiently secure the sail with the sail ties. The 8-foot waves pummel us every 8 seconds, making the maneuver difficult, but it's not nearly as discombobulating as the wave trains we experienced in Mendocino.

And just like that, we've taken down the mainsail safely. Perfectly coordinated and executed. Exactly as well as we've done it hundreds of times this year in smoother conditions.

We watch *Ana María* settle into this new configuration as we eat the dinner I prepped earlier today. We've lost 1 knot of speed, but the genoa has enough power on the whisker pole to keep us riding the tops of the waves. With the comfortable angle of the seas and without the risk of a dangerous jibe, we begin to breathe sighs of relief. *Ana María* is settled for a while, so it's time to start the watch schedule. I go below to crawl into the comfort and safety of the sleeping bag and lee cloth, which acts as a safety net to keep me from toppling out of bed.

Andrés wakes me up three hours later so I can take over. He reports that *Ana María* has done great under the poled-out genoa. We discuss tactics in preparation for the next four hours. Slow down if I can; otherwise, it will be a nighttime arrival into Santa Rosalía.

Slow down? No way. The winds never subside. Instead, I see 38 knots show up on our wind instrument. Definitely higher than forecasted.

They call this a "sleigh ride"? This does not remind me of the horse-drawn sleigh ride we took on our honeymoon in Park City, Utah. No, this reminds me of the best sledding of my life. As a teenager, my church youth group used to drive to the backwoods of Eminence, Missouri every winter to go spelunking. If we were really lucky, a fresh snowfall would cancel the caving and we'd spend the day sledding down a 100-yard steep icy hill. All day long, we'd climb up that hill then look down. We'd make the brave decision to go for it. And we'd hold on as hard as we could, desperately steering away from the trees, and holding our breath until we could skid safely to the bottom. This sail reminds me of those days.

We're still sailing at 8 knots, surfing every wave that hits our stern. The Monitor windvane is keeping up with the wind and seas. The steering adjustment we made to the system after last year's incident is working reliably. *Ana María* feels like she may even be enjoying this ride.

I turn on the *Hamilton* soundtrack and dance and sing along in the cockpit. The upbeat music keeps me energized and the plot line keeps me awake until it's time to round Cape Virgenes. We'll have to turn even farther downwind after the cape. I don't want a repeat of last year's entry into Monterey when I was too slow to respond to a wind shift, missed the point, and Andrés was forced to spend the next three hours tacking upwind to get us into the bay.

This time I am focused on tactics. I don't have to worry about jibing the boom, but I have a poled-out genoa, so I am constrained to sailing at 150° off the wind on either tack. Every 15 minutes, between *Hamilton* songs, I make slight course adjustments in an effort to avoid any more sail changes for the trip.

By the time Andrés wakes up for a watch change, it looks like my tactical efforts were successful. We should be able to maintain this course until we can pull into safe harbor. I once again go below to rest up before our arrival.

Only an hour later, Andrés wakes me up: "I need your help. We're arriving in Santa Rosalía." I look at my phone, 3:06 a.m. Despite our best efforts, we're making landfall in the dead of night.

I'm sure all the sailors are thinking "Why would you ever go into a marina at night if you can help it?" They're right to ask. All kinds of things can happen when you can't see. We've read the stories, heeded the warnings. But there is no safe anchorage between San Francisquito and Santa Rosalía where we can pull in to get protection from these 35-knot winds. We can either sail 40 more miles on this midnight sleigh ride or we can try for safe harbor.

As sailors, we are sometimes forced to make the *least dangerous* decision.

I come up to the cockpit, binoculars in hand, to help Andrés furl in the genoa. Thankfully, we're now in the lee of Cabo Virgenes, so the wind has died significantly. We get out all of our charts, both the Mexican Navy charts and the Aqua Maps charts, and start looking for navigation lights.

The cruising guide was right. The bright lights of the town make it difficult to discern the two pairs of green and red lights that mark the entrance to the harbor. It's like a high-stakes game of *Where's Waldo?* We're staring at thousands of twinkling white lights, scanning, scanning, scanning for one green and one red among the sea of distractions.

After a couple of minutes staring through the binoculars, I see a green one. I point it out to Andrés. "I don't think that's it. It doesn't make sense." We pull up the various charts, trying to get our bearings. We look for other references, such as the big red flashing lights on the antenna on the hill behind it. Does the relative position of the green light make sense against that antenna? Yeah ... yeah, actually it does. But then where's the red light that should be next to it? Ooo, maybe that's it? Was that a blinking red light or is that a traffic light?

We edge closer to the green light, cautious. Many boats have run aground coming into marinas at night because they were just absolutely sure *that* was the light they were looking for. Captain Phyllis, our sailing instructor, drilled into us to check and double-check and triple-check and keep looking for supporting or disproving evidence of our position.

As we get closer to the green, the red becomes increasingly obvious. Our radar begins to pick up the shape of the harbor breakwater, the port, and the marina. Growing more confident, we make the turn into the channel and are relieved to see the two blinking white range lights. All we have to do is line up with those lights and we'll have safe entry into the harbor.

Once through the channel, exchanging one stress for another, we begin to scout for a place in the marina. We've heard that the marina is packed, so we might not have a slip. We finally spot one at the very beginning of the fairway. It's a starboard tie and we have an off-the-dock wind. There are complicated physics involved in that bad news, but basically it means this: Starboard tie + Off-the-dock wind = Boat mechanics and nature are actively working against us to push us away from the dock.

Andrés steers us back into the harbor so we can prep *Ana María* to dock. As I tie fenders to both sides and get all five dock lines ready, I'm transported back to the last time we had this same challenge.

Just over a year ago, before we even sailed out of the Strait of Juan de Fuca and made the Big Left Turn into the Pacific, we accidentally arrived at the Port Angeles marina at night after a rough sail. We struggled to navigate and communicate with the big yachts arriving at the same time. (We later discovered that we had been using a broken radio the whole time.) We narrowly pulled into a starboard tie with an off-the-dock wind. The wind blew the boat down toward our neighbor and we had to use a boat hook to avoid a collision. We forgot to put the boat in forward, so we had one useless line keeping us on the dock. No damage was done, but the stress was enough to keep us in bad moods for two days.

And here we go again a year later.

As Andrés steers us back toward the dock, I crawl over the lifelines, holding onto the shrouds, calling out distances to the dock, before stepping back off the boat and slipping the spring line around the aft dock cleat. "Boat is stopped," the captain announces. I complete the cleat hitch and then grab the bow and stern lines to snug *Ana María* up against the dock.

We just docked without even waking up our dockmates. We sailed without panic, without fights. We sailed without hurting ourselves or *Ana María*.

I realize that we are more confident and more competent sailors.

Our friend Mille posted pictures of her little two-year-old boy: one from this Halloween and one from last Halloween. She posts pictures throughout the year, so I've seen him grow gradually from a baby into a toddler, but, from month to month, I don't see much of a difference. In these two pictures side by side, however, it's hard to believe he's the same little boy. He's grown so much in a year.

Tonight's conditions and challenges mirrored the ones we faced last year. We've sailed all year long. From one sail to the next, it doesn't feel like we've changed, yet tonight I see how we've grown. We've developed. We're the same people, but we've become better sailors, better partners.

What a difference a year makes.

THE HIGHLIGHT

Santa Rosalía, Baja California Sur, México
27° 20' 14" N 112° 15' 40" W

We find ourselves in Santa Rosalía, already our favorite little town in Baja, for the town's 137th anniversary celebration.

It's happenstance as the party was rescheduled for this week due to hurricanes this summer. We can't believe our luck! It is *the* event of the year. The streets are full of carnival rides and games. The ranches and restaurants from all over the state are serving the most delicious regional foods for the celebration. We dine on spit-roasted tacos al pastor and thirstily drink agua fresca with bits of guayaba. We stand shoulder to shoulder with the crowd to watch the indigenous dancers, the crowning of the town queen, and each village's own folk dance and song on display.

We're immersed in the culture as our group of 25 cruisers are the only gringos present. The town is jam-packed with every resident in a 100-mile radius. Women wearing their nicest makeup and jewelry chat enthusiastically with friends. Men in starched shirts and polished cowboy boots exchange warm handshakes as they recognize neighbors. Little boys carry prizes they've won in the rifle shoot-out. Little girls with bows in their hair joyfully dance on stage. Teenage girls dressed in the trendiest outfits they own pretend to ignore the packs of teenage boys spraying each other with silly string. It's a familial and festive atmosphere. The locals dance to the live music until 6:00 a.m. each morning, long after us gringos retire to bed.

THE ENTERTAINMENT

It's nerve-racking to be on constant alert that our boat, our only home, could run into something, the ground, another boat, or the dock. It's also nerve-racking to know something, another boat, a panga, anything, could run into our boat, our only home.

For a year, our pack of cruising companions has lived with this stress every time we enter a marina or anchorage, so when we spot the bumper car ride at the anniversary fair, we eagerly pay the $3 and play a round together.

The carny turns on the ride, and it's as if everyone's nerves from the past year EXPLODE all at once.

I guarantee you've never seen a group of mature, responsible adults ram into one another with such glee and reckless abandon. To hit each other over and over with no consequences and no insurance claims leads to pure, unadulterated delight.

THE WILDLIFE

It's shrimping season here, so the sea is full of shrimp boats. Friends advised us to bring cigarettes and Coca-Cola aboard so we could trade them for fresh shrimp, but we're still looking to make the trade.

THE LINGO

"One, two, three, and, five, six, seven, and, one, two, three, and, five, six, seven, and!"

"Let's do a salsa class! You can teach us all how to dance. Even Max!" exclaimed Karen from last month's magical adventures on *Lusty*, when I let it slip that Andrés is a fantastic salsa dancer.

When we made it into the Santa Rosalía marina, everyone was already anticipating our arrival. "Oh, you're Andrés on *Ana María*? Karen said you're going to teach us how to salsa!"

Not wanting to disappoint others, we made a deal with Max and Karen: you gather the cruisers and bring a speaker, and Andrés will teach the class.

Gather the people they did! Twenty-two cruisers showed up to learn the moves. They showed up ready to laugh, have fun, and tear up the dance floor.

Andrés, for his part, gave them a great introduction to salsa: teaching the rhythm ("One, two, three, and, five, six, seven, and ..."), forming a dance train, showing them how to dance with a partner, and making them rotate partners often enough that they danced with almost everyone.

"That was a great night! I danced with 10 different women," remarked one happy customer, Mike on *Reverence*.

After much prodding from the crowd, Andrés ended the class with a demonstration of his moves, his fancy footwork, and his twirling me around the dance floor. Meredith, our new friend on *Jackdaw*, was sweet to tell us at the end of the night, "As much fun as it was to watch you dance, the best part was watching you two look at each other throughout the night. There's clearly a lot of love there."

swoon

THE GALLEY

"What do you eat out there? You're not still eating freeze-dried backpacking food, are you?" I get this question a lot.

We've gotten the hang of provisioning for 28 days between grocery store trips. It's been a challenge with no freezer and a tiny fridge, but we've only lost a cucumber and sweet potato to spoilage. Here's what we ate during our month in the remote northern Sea of Cortez.

Lunches: tuna melt*; avocado chicken salad; black bean, corn, and tomato salad*; black bean avocado quesadillas*; curried chickpea wraps; black bean tuna salad*; cucumber chicken salad; chickpea tuna salad*; chickpea masala*; chicken verde; sofritas bowl; salsa chicken; chicken tomato couscous*; and ham & cheese sandwiches.

Dinner: chicken primavera; Mexican zucchini skillet*; chicken fried rice; Carolyn's gazpacho*; sesame chicken*; hamburgers à la Mark Rhoades; eggplant chickpea tagine; black bean sweet potato hash; spicy zucchini casserole*; spaghetti Bolognese; black bean burgers; rice and beans*; Greek pasta salad; vegetable salad à la Que Tal*; grilled brats with Japanese cucumber salad*; stuffed pepper soup; lentil soup; tacos al pastor; Colombian bandeja paisa; minestrone pasta salad*; black bean-stuffed sweet potato; Mexican casserole dip*; ropa vieja; grilled pizza*; sausage and potatoes*; chickpea shakshuka; stovetop tuna penne*; tofu stir fry.

*Recipes from *The Boat Galley Cookbook*

THE CHALLENGE

Remember when I said how crucial and reliable our watermaker is? Well, it broke. Completely broke. We have enough drinking water to get us to Puerto Escondido where we'll spend a day hauling water from shore to *Ana María* to fill our water tanks to the brim.

THE HORIZON

We'll hop from one snorkel spot to the next en route to La Paz, Mexico, where we need to figure out the potable water situation.

This Thanksgiving, may you find your life full of things for which you can be thankful.

Fair winds and following seas,

Katherine

El Mezteño, Isla Espíritu Santo,
Baja California Sur, México
24° 30' 56" N 110° 23' 27" W

VOLUME 2, ISSUE 4: ARE WE REALLY GOING TO DO THIS?

December 28, 2022
El Mezteño, Isla Espíritu Santo, Baja California Sur, México
24° 30' 56" N 110° 23' 27" W
Wind: N 18 knots
Weather: 70°F Partly cloudy

"**D**o you see anything?"

I try to detangle myself from the thorny bush I thought might be hiding the trail before yelling back, "Nope! Trail's not over here."

We're here looking for the trailhead that supposedly leads to the best lookout in all of Isla Espíritu Santo. "The view, if you can find the trail, is worth the long and strenuous climb," read the review that inspired today's adventure.

Most of the hiking we've done together has been on the well-maintained trails in Washington State. Yes, you may climb 3,000 feet in 3 miles, but all you have to do is continue to put one foot in front of the other all the way to the top. On this "trail," it looks like we're in for a long afternoon of searching for a loose series of markers left by kind hikers who've blazed the trail for us.

Finally, we see a cairn, a manmade pile of rocks marking a route up the canyon. Lifting our feet over cacti, we make it to the first cairn and immediately begin scanning the canyon for the next. The cairns camouflage themselves among the surrounding rocks of the same shade. Only its unnatural shape reveals its role as a trail marker.

Andrés spots the next cairn about 20 feet in front of us and 5 feet above us. He climbs toward it with me following a couple feet behind.

A rhythm emerges as he navigates the trail. "Cairn!" He yells every couple of minutes, indicating we're on the right general path. Climb. Climb. Climb. Look. Look. Look. There! Another cairn!

Climb. Climb. Climb.

Look. Look. Look.

Cairn!

I fall in step behind him, and my mind begins to wander to last night's discussion. We've been poring over Jimmy Cornell's *Ocean Atlas* to prepare to cross the Pacific Ocean this winter.

In typical boating fashion, crossing an ocean is less than straightforward. There is no Google Maps app where we can enter our current location as our starting point and "French Polynesia" as our destination. Instead, we have the pilot charts with some general directions on how to get across the biggest ocean in the world.

Do we leave Mexico in February and risk not giving the famous trade winds enough time to fill in?

Do we leave in March and risk battling an additional 300 miles of the infamous doldrums before we make landfall?

Do we cross the Equator at 120°W as recommended in *World Cruising Routes*? Or at 125°W mentioned in the pilot charts? Or at 130°W like our friends did last year?

"Cairn!" My thoughts are interrupted by Andrés' confirmation that we're on the right path.

Climb. Climb. Climb. Look. Look. Look. Cairn! Up, up, and up we go, one cairn at a time.

We've been at it for an hour, bouldering more than hiking. The rocks in the arroyo have gotten bigger and bigger as we climb.

Right hand reaches up, feeling for a strong handhold. Left foot finds a toe hold. Left arm up to hoist my body up through the crevice. Step up, reach, pull, hoist, rinse, repeat.

The smell of our own sweat is thankfully overpowered by the whiffs of eucalyptus plants tucked into the rocks.

We get much needed refreshment as the northern winds spill over the top of the island, whistling through the nooks and crannies of the canyon, rustling the branches of the few trees that can survive here from one rainy season to the next. The winds tickle our faces, imparting a bit of motivation to continue the climb.

"How much of the trail have we done?" I inquire of my navigator Andrés. He pulls out the photo of the trail map we snapped from our cruising guide. "I'd guess, maybe a quarter of the trail?"

Long and strenuous. The trail reviewer was right.

Abruptly, our rhythm is disrupted:

Climb. Climb. Climb. Look. Look. Look. ... Look. Look. Look. Climb. Climb. Climb. Look. Look. Look.

No cairns in sight.

We look left, pretty shrubby. We look right, pretty hefty boulders.

We've lost the trail, having seen the last cairn a full 15 minutes ago. "Let's split up. I'll go left and climb up for a better view," Andrés proposes. I continue in our general direction. Dead end. Move to the right. Another dead end.

I've started to double back to our last known cairn when I hear Andrés a couple hundred feet above me. "Cairns! I see them up ahead of you. Can you get to where I'm pointing?"

All I see are large boulders, but if I cross this rock to the right and heave my body over that rock, I think I can make progress. "I'll try!" I yell.

Climbing boulder after boulder, I consider one of the most pressing challenges of an upcoming ocean crossing. Our current plan hinges on getting a six-month visa from the French government. The visa has been a headache, a problem we've not been able to solve.

What if we can't get the six-month visa?

Should we still try to sail to French Polynesia even if we only have 90 days to explore it?

Should we stay only 90 days then sail for Hawaii?

Should we rush through the islands in the three months and hope one of the more western island groups will give us an extended visa?

We prefer linear decision-making processes, but our discussions this week have been circular. We consider, discuss, decide ... then double back to reconsider, re-discuss, re-decide. Back and forth, round and round we go.

If a six-month stay in French Polynesia isn't an option, where's our sign indicating we're on the right path? We're desperate for something we can point to one day and say, "We followed the path laid out before us."

Thankfully, I lift my body over a boulder to find myself standing next to the cairn. We're back in business, but we're making progress at a snail's pace.

No wonder when we look again at the map 20 minutes later, we're still only a quarter of the way through the trail. Have we made any actual progress? Are we ever going to make it to the top?

The boulders have thinned out, and we're trekking along at a faster clip on a flatter path. The smaller rocks mean less crawling up and over mammoth boulders, but it also means we are traveling on a less stable foundation.

The ground shifts below our feet. That rock is not as stable as it looks.

The sound of rocks sliding reaches my ears and my entire body braces itself before I realize it is the rocks under *his* feet.

"You okay?" I check on Andrés up ahead. "Yeah," he replies, regaining his footing.

It's been an hour since we last looked at the trail map. The trail has to end soon, and we're pretty sure it ends on top of a ridge. The reviews warned us that it's hard to find the crossover between this arroyo where we've been climbing and the ridge with the final viewpoint.

The trail map indicates we should keep going on this arroyo, but is that a cairn on the ridge to our left? A cairn or a coincidence?

Do we stay on the "trail" or trust our gut and go for the ridge?

Andrés finds a relatively clear path and climbs to the top to scout it out.

I continue hiking the slippery arroyo, careful not to twist an ankle, and I start to weigh our options for an ocean crossing. We're in a La Niña year now, which is forecasted to transition into neutral conditions in March and then into El Niño at the end of 2023. Conventional wisdom says that La Niña conditions make for a much more pleasant experience in French Polynesia, though it also makes the ocean countercurrents stronger. Do we rush our departure and shoot for a La Niña arrival in French Polynesia, or do we wait and avoid an epic battle against the currents?

If we rush, we'll set off on the passage exhausted from all the preparations. If we linger, we may close the door on the option to sail to Hawaii after French Polynesia.

It's always a balancing act to weigh the advice of trusted sources with common sense that considers our personal situation and the actual weather we encounter.

IT'S ALWAYS A BALANCING ACT TO WEIGH THE ADVICE OF TRUSTED SOURCES WITH COMMON SENSE THAT CONSIDERS OUR PERSONAL SITUATION AND THE ACTUAL WEATHER WE ENCOUNTER.

A couple minutes later, Andrés interrupts my rumination, "This is the ridge! I can see those reefs we tried to snorkel last year. It's way easier to hike up here!"

I climb up to the ridge through the brambles, trying to avoid the worst of the thorns. Up top, he's right. We clearly made the right decision to leave the trail and traverse the ridge given the solid ground and little vegetation under our hiking boots.

And then there it is.

Wow!

We're at the top of Isla Espíritu Santo with a 360° view of the island and a bird's-eye view of Caleta Partida cradling nine boats in the anchorage below.

The view is breathtaking. We're standing on the southern rim of what was once a volcano whose crater on the east and west sides has eroded into the sea. We marvel at the rippled sandbanks caused by the alternating waves and daily tide changes. Vultures effortlessly ride the thermals around us, perhaps waiting for less fit hikers to attempt the trek. The mountains of the Sierra de la Giganta stand guard over the peninsula to the west.

This has to be the best hike with the best view we've done in Mexico.

Reluctantly we turn our backs to the view so we can scuttle back to *Ana María* before it's dark.

"You know, I almost gave up," Andrés calls back to me as we pick our path back down the arroyo.

"Oh yeah? When?"

"When we checked and were a quarter of the way to the lookout but then lost the cairns only to find them again and realize 20 minutes later that we were still only a quarter of the way."

In my mind, I start to catalog all of the days we've come *this close* to quitting sailing: the day the epoxy caught on fire and we realized boat work was harder than we ever dreamed it would be. The day I sailed into Bodega Bay with a broken leg. The day after we rolled all night in the Los Gatos anchorage. The day we found out about Dad's lymphoma. The day just last week when the mere idea of an ocean passage overwhelmed us both.

"That was worth it," he calls back again, still thinking of the view from the top.

"Yes," I agree. "So worth it."

THE HORIZON

We've decided to go for it. We're gonna try to cross the Pacific Ocean this winter. Lots can happen between now and then and during the actual crossing, but for now, here's the plan:

We'll look for a weather window between mid-February and early April to sail from La Paz, Baja California Sur, Mexico to Hiva Oa, Marquesas, French Polynesia.

We'll sail the 2,700-nautical-mile, trans-equatorial route on our 34-foot Pacific Seacraft. Given our 100-mile-a-day average and the windless doldrums midway, we expect the passage to take 30 days of non-stop sailing.

We also expect this to be the hardest thing we've ever done. As a double-handed crew with one of us always needing to be on watch, it will be quite the challenge of endurance and sailing strategy.

We have it on good authority, though, that when it comes to the magnificent cruising grounds of French Polynesia, the view is worth the climb.

French Polynesia will give us 90 days to explore the islands. After that, well, we'll balance conventional wisdom with weather conditions and our personal circumstances to make the next decision.

THE HIGHLIGHT

La Paz, Baja California Sur, México
24° 13' 04" N 110° 17' 60" W

We loved hosting our sisters Paula, from NYC, and Anne Marie, from Philly, as well as our friend Annie, from Bellingham, and showing them around La Paz.

THE WILDLIFE

We were pretty proud tour guides when, on our sail with Anne Marie and Annie, we found ourselves surrounded by a pod of big bottlenose dolphins. "Dolphins! Dolphins!" we shouted. Unfortunately, in trying to be good tour guides, we had given our guests Dramamine to fight seasickness. They could barely rouse from their Dramamine-induced slumber to catch a glimpse, murmuring, "... Yeah, dolphins ... ," before falling right back asleep.

THE ENTERTAINMENT

We spent a month in La Paz so we, I mean, Andrés, could watch the World Cup. We loved joining the local fans at the bars on the *Malecón* to watch Mexico play the early games and to watch Messi finally clinch a World Cup victory.

THE CHALLENGE

The French truly take bureaucracy to a whole new level. We've been battling for three months trying to get an extended visa but, so far, no luck. *Merde!*

THE GALLEY

We spent a non-traditional Christmas in El Mezteño, so we went for a non-traditional holiday meal of homemade pizza and bocadillo. Andrés first made this Colombian dessert for me on our second date, baking a very ripe plantain in the oven before topping it with guava paste and queso fresco. ¡*Delicioso!*

THE LINGO

¡Ven a nuestras almas! ¡Ven no tardes tanto!

Colombians celebrate Advent with nightly readings, prayers, and songs called *La Novena*. We celebrate with fewer tambourines and maracas than is traditional, but it's still nice to keep the tradition alive on our travels.

Fair winds and following seas in 2023!

Katherine

La Paz, Baja California Sur, México
24° 09' 28" N 110° 20' 03" W

VOLUME 2, ISSUE 5: ANCHORS AWEIGH!

February 8, 2023
La Paz, Baja California Sur, México
24° 09' 28" N 110° 20' 03" W
Winds: N 25 knots
Weather: 73°F Sunny and clear

"There are two kinds of sailors in the world: those who've run aground and those who lie about it."

We're heading back into La Paz for one final push of preparations for our Pacific passage. We're searching the crowded anchorage for a safe place to anchor for one night before our marina reservation tomorrow. It's tough because so many boats are stuffed between the banks of downtown La Paz and the ever-shifting sandbanks.

As we head to the same safe spot where we anchored last time, a new spot, a closer spot, becomes visible. This spot is 20 minutes closer to the marina where we'll go tomorrow morning.

"Let's try it," we agree as Andrés turns the boat to port to survey the spot.

"Katherine, can you go to the bow and check the sea bottom for me?"

I head to the front of the boat to look for rocks or coral that could foul our anchor, but the water is murky. The murky water under the overcast sky prevents me from seeing the bottom at all even though we should only have about 6 feet of water below us.

Suddenly, I glimpse white sand perfect for our anchor. It's a relief for a split second before I realize how close it is.

"Ground! GROUND! I SEE GROUND!" I yell in panic.

Andrés makes an abrupt turn to starboard to avoid hitting it, but instead, he feels the boat slide gently onto the sandbank.

He immediately revs the engine to 1500 rpm, but our instruments show

"0.0 knots speed over ground."

We're aground.

We can't stay aground. It's not safe. The wind and seas could pick up and start bashing our *Ana María* against the seabed.

I watch as Andrés performs the obvious and easiest fix by throwing the transmission into reverse and trying to back off the sandbank. I watch his face fall when he realizes it's not going to work. We're stuck.

A quick evaluation of our predicament gives us some good news. We're definitely on a rising tide, not a falling tide. So, worst-case scenario, we'll just wait an hour for the water to rise a bit and the boat will naturally lift off the sandbank.

I rattle off some options— "Do we need to call on the VHF for someone with a dinghy and a heavy-duty outboard to come kedge us off? Or should we deploy the kayak and go set a kedge anchor ourselves?"—but Andrés has some less extreme solutions to try first. I'm suddenly grateful that we completed our sailing certification courses where we learned what to do in these situations.

"I calculate we're only aground by 2 inches. Let's use the weight of the boom to try to heel the boat away from the sandbar and see if the leaning doesn't give us those 2 inches to move off."

We push the boom out all the way to starboard just as our *Basic Keelboat* textbook taught us.

"Do you want to go on the boom, or do you want to run the engine?" I consider his question as the picture from the textbook comes to mind, which shows cute little blond teenage girls sitting on the boom of a 20-foot Catalina, where they smile and dangle their legs above the water. This feels more stressful than the textbook insinuates. I let him go on the boom while I take position at the helm.

Andrés climbs out onto the boom as if it's a sturdy limb on a great climbing tree. With him settled, I put the transmission into forward and rev up. 1100 rpm. 1400 rpm. 2000 rpm. Still 0.0 knots speed over ground.

I try again, pushing the tiller hard to port. 1100 rpm. 1400 rpm. 2000 rpm. 2200 rpm. Nothing.

"I need more leverage on the boom to effectively heel the boat." I nod at his assessment and put the gear back into neutral so he can climb back onto the boat. He turns around and this time treats the boom like monkey bars, hanging onto the bottom of the boom and using momentum to swing his body out to the end.

"Oh Lord, please help this to work," I mutter under my breath as I slide the engine into gear. 1100 rpm. 0.0 SOG. I rev up. 1400 rpm. 0.0 SOG.

1800 rpm. 0.0 SOG. Wait! 0.1 SOG!

0.3 SOG. 0.6 SOG.

"It's working!" I yell to my husband who is hanging at the end of the boom, off the side of our now moving boat.

We're off the sandbank, but I can't stop yet in case we get pushed by the current or wind right back onto it. I slow down to let the boat continue to glide when I realize our second predicament.

Now that we're off the sandbank, how do we get Andrés back on the boat?

He looks at me, and I know he is thinking the same thing. He's been hanging there for a full minute, all his strength spent on maintaining his grip on the boom. He doesn't have the strength to swing his body back to the side deck.

Clips of contestants on *American Ninja Warrior* flash through my mind and I know what's about to happen. His face tells me he knows it too.

His fingers start to slide and slip and suddenly ...

SPLASH!

Our ran aground situation has now become a man overboard situation.

Andrés' head quickly bobs out of the water, and I am relieved to remember we are only in five feet of water. Still, there is a current, so we want to get him back in the boat as quickly as possible.

The transmission is in neutral, but we're still gliding. I can't put it in reverse to stop the boat because Andrés is close to the propeller. Recovering from the shock, he starts to swim toward the stern of the boat.

He gets about a foot away and reaches for the Monitor windvane mounting pole on the stern. The boat pulls away. He reaches again and again misses it by an inch.

My eyes go to the LifeSling device mounted on the stern, which we bought for just such an event. Once again, I'm thankful that our sailing certification curriculum included a LifeSling drill. If he doesn't get ahold of the boat with one more try, I'm deploying the LifeSling.

But no need. He musters up one more burst of energy and gets a firm grip on the Monitor windvane. I check our surroundings. We're in a safe place, not in danger of running aground or into other boats, so I set up the boarding ladder. He keeps a grip on the boat as he comes around to the ladder, but instead of climbing up, he asks, "Can you give me my mask and snorkel? I'm already wet. I might as well check the keel."

I hesitate, nervous about the currents, but give in knowing we won't be able to stop worrying about possible damage to the keel. With a mask and snorkel, he disappears below water.

My eyes rotate between the GPS position of our boat, our relative position to other boats, and my husband's snorkel. My blood pressure rises a bit when he doesn't surface right away.

Where is my husband? Why is this taking so long?

Right before full-blown panic sets in, he surfaces and climbs the boarding ladder, his Salty Dog t-shirt and shorts sopping wet.

"We ran aground on sand, not a rock in sight. I checked the keel. I didn't see any damage." With my husband safely back aboard and the structure of our boat apparently still intact, I breathe a big sigh of relief.

Andrés starts to dry off and begins to count our blessings. "I hate that we ran aground, but it could have been way worse. We were on a rising tide instead of a falling tide. We ran aground on a pure sand bottom. There was no wind or waves. I was only going about half a knot when I hit the sand."

"Yes, and if it's true that 'you're not a real sailor until you've run aground,' I'm glad we got that over with in such benign conditions."

"Yeah, let's just never do it again."

I smile back at my husband and agree.

THE LINGO

Running aground is never a good thing. Running aground can cause structural damage to the hull, the keel, and the joint between the two, not to mention the damage done to your sailor's pride.

One way to get the boat unstuck once it has run aground is to heel it. Normally, the boat heels or leans to the side as we sail. Leaning the boat over sideways reduces its draft, so it's a technique that can be used to get a boat floating again.

THE ENTERTAINMENT

We've been in Marina de La Paz this month to provision and prepare for the Pacific passage. We heard it is the best marina in Mexico, and now we know why—the community.

Every evening when the sun begins to set, the cruisers on Dock B set up the folding chairs for the nightly Captain's Hour. We know it's time to wander out to the dock when we smell the cigar smoke and hear the wine and whiskey being poured into glasses.

I can't shake the feeling that we've found ourselves in an Agatha Christie novel, with all the larger-than-life characters placed in a temporary but intimate situation. We have Bob and Karla, the warm retirees from Seattle. Garth and Kimberley, the Canadians planning a cruise through the Panama Canal and the Mediterranean. Robert, the 84-year-old former financier from France. Eva and Kim, the indigenous snowbirds from Alaska. And John Davidson, the actor who played opposite Sally Fields on *The Girl with Something Extra* and the host of *Hollywood Squares*. In their eyes, we are the "young techies here away from jobs and Social Security contributions."

We sit around each night to talk about boat work travails and cruising dreams. John Davidson pretends it's one of his floor shows in New Hampshire, peppering the discussions with songs, stories, and jokes.

Nightly kinship and entertainment—it'll be tough to leave this magical dock.

THE GALLEY

When I was eleven, I went with my mother to attend a baby shower where the mom-to-be proudly announced that she had calculated the exact number of diapers she would need during the baby's life. Even as a kid, I understood the futility of calculating such an unpredictable figure.

This week I feel a bit like that mom-to-be as I try to plan what we'll eat on our 30-day Pacific crossing. I have no idea what's realistic, but I had to buy something for us to eat. I scouted out all our food options at the nine *supermercados* in walking distance of the marina and here's the food plan I landed on:

- 4 days of seasick-prevention meals (no grease, no spice, no acid) to eat pre-passage
- 10 days of American freeze-dried foods for bad sea state conditions
- 10 days of no-chopping, heat-in-pot meals
- 10 days of simple meals requiring minimal chopping
- 20 days of extra canned meats and grains in the event of a really slow passage
- 30 days of emergency rations (originally purchased before we left Washington State)
- 3 days of military rations in the ditch bag (also purchased before we left Washington)

THE HIGHLIGHT

For a brief respite from the non-stop boat work and passage preparations, we left *Ana María* at Marina de la Paz and met Andrés' parents and aunt in his hometown, Medellín, Colombia.

THE CHALLENGE

Exactly one week before we planned to depart for French Polynesia, the ratcheting block we use to furl and unfurl our headsail disintegrated. There was none to be found in La Paz nor in all of Mexico. We scrambled for a solution that would continue to allow us to single-hand a sail change.

Suddenly I needed all the tricks and skills from my days as a procurement lead. Within three days of realizing we needed the blocks, they were ordered, cleared through customs, and delivered into our waiting hands.

THE HORIZON

This week we will weigh anchor to sail 2,700 nautical miles (3,100 miles) from La Paz, Mexico to Hiva Oa, Marquesas, French Polynesia. We anticipate that the journey will take about 30 days.

Everyone says the trip will be days of boredom punctuated by moments of intense fear and exhaustion. Wish us luck!

Fair winds and following seas,

Katherine

SPECIAL EDITION: PACIFIC CROSSING

La Paz, Baja California Sur, México
24° 09' 19" N 110° 19' 37" W

DAY 0

February 9, 2023
La Paz, Baja California Sur, México
24° 09' 19" N 110° 19' 37" W

We're supposed to leave La Paz today to sail slowly to Cabo San Lucas, where we'll start our 30-day crossing. Alas, because of the 40-knot winds blowing from the north, the port captain won't give us permission to leave.

It feels like we're about to play game 7 of a tied 3-3 World Series, but there is a rain delay.

Like baseball players chew tobacco, I am chewing Tums, sticking whole wads of them in my mouth, trying to dampen the heartburn shooting up from the ball of anxiety that seems to have set up permanent residence in my stomach.

DAY 0...AGAIN...

February 10, 2023
La Paz, Baja California Sur, México
24° 09' 19" N 110° 19' 37" W

After waking up to the early alarm we set, I stumbled out of the v-berth to turn on the VHF and bring the handheld radio back to bed. Not quite asleep and not yet awake, we listen as the ferries call the port captain. Since they are much larger vessels and not subject to the same restrictions, I can't tell whether we, too, will be able to leave.

The winds are letting up after three full days of blows. If the port captain opens the port today, we can still catch the ideal weather window we see forming west of Cabo, but the port captain won't make the official announcement on the VHF until late morning. We listen to the radio chatter in case someone asks him ahead of time.

Finally, we hear a fishing panga ask timidly and hopefully, "Is the port open?" "No, port is closed until tomorrow." Welp. There goes our ideal weather window. We'll have to wait at least another five days.

DAY 0...NO, REALLY THIS TIME!

February 15, 2023
La Paz, Baja California Sur, México
24° 09' 19" N 110° 19' 37" W

At last! We've cast off from the dock to the chorus of well wishes and celebratory foghorn blows from Patrick and Christine on *Clare de Gouet*.

Our excitement quickly wanes when the autopilot suddenly becomes possessed, choosing its own course and jerking back and forth wildly, as we exit the La Paz channel. Visions of hand-steering across the ocean nearly make us faint, but a little fiddling with the compass seems to have fixed it.

We're anchoring tonight in Isla Espíritu Santo so we can have a downwind-only sail tomorrow. We've been preparing for today for the past five years, but now we find ourselves more hesitant than excited.

It's like that day when my friends Ashley and Leah and I decided to go to Six Flags in St. Louis. All summer, the average attendance at the park had been 9,000. We picked the only day when 20,000 other people showed up.

We waited in line for over an hour to ride our first roller coaster, chatting merrily, until we were next in line. "Uh oh, we're not youngins anymore. Are we too old to ride a roller coaster? Are we going to be able to walk afterward, or will we have to crawl off the ride thanks to vertigo?"

No one is forcing me to do this. I can just leave right through the exit. I'm tempted, but I stay. I just waited an hour in line for this ride. I hop into the seat, lock the seatbelt, check the lock, then check it one more time. The 16-year-old theme park employee comes by for a cursory check of the locking mechanism, but I think he should check it one more time. I want to call out to him, but it's too late. He just pressed the big green button.

Ready or not, here we go!

T-4

February 16, 2023
Canal Cerralvo, Sea of Cortez, México
24° 17' 14" N 110° 00' 57" W

We're getting thrashed in the Cerralvo Channel headed south to Cabo where our 30-day passage will actually start.

All day we've had 30-knot gusts with 8-foot seas hitting us every 6 seconds. Occasionally a 10-foot wave hits our stern, shoving us violently down the wave. We have read several accounts of the Pacific crossing where the maximum wind sailors encounter is 30 knots, so these may be the toughest conditions we will see.

My arms will be sore tomorrow from holding so tightly onto the boat. It feels like being in a car with a teenage driver, and you keep patting your chest and your lap to make sure your seatbelt is securely fastened. I find myself instinctively doing this all day, but there are no seatbelts on a boat. Another wave hits the stern and I think "Shouldn't I be strapped into a jump seat or something?"

T-3

February 17, 2023
Bahía de los Muertos, Baja California Sur, México
23° 59' 27" N 109° 49' 40" W

Today is a day of great relief.

For one, we have much better conditions. The waves are half as high as yesterday's, the winds not quite as gusty.

Secondly, we have ruled out an imminent threat to our voyage. The bilge was full of water last night when we checked. Andrés settled on two possible causes: a leak in the rudder post's packing gland or a crack in the skeg.

We felt sick as we considered our predicament. If it's a crack, it could get a whole lot worse as we cross the ocean. The right fix would be to return to La Paz to haul the boat out of the water, drop the rudder, and do a proper fiberglass repair. The process would take weeks. Alternatively, we could try to cover the crack with epoxy here in the water.

Andrés perfectly captured our doubts about using epoxy to fix a crack while in the water: "It's like finding a rip in your parachute right before you jump out of the plane and wondering whether duct tape would be enough to hold it." The epoxy fix may hold for the beginning of the passage, but it could easily fail by the end of it.

We may be dumb enough to cross the world's largest ocean on a tiny boat, but we're not stupid enough to cross it on a sinking boat.

In despair, Andrés asks me, "Can we do this?"

WE MAY BE DUMB ENOUGH TO CROSS THE WORLD'S LARGEST OCEAN ON A TINY BOAT, BUT WE'RE NOT STUPID ENOUGH TO CROSS IT ON A SINKING BOAT.

I learned this summer in *Atlas of the Heart* by Brené Brown that when we're overwhelmed with anxiety about uncertainty, we strive to make decisions that will bring certainty. Unfortunately, when we are this overwhelmed, our decision-making abilities are considerably handicapped.

I imagine us motoring back to La Paz, putting *Ana María* on a cargo ship, and shipping her back to Washington. That path feels certain, but surely we're not in the right frame of mind to make that kind of decision.

"Let's wait," I say. "We'll watch tomorrow and see if we can't pinpoint the source of the leak."

Today, only a couple hours into our sail, we spy water gushing from the rudder packing gland as we surf the waves. There's no indication of a crack in the hull.

Thank goodness! It's a relatively easy fix with materials we squirreled away for just such a repair. We're back on our way.

T-1

February 19, 2023
Los Frailes, Baja California Sur, México
23° 22' 54" N 109° 25' 13" W

Today we made bets on when we would arrive and when we would cross the Equator. We both chose March 22 for arrival in Hiva Oa, French Polynesia. I say we will cross the Equator on March 14. Andrés thinks March 15.

Our thriftiness with fuel has paid off. We've used less than 2 gallons of diesel to travel 120 miles, so we can skip the hassle of a fuel stop in Cabo San Lucas. We'll jump off from our anchorage here in Los Frailes.

Since we can leave from this anchorage and the weather forecast indicates we can leave tomorrow, our departure is imminent. I find myself back on the roller coaster, on the excruciatingly slow climb at the beginning. I can hear the gears and pulleys ratcheting, yanking me higher and higher.

Don't look down.

Don't look down.

Whatever you do, don't look at the 2,700 nautical miles to go until Hiva Oa.

Just as I reach the top, my stomach begins to drop as the train cars gather speed and barrel down the rails.

The only thing I can do now is hold on tight and enjoy the ride.

Day 17

Current Location:
2° 07' 04" S 130° 17' 01" W

THE
CO-CAPTAIN'S LOG
Pacific Crossing

Distance sailed: 119 nm
Total distance sailed: 2,046 nm
Distance to Hiva Oa: 630 nm
Wind: E 5 kts
Weather: Sunny becoming squally
Sail plan: Spinnaker from first light to sun down then wing-on-wing
Fuel remaining: 37gal

Listen to today's logs

Crossing an ocean on a small sailboat is a lot like playing the game Settlers of Catan.

Well, okay, it's like playing Settlers of Catan outside in a thunderstorm on a tilt-a-wheel carnival ride while sleep deprived …but stay with me.

There are the obvious similarities in the basic nature of any strategy game, e.g. it matters where you start, it matters how you move across the board, etc.

What makes Settlers of Catan so much like an ocean passage, though, is the paramount importance of managing resources. In the game, whoever maximizes the use of their bricks, wood, iron, wheat, and gold wins the game. Out here, the sailor who maximizes the use of the sails, current, fuel, solar

STOP!

You can continue to read the book here …

or …

you can pause and cross the Pacific Ocean with us,
following along day by day as we sail to French Polynesia.

For the duration of our passage, you'll receive a
free daily email that features:

~~~~~~

Daily updates from our passage with our location pinned on a map

~~~~~~

The Co-Captain's Log

~~~~~~

Introducing The Captain's Log

~~~~~~

Audio recordings of both logs

~~~~~~

Photos and videos from the passage

~~~~~~

To join us for the journey of a lifetime, scan this QR code
or visit www.cocaptainslog.com/crossing

Are you sure you want to keep reading here? The email experience will be richer and the rest of the story will be here waiting for you after we've arrived in French Polynesia.

To come aboard *Ana María* for the Pacific Crossing, scan this QR code or visit www.cocaptainslog.com/crossing

PACIFIC CROSSING

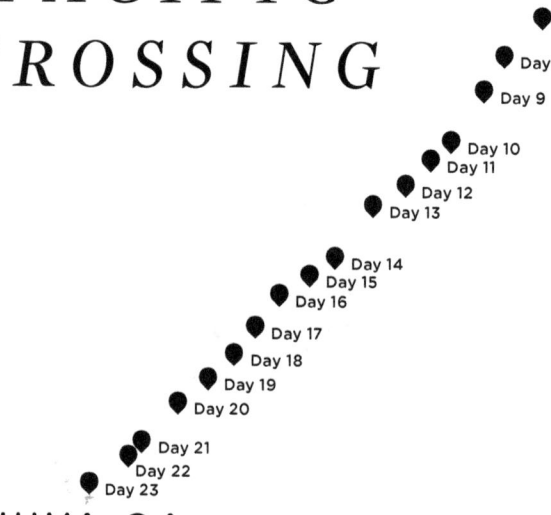

HIVA OA

*FRENCH
POLYNESIA*
(FRANCE)

DAY 1

February 20, 2023
Distance to Hiva Oa (as the albatross flies): 2,650 nautical miles
Winds: N 15-20 knots
Weather: Partly cloudy and chilly
Sail plan: Wing-on-wing at 150° then close reach at 60°

Today we've made silly mistakes. Maybe it's the adrenaline. We need some adrenaline to counteract our fear, but right now we have too much and it's making us jittery.

First, when leaving the anchorage under sail (we need to save every ounce of fuel!), I tried to backwind the genoa to tighten our turn and avoid hitting our neighboring boats. Trying to do it by hand without a winch, however, was stupid, and the genoa flogged before Andrés got it under control. Luckily, the turn was tight enough that we didn't hit any boats.

This afternoon the wind weakened enough to shake a reef, which we've done a thousand times. This time, though, the mainsail was caught on the gooseneck assembly, causing a slight tear in the sail. Fortunately, we have a sail repair kit on board, and we were able to patch it.

Both were minor mistakes and fixable, but they are mistakes we can't afford out here.

We just need to settle now. Settle into the rhythm of sailing. Settle into the motion. Settle into the watch schedule.

Settle down, Katherine. Settle down.

THE WILDLIFE

The echoes of the whales calling to one another in Bahía Los Frailes kept me awake our last night at anchor. It's hard to be mad about lost sleep when the sound reverberating through the hull is so other-worldly and magical. The whales escorted us for the ride from Los Frailes to Cabo. A pretty nice send-off!

DAY 2

February 21, 2023
Distance sailed: 106 nautical miles
Total distance sailed: 106 nautical miles
Distance to Hiva Oa: 2,499 nautical miles
Winds: N 12-15 then 15-25 knots
Weather: Clear skies. Chilly enough for full foul weather gear during night watches. Rain during the day.
Sail plan: Genoa, staysail, and first-reefed mainsail at 60° close reach

It's an hour into my night watch, and the lights of Cabo San Lucas and San Jose del Cabo are fading behind us.

The lights we expected to see, the red and green lights on the army of fishing boats that swarm around Cabo, are nowhere to be seen. They must have rounded the peninsula to fish the shallow reefs. No floating-city cruise ships are ferrying tourists from Cabo to Puerto Vallarta. Only one cargo ship is showing up as an AIS target, but she is 37 nautical miles away and moving fast toward the Panama Canal.

The only light now comes from the dim backlighting on my instruments and the brilliant sparkling night sky. With no clouds and no moon, it looks like the entire universe is visible. Some constellations I recognize, but many stars I am surely seeing for the first time tonight.

Should I try to count them? No. Impossible. There are millions of 'em. I just want to enjoy them.

It's this view that has called humans to pursue space travel rather than deepwater exploration. Out here, the motion of the ocean dominates the senses, rocking my whole body back and forth, but it's the stars that capture all my attention.

THE CHALLENGE

You'll often read about what happened on "this watch" and "that watch." On a passage like this, we sail nonstop, so someone must always be on watch to look for ships, adjust the autopilot for wind shifts, and monitor for changing conditions. With a two-person crew, this means one of us is always awake while the other sleeps—and both of us are always tired.

Normally we do 3- or 4-hour watches. For this long passage, we've worked in a 6-hour sleep for each of us to help manage fatigue. Here's our current watch schedule: 6:00 p.m. – 10:00 p.m. Katherine, 10:00 p.m. – 2:00 a.m. Andrés, 2:00 a.m. – 8:00 a.m. Katherine, 8:00 a.m. – 2:00 p.m. Andrés, and a 2:00 p.m. – 6:00 p.m. Dogwatch when we'll take short naps as needed, shower if conditions permit, make and eat dinner together then prepare for the night watches.

DAY 3

February 22, 2023
Distance sailed: 118 nautical miles
Total distance sailed: 224 nautical miles
Distance to Hiva Oa: 2,384 nautical miles
Winds: 7-10 knots, becoming fluky
Weather: Overcast and chilly
Sail plan: All three sails were out but too much slatting so a spinnaker day it is.

I have an idea!

Let's play a game called Dodge the Cargo Ship.

I'll be a tiny sailboat struggling with fluky winds. You be the Panama Canal.

As soon as it gets dark, you rapidly shoot as many cargo ships and tankers as you can straight toward me, and I'll see how many I can dodge.

Fun game, right?

Maybe for you.

Nevertheless, tonight's score was *Ana María* 13, Panama Canal 0!

Hooray for the home team!

THE LINGO

We have a priceless tool in our battle against cargo ships: automatic identification system or AIS. I can't google it out here to tell you how it works, but I can tell you how we use it.

We have an AIS receiver and transponder. When another vessel with AIS comes into range, between 5 and 50 miles, depending on the vessel, a boat icon pops up on my Cortex handheld device. That icon tells me the vessel's relative position, course, speed, and the most useful data when I'm sleep-deprived: when and how closely we'll pass the vessel.

Our device even shows us whether we need to steer up or turn down to increase the passing distance between us. Our transponder sends our position, course, speed, and vessel name to the other vessel. This is helpful because we know they see us even if we are the size of a speck of dust compared to them.

Tonight at 2:00 a.m., we heard over the radio *"Ana María, Ana María, Ana María.* This is tanker *Weisshorn Explorer* on your port bow. We cannot see your lights yet, but we see you on AIS. Is it your intention to maintain course and speed? If so, you can pass us on our bow, and we will pass astern of you." Marveling at the courtesy of this captain, we hailed back, "Correct, we will maintain course and speed so you can pass astern of us."

DAY 4

February 23, 2023
Distance sailed: 119 nautical miles
Total distance sailed: 343 nautical miles
Distance to Hiva Oa: 2,295 nautical miles
Winds: NNW 10-15 knots
Weather: Overcast
Sail plan: Wing-on-wing-on-wing ... as in our normal wing-on-wing with the main pulled out to leeward and the genoa pulled to windward on the whisker pole plus the staysail out and sheeted in tight to act like a riding sail. We'll try anything to get some stability with the Pacific swell on our beam.

I'm just settling in for my first watch of the night, having taken down the spinnaker and set up wing-on-wing-on-wing with Andrés. He's given standing orders: "If the wind dies completely for 20 minutes, do a line check and start the engine. Motor at 2000 rpm on a course of 202°True for three hours. Might as well run the watermaker while the engine is pumping out energy."

My favorite podcast is queued as I expect a long watch of trying to keep the boat moving in dying winds.

SPLASH!

What the heck was that? I turn to the stern of the boat. If that's a whale, he is way too close for comfort.

SPLASH!

This time on my starboard side.

SPLASH! SPLASH! SPLASH!

Dolphins everywhere! They're smaller than those we've seen in the Sea of Cortez. Maybe 3-feet long? They have funny-looking bodies, as if all their tails are chopped off.

With the backdrop of the neon red band of the setting sun separating the blue ocean and the gray overcast sky, they put on quite the show for me. Jumping. Dancing. Twirling. Swimming right alongside me.

What delightful company to have on my watch this evening!

THE ENTERTAINMENT

Many of you shared Spotify playlists with us, and some of you even made playlists for us. Your efforts keep us awake during watches, so thank you! I've been enjoying Malia Norman's "Songs to Sail To" and Ryan Martin Brown's "50 Songs to Cross an Ocean."

DAY 5

February 24, 2023
Distance sailed: 128 nautical miles
Total distance sailed: 471 nautical miles
Distance to Hiva Oa: 2,172 nautical miles
Winds: N 15-25 knots
Weather: Partly cloudy, getting too warm for my Smartwool long underwear underneath my full foulies (yay!)
Sail plan: Wing-on-wing at 150° with a first-reefed mainsail

My confidence took a hit today.

We jibed the boat, a complicated ordeal given the strong winds and steep swell on our beam. I know how to jibe. I can tell you each and every step of a safe jibe. But recently, panic has mutinied against logic mid-maneuver. Andrés has been working with me to make my steering decisive in heavy seas and to ensure I don't allow the boat to round up to a beam reach, risking a knockdown.

So strong was my focus on decisive steering and not rounding up that I choked and messed up the most basic step of the maneuver: I pushed the tiller the wrong way. Luckily, Andrés realized it and quickly corrected me. Together we still managed to jibe gracefully.

I felt ashamed. Ashamed for making such a simple mistake. Ashamed that I can't seem to control my panic. Am I more of a liability to Andrés than an asset on this passage?

My shame lingers through to my first night watch. Seas are heavy. Winds pipe up then slow down. The Monitor windvane, our non-electric, mechanical autopilot, is misbehaving. Our current course would take us to Peru.

"Cast not away thy confidence," Dad would tell me if he was here, so I start listening to John Maxwell's "Winning Is an Inside Job." I've loved John Maxwell ever since Jolie, the refinery manager where I used to work, showed us his video "Law of Influence."

Only a few minutes in, my morale starts to lift. I can apply some of these lessons right now:

1. **Take responsibility.** I am not just a warm body here in the cockpit. Andrés does such a great job routing us. While he rests, I need to take the helmsman's responsibility seriously and figure out a way to get us headed back to Hiva Oa on a course of 190-200°True.
2. **Listen and learn from other successful people.** What did I observe Andrés do this afternoon to adjust course and tune the Monitor windvane? He adjusted the windvane control line up and down. He tightened the tiller control lines. He loosened them. He tightened one and loosened the other. He studied the impact of each adjustment and tweaked and tweaked. I can do that. I can adjust the windvane control line. I can play with the tension on the tiller lines. I adjust and watch and adjust some more. It takes 30 minutes, but I finally get us on a course of 195°True with the Monitor windvane behaving reliably.
3. **Learn from your mistakes.** Don't "try, try, try again." Instead, try, then stop, and think. Then try again. If all goes according to plan, we won't have to jibe again for several days. Instead of just hoping I don't panic again, I'll think of ways to get my panic under control. Maybe do a dress rehearsal before the jibe so I have muscle memory?

When Andrés comes on watch, I give him a status report and a summary of my work with the Monitor windvane. "Good!" he says. "195°True is the ideal course, and I think even I would have struggled to get the Monitor windvane set to that. Great job."

I am not a great sailor *yet,* but I am committed to becoming a better one.

DAY 6

February 25, 2023
Distance sailed: 136 nautical miles
Total distance sailed: 607 nautical miles
Distance to Hiva Oa: 2,045 nautical miles
Winds: N 20-28 knots apparent
Weather: Partly cloudy
Sail plan: Second-reefed mainsail and genoa pulled out on the whisker pole. Sailing at 130° apparent wind angle. End-boom preventer in place. When we do little day hops from one bay to the next, we use our boom vang as a preventer to keep the boom in place and prevent a dangerous accidental jibe. On days like today with the relentless wind stressing the rig and the tall swells nearly touching the boom, we use the heavy-duty, end-boom preventer system Andrés designed. It is a hassle to set up, but it more effectively protects the integrity of the rigging. We've heard horror stories of Pacific Seacraft 34s without an end-boom preventer breaking their booms in two. That would be a catastrophe out here.

The turf war has begun.

We read about the turf war between boobies and sailboats in Rick and Cindy Patrinellis' account of crossing the Pacific on *Cool Change*, a Pacific Seacraft 31. They had several boobies land on their bow for a free ride. One attacked Cindy in the cockpit—something straight out of the movie *The Birds*—thinking she had stolen the fish the boobie had caught for a midnight snack.

Admittedly, we are the aggressors in the turf war—*we* have entered *their* territory, though we do wonder why they have chosen offshore for their home. They must fly against 30 knots of wind and fish in huge swell with nary a place to rest. They probably study us and wonder "Why would humans choose to come out here, battling 30 knots of wind, horrendous cross swell, and nary a safe harbor?"

We find ourselves together out here, yet there is no camaraderie, despite misery loving company.

Once we entered their turf, they considered all our turf fair game. They circle and circle and circle *Ana María*, trying over and over to land.

Now, we're not monsters. We know spotting *Ana María* must feel like a miraculous provision of much needed respite, so we proposed a peace treaty: You can land and ride on the bow from here to Hiva Oa. You can ride on the warm radar or the perfect little perch next to the radar. The whisker pole is also fair game. But NO sitting on the solar panels!

And how did our adversaries respond to such a proposal? They laughed in our faces. Actually, they didn't laugh. They did what birds do when they want to spite you: They dropped a gallon of poop on our precious solar panels. I cannot believe how much poop came from such a small bird.

With my resentment still seething, I had settled into my night watch when they sent a peace emissary. They should have sent one with a bit more tact.

I was all alone in the middle of the ocean, minding my own business, when a boobie dove between the stern pushpit and the bimini, landing in the cockpit right next to me, squawking and flapping like a bird possessed. It nearly scared me to death.

It took me a good five minutes and a number of tactics to send him on his way.

This morning Andrés and I spent 20 minutes cleaning up the solar panels. It was the first time on the trip … but I doubt it will be the last. The battle wages on.

THE CHALLENGE

We are uptight about our solar panels because they are the only source of energy we can afford on the boat. Many passage makers run their engines for an hour or two each day to top up their batteries and ensure the fridge can continue to keep food cold. *Ana María* can't carry enough fuel for that, so we rely on our two solar panels to charge our batteries and power our instruments, lights, radar, fridge, and electric autopilot. We foresaw this challenge and followed Don Casey's unpopular but sound advice in *This Old Boat*: we filled in our spacious fridge with insulation, converting it into a tiny but efficient fridge. We're pleased as punch with the panels and system performance, our fully charged batteries, AND our cold food.

DAY 7

February 26, 2023
Distance sailed: 152 nautical miles (without current!!!!!)—a record day for *Ana María*
Total distance sailed: 759 nautical miles
Distance to Hiva Oa: 1,871 nautical miles
Winds: NNE 22-32 knots apparent, 40 knots true
Weather: Clear and sunny
Sail plan: Second-reefed mainsail and genoa pulled out on the whisker pole then poled-out genoa only. Sailing at 160° apparent wind angle. End-boom preventer in place.

A TALE OF 3 WISE MEN ... OR 2 WISE MEN AND A WISE WOMAN

"How is the Monitor windvane doing?" I asked Andrés just before he headed down for a nap. "She's doing great."

So, I am surprised to see only 10 minutes later, she isn't doing great at all. She keeps rounding upwind, and I must scramble to bring the boat back downwind to avoid getting these 10-foot swells on our beam. I adjust all the control lines, but still, she's rounding up. I glance back at the Monitor windvane itself and ... oh ... my ... gosh ... the paddle has come off the Monitor windvane, and it's trailing behind us, hanging on by a literal thread, as we surf these waves at 9 knots!

"I NEED YOUR HELP!" My call down to Andrés must have had the right amount of urgency because he poked his head up almost immediately.

"The paddle! It's come off!"

"I gotta get dressed and get my life jacket."

"Hurry!" This is no time to dillydally. We don't have a spare. If we lose that paddle, it will be four days of hand-steering in 2-hour shifts. With my hand now on the tiller to steer the boat, I know how miserable that would be.

Andrés climbs to the stern, clips his tether to the boat, and tries to grab the paddle. "Oh sh*t, that guy was right!"

"That guy" would be Bruce, of Bruce and Gina on *Dream Catcher*. He saw our Monitor windvane and wisely cautioned, "You need a spare sacrificial tube for that thing. Mine broke early on in a passage and it took me a couple of rough days to fix it. Put some penetrating oil on there in case you need to take the broken one off."

Now, if we carried a spare for every item someone said broke on a passage, we would essentially need to tow another Pacific Seacraft 34 behind us. However, we checked our spares and, sure enough, we have an extra sacrificial tube stowed with the emergency rudder.

The sacrificial tube on the Monitor windvane acts like a fuse in an electrical circuit. The tube is designed to snap if subjected to a certain amount of force, breaking the mechanical links of the Monitor windvane and preventing that strong force from ripping the Monitor windvane from the hull and creating a hole in the boat.

"The sacrificial tube broke?" I cry incredulously. That would require enormous pressure!

"Yep."

Looks like I'll be hand-steering while Andrés tries to fix it. The wise advice of Emma Davis, a fellow sailing pupil of Captain Phyllis Woolwine and who made this passage last year on her Pacific Seacraft 37, comes to mind: "Just remember all that Phyllis taught you and you'll be fine."

With one hand firmly gripping the end of the tiller, I am transported back to our 2019 Bareboat Cruising course with Captain Phyllis when we crossed the Strait of Juan de Fuca in 35-knot winds and 7-foot seas crashing on the stern.

All day as we hand steered, Phyllis would coach, "Pull the tiller! Pull, pull! Okay, now push! Push, push the tiller so you don't jibe. Okay, now pull hard! Pull hard so you don't broach. Pull!" When we arrived at the anchorage that night, I felt like I had ridden a mechanical bull across the strait.

It's Phyllis' voice in my head now telling me to push and pull, pull and push. Today we "only" have apparent wind to 32 knots, but we have 10-foot swells topped with crashing wind waves. I pull, pull, pull to avoid catching one of the waves on our beam, then push, push, push as we surf down the waves at 9.6 knots. It's going better than I would have expected. No sense of panic, just focus.

Steering requires all my attention, but out of the corner of my eye, I can see Andrés is making good progress. Just over an hour after I called him up, he is dropping the paddle with a new sacrificial tube down into the water and setting the Monitor windvane to steer.

"Wow! You're finished already? I am impressed! Bruce had made it seem really difficult to get the tube out."

"Yep, I suspect it broke because there is too much weather helm. We have too much sail up for the 40 knots of true wind behind us. Let's take down the mainsail. It should be easier for the Monitor windvane to keep up without breaking."

Then as we are tethering to take down the mainsail, he turns to me, "Can I tell you a secret?" And with a twinkle in his eye, he admits, "Back when Bruce told us his story, I put penetrating oil on the sacrificial tube on the paddle of the Monitor windvane just in case this happened. Today I pulled the broken tube out, no problem."

What a wise man he is!

THE HIGHLIGHT

The best thing about the passage so far is that it's been incredibly fast. Lucky for us, the famous trade winds filled in earlier—yay!—but are stronger—uh oh!—than expected. We're exhausted from the intensity of sailing constantly in the strong winds and heavy seas, but boy, are we making great time in the trade winds! The trade winds have been used by sailors for centuries to travel reliably across the oceans, allowing transoceanic trade, hence the name. We're galloping toward the Equator with the northeast trade winds filling our sails. Once we cross the Equator, the southeast trade winds will push us to the Marquesas.

DAY 8

February 27, 2023
Distance sailed: 132 nautical miles
Total distance sailed: 891 nautical miles
Distance to Hiva Oa: 1,742 nautical miles
Winds: 10-40 knots—Variable depending on the squalls
Weather: Squalls
Sail plan: Wing-on-wing with genoa on the whisker pole and staysail to leeward, sailing at 130° apparent wind angle

We learned our lesson.
 Never say "After these relentless trade winds, the ITCZ will be a welcome change," loud enough for Neptune to hear you. He gave us a taste of what's to come next week. A whole night spent attempting to dodge squalls, mostly unsuccessfully.

I'll take the consistent 25-knot trade winds any day over the frightening lightning, clocking winds, and downpours of the squalls.

THE CHALLENGE

We're stuck in the ITCZ or Intertropical Convergence Zone. This ever-metamorphosing area north of the Equator is the meeting place and dueling grounds for the weather systems in the Northern and Southern Hemispheres.

If the trade winds are famous for steady, reliable winds, then the ITCZ is infamous for its unpredictable weather, squalls and storms, and oscillation between extreme conditions and dead calm. It's not a place you want to linger.

You may have heard it being called the doldrums. Honestly, we're not sure what the difference is, if there is any, as we've seen the terms used interchangeably.

We once read about a German couple making this crossing. At about our current position, the captain put out a request for help to the Pacific Puddle Jump Rally: "My crew is done with this passage and wants off this boat immediately. She says the ITCZ is too much for her. Can anyone pick her up?" The woman was ridiculed for making such an unrealistic demand and the captain ridiculed for even entertaining the idea. Though she was crazy for thinking she could quite literally jump ship, now having experienced the ITCZ for myself, I can honestly say that I don't blame her.

DAY 9

February 28, 2023
Distance sailed: 128 nautical miles
Total distance sailed: 1,019 nautical miles
Distance to Hiva Oa: 1,632 nautical miles
Winds: NNE 22 knots with 40-knot squalls
Weather: Sunny between squalls
Sail plan: Wing-on-wing with poled-out genoa to windward and staysail to leeward

Just when I thought living on a boat couldn't lower my standards any more than it already has ...

It took us one night to lower them yet a couple more notches when our foul weather gear got so drenched by the squalls that they stopped keeping water *out* and began keeping water *in*. We spent a miserable night sitting in the pools of water created by our accidental rain catchment devices.

Why are we getting soaked, staying soaked, going inside with soaked clothes, drying off, and putting on soaked clothes to come back out, only to get soaked again?

Then an epiphany: We are a married, two-person crew without a YouTube channel. Why are we messing with clothes? In this squally weather, we've exchanged our foul weather suits for our birthday suits.

Classy, I know.

THE GALLEY

Despite the 10 days of hectic wind and the rough swell on our beam, there have only been three days when all I could muster in the galley was boiling water for the freeze-dried food. Otherwise, we've eaten well, working our way through the fresh produce while it lasts. Besides the Mountain House backpacking food, we've enjoyed homemade chicken pepperoni pasta, salmon pesto pasta, chicken with peach sauce, stovetop tuna penne, taco soup, and chicken tomato couscous.

DAY 10

March 1, 2023
Distance sailed: 126 nautical miles
Total distance sailed: 1,145 nautical miles
Distance to Hiva Oa: 1,524 nautical miles
Winds: N 18-27 knots
Weather: Sunny with a break from the squalls (and a quick end to our short-lived nudist lifestyle)
Sail plan: Genoa pulled to windward on whisker pole

How do you sail 2,700 nautical miles? This is how I do it:
Every 20 minutes, the music stops.
Then I ...
Stand up in the cockpit and look at the horizon in every direction for any lights of cargo ships, tankers, or fishing boats.
Check the AIS map for any targets within 50 miles.
Turn on the radar with a radius of 8 miles to check for squalls or vessels without AIS.
Compare the current course over ground with the captain's desired course over ground and adjust the windvane or autopilot accordingly.
Use the red light on the headlamp to check the decks, the sails, the sheets, and the windvane lines for problems or fouling.
Set a timer for the music to stop again in 20 minutes.
Press "play" on the Spotify playlist.
Repeat approximately 2,160 times or until I reach Hiva Oa.

DAY 11

March 2, 2023
Distance sailed: 131 nautical miles
Total distance sailed: 1,276 nautical miles
Distance to Hiva Oa: 1,370 nautical miles
Winds: NNE 15-20 knots
Weather: Clear, sunny, hot
Sail plan: Wing-on-wing with first-reefed mainsail and genoa. End-boom preventer in place.

After five days of intense wave after intense wave, we are finally getting wave after wave of relief.

Relief that we can finally raise the mainsail.

Relief that all three of us survived the trade winds more or less unscathed.

Relief that we've already traveled more than 1,200 miles and only 9 of them required using our engine.

Relief that we were finally able to replace the chafe guard on the genoa, add a chafe guard to the second reefing line, change out the composting head, and empty the bilge of salt water.

Significant relief that we had spare screws for the two screws that went missing on our genoa furler in the heavy weather.

Relief that, instead of the barrage of squalls that have filled the horizon the past few nights, the night sky is clear and full of stars.

Relief from the nice warm water and raspberry-scented shampoo washing off five days of salt and sweat.

Relief for our rear ends that we can finally bring out the cockpit cushions, saving us from having permanent tattoos from the rough, non-skid-covered fiberglass in the cockpit.

Relief that we've gone from galloping wildly to trotting at a nice clip of 5 knots on a great course toward our destination.

Relief that tonight the Pacific is finally living up to its name and granting us a peaceful night.

THE LINGO

"Reefing" means to shorten sail or reduce sail area. As winds get stronger, we need less sail up to move the boat. As winds gets stronger, having less sail up keeps the boat balanced. Reefing isn't for wimpy sailors but for clever ones. A properly reefed sail can often improve our course without sacrificing speed.

On *Ana María* we say, "Reef early. Reef often," and we've been reefing often in these squalls. We use two reef points on our mainsail: the first reef reduces the sail by ~25 percent, and the second reduces the sail by ~50 percent. We could reef our headsails, but we avoid it to spare the pressure on the furlers.

DAY 12

March 3, 2023
Distance sailed: 120 nautical miles
Total distance sailed: 1,396 nautical miles
Distance to Hiva Oa: 1,277 nautical miles
Winds: NE 15-20 knots
Weather: Squally
Sail plan: Wing-on-wing with genoa and second-reefed mainsail. End-boom preventer.

"We were as far as we could get from anywhere without getting closer to somewhere." –Ulys K. Smith

We've made it halfway! Maybe not time-wise, but distance-wise, we've already completed half our journey.

We'll eat Colombian chocolate tonight to celebrate.

THE LINGO

Sailors for decades have called this passage the Pacific Puddle Jump with no small dose of irony. We joined the Pacific Puddle Jump Rally to benefit from the wisdom and help of the rally organizers, the discounts, and the ability to see the live position and daily updates of all the other boats crossing. We've loved reading the updates of the boats who've just finished the passage, saddened to read some passages are canceled due to flooded engines, and eager to welcome the fleet of boats who will start the passage in March and April. You can google Pacific Puddle Jump Rally and see on its website a list of all the boats participating. Though we did qualify as a "micro-boat participant," (the median length of the fleet this year is 44 feet—10 feet longer than *Ana María*) we were not, to Andrés' disappointment, the smallest boat in the rally this year.

DAY 13

March 4, 2023
Distance sailed: 131 nautical miles
Total distance sailed: 1,527 nautical miles
Distance to Hiva Oa: 1,145 nautical miles
Winds: NE 18-22 knots
Weather: Squalls and rain with 100% cloud cover
Sail plan: Wing-on-wing with genoa and second-reefed mainsail. End-boom preventer.

"Will we be seasick like this for the entire 30 days?" we wondered in the Cerralvo Channel at the start of this passage.

"Will this 12-foot swell crash onto our beam the rest of the 2,600 nautical miles?"

"Will we have these 32-knot winds pummeling us for the next 20 days?"

"Will every night from now on be a continuous train of 40-knot squalls, lightning, and torrential downpour?"

And today ...

"Will we ever see the sun again or will it just be 100 percent cloud cover from now on? Will our batteries ever get charged again? Will it ever stop raining? Will we ever get out of the ITCZ?"

In coastal passage making, you know that whatever discomfort you're experiencing will be short-lived. You'll be safely anchored by sundown. You'll be docked in a marina tomorrow. Safe harbor is only two days away.

Out here, it feels as though the discomfort of the moment could last an eternity.

After I broke my leg, while convalescing, taking pain meds, and wondering "What in the heck are we going to do now?" I read *Option B: Facing Adversity, Building Resilience, and Finding Joy* by Sheryl Sandberg and Adam Grant. The book introduced me to Dr. Martin Seligman's research on optimism and his theories on our responses to adversity when we feel it's personal, pervasive, and permanent.

On an ocean passage, every adversity feels permanent.

Dr. Seligman's research inspired me to spend all of 2022 studying, contemplating, and practicing hope. While I discovered that optimism and hope are not one and the same, they both share this confidence: it will not be this way forever.

So today while it rained for hours on end and our solar panels made exactly zero power to charge the batteries, we did something we have never done before while sailing. We verified that there were no ships within 50 miles, set up the Monitor windvane to steer for us, and we both crawled inside the cabin, into warm, dry, comfortable sea berths where we read a cruising guide to all the delights that await us in the Marquesas. A land flowing with milk and honey.

And that gave us hope.

We will not be floundering forever in the ITCZ, but God willing, we will make landfall in Hiva Oa in the next two weeks.

We will not be confined to this boat forever but will soon be hiking up to see French Polynesia's biggest waterfalls.

We will not eat ham sandwiches and granola bars forever but will soon be eating *poisson cru* and fruit plucked right off the trees.

We will not be washing our shirts and underwear in the sink forever but will be able to pay the laundry lady to wash, dry, and fold our clothes and sheets.

We will not be surviving on four-hour naps forever but will soon get a full night's sleep.

We will not be stuck under these clouds forever, but we will see the sun again. Maybe not tomorrow. But hopefully the next day.

And it will feel oh so glorious.

THE WILDLIFE

We haven't seen much wildlife since we left Socorro Island in our wake. Whereas we now see only the occasional boobie, we see tons and tons of flying fish.

To my surprise, flying fish actually fly! Did you know that? Their name is not just hyperbole. They have real wings and are constantly leaping out of the water and flying over the swells. Some miss their intended destination and land on our decks instead. Every morning we pick up a few and throw them back into the sea.

DAY 14

March 5, 2023
Distance sailed: 131 nautical miles
Total distance sailed: 1,658 nautical miles
Distance to Hiva Oa: 1,005 nautical miles
Winds: NE 15 knots sustained, squall gusts to 40 knots
Weather: Overcast and squally
Sail plan: Wing-on-wing with genoa and second-reefed mainsail. End-boom preventer. Ran engine for 3 hours.

I'm very tempted to simply write "No good, very bad day" and leave it at that. But if you can't join us in our sufferings, how can you join us fully in our celebrations?

The things that went poorly today:
+ 40-knot squalls all night and all day, meaning, we spent 24 hours either cowering below, hoping the sails wouldn't rip to shreds, or outside in the cockpit sopping wet.
+ The squalls messed up our watch schedule, so we're running on fumes.
+ The squalls pushed us into a gigantic no-wind zone and left us there to languish in squall after squall.
+ We were forced to use some precious fuel to motor west to find some wind.
+ We ran the watermaker while running the engine. The heel (or tilt) of the boat and the level of the tanks forced water to flood the bathroom—at least it was fresh water!
+ As we were motoring, a random fishing boat without AIS passed less than 2 nautical miles in front of our bow.
+ The minute the fishing boat passed us and we thought we could relax a bit, we realized our wind instrument, which tells us the direction of the wind and its strength, was broken. This is the second instrument to break on this trip.
+ Fixing the wind instrument meant hoisting Andrés 45 feet out of the safety of the cockpit to the top of the mast.

The things that went well today:
+ The bearings of the wind instrument had gotten clogged when the dust from a year in the Sea of Cortez mixed with the rain from the ITCZ squalls and then dried in clumps. Andrés was able to clean them and grease them up. The wind instrument is back in business!
+ Our batteries are mostly charged.
+ Our water tanks are full.
+ We ate a great lunch of potluck burgers and rice.
+ We did not catch any of the fishing boat's nets in our propeller.
+ We have a great direct course to Hiva Oa, averaging 6 knots.
+ Right now, we have no structural damage. We're not sinking. Our rig and sails are in good shape. Our engine still works. Our autopilots are working. Both crew members are healthy and still *mostly* sane.

THE ENTERTAINMENT

Audiobooks help the watches pass quickly. I finished *The Alice Network* (thank you, Sissy!) and am loving *Project Hail Mary* (thanks for the gift, Alexandra, and the recommendation, Matt!). Andrés is listening to *The Help* (thanks Mom and Dad!).

DAY 15

March 6, 2023
Distance sailed: 142 nautical miles
Total distance sailed: 1,800 nautical miles
Distance to Hiva Oa: 870 nautical miles
Winds: SE 12 knots ... from the south!! Could we be out of the ITCZ???
Weather: Hot and sunny
Sail plan: Mainsail, genoa, and staysail sailing at 80° apparent wind angle

I sit here in the cockpit in the last two hours of my second night watch, amazed at the sight.

Nearly due west, the glowing yellow full moon is setting on the horizon after I watched it unfettered by squalls cross the starry sky last night.

To the north, thankfully at some distance, I watch an electric lightning display as all those squalls we left behind continue on their northwest rampage.

Opposite the moon and framed by the stern pushpit and bimini, the sun is rising in the east, turning the horizon bright orange, a stark contrast to the dark gray but harmless wispy clouds.

Completing the circle, I look to the south across our port beam. I can't see it. There is no sign pointing to it, but I know it's there ...

The Equator.

DAY 16

March 7, 2023
Distance sailed: 127 nautical miles
Total distance sailed: 1,927 nautical miles
Distance to Hiva Oa: 739 nautical miles
Winds: SE 5-10 knots
Weather: Sunny and hot
Sail plan: Spinnaker and mainsail

Today was *supposed* to be the day we would celebrate our equatorial crossing, but yesterday morning, Andrés looked at the charts and forecasts and announced we would cross the Equator in the middle of the night last night, a full week before either of us predicted at the beginning of the passage.

"I guess that rules out an equatorial swim for you, but we could celebrate at breakfast or lunch tomorrow. What do you think?"

I don't have any special breakfast makings, so I replied, "Let's do it at lunch. I have a celebratory dish I can make."

At the end of Andrés' afternoon nap yesterday, I was playing around in the charts, looking at how far we've sailed, looking at how close Hiva Oa is, looking at our current position, and I realized something.

"Guess what!" I exclaim when he rouses.

"What?"

"We're 4 miles from the Equator! We're not going to cross it in the middle of the night. We're going to cross it at dinnertime."

Ditching the mundane dinner plans I had in mind, I prepare a bit more festive meal for this hot weather party: tacos al pastor. Pork cooked in pineapple juice. Salsa casera. Pineapple chunks. Freshly squeezed lime. Wrapped up in a tortilla. Yum. Yum. Yum!

I hurry to clean up dinner because we must be getting close. "How much time until we cross?" I ask Andrés as I dry the last of the dishes.

"Probably 10 minutes. I'll put the GPS position on my phone so we can track it. ... Ooooh! Look! 0°0'0"! We're here! We're at the Equator!"

"Woooohooooo!' I add my hollers to the jubilation, jumping up and down, giving him high fives.

Good thing I put the champagne to chill in the fridge just in case. I grab the small bottle, two champagne flutes, and the treat I picked up in Medellín for this occasion before making my way into the cockpit.

Andrés pops the cork, pours us each a glass, and sprinkles the rest into the sea as the traditional gift to Neptune.

We sit side-by-side, savoring the sensation of the cold champagne tingling in our mouths, nibbling on the dark chocolate açaí bites, giddy with excitement. Crossing the Equator on a sailboat is a big deal. Crossing the Equator after 1,800 hard-fought nautical miles feels like a victory.

Instead of an anticlimactic nighttime crossing, we're smiling together in the warm cockpit, the mainsail shading us from the sun's harshest light. All three sails are out, pulling us at a gentle 5 knots into the Southern Hemisphere. This is about as perfect a celebration as it gets.

Once we fêted, washed and put away the flutes, set the sails for the night, and tucked Andrés into the sea berth below, I sat quietly in the cockpit, marveling at the sights.

My view was almost the exact opposite of yesterday morning's. The sun set slowly and brilliantly in the west as the full moon rose straight up from the east. The Northern Hemisphere and the Equator disappeared in *Ana María*'s wake while Hiva Oa beckoned sweetly from less than 800 nautical miles away.

For the first time in several days, I didn't want to escape my surroundings, preferring to immerse myself in an audiobook. I wanted to be fully present to memorize every sensation, to etch into my soul the joy and pride of the accomplishment.

What a night! A night I'll treasure the rest of my life.

THE LINGO

No longer shall we be called "Pollywogs." Henceforth, having crossed the Equator under sail, we shall officially be called the long-honored "Shellbacks."

DAY 17

March 8, 2023
Distance sailed: 119 nautical miles
Total distance sailed: 2,046 nautical miles
Distance to Hiva Oa: 630 nautical miles
Winds: E 5 knots
Weather: Sunny becoming squally
Sail plan: Spinnaker from first light to sundown then wing-on-wing

Crossing an ocean on a small sailboat is a lot like playing the game Settlers of Catan.

Well, okay, it's like playing Settlers of Catan outside in a thunderstorm on a tilt-a-wheel carnival ride while sleep-deprived ... but stay with me.

There are the obvious similarities in the basic nature of any strategy game, e.g. it matters where you start; it matters how you move across the board, etc.

What makes Settlers of Catan so much like an ocean passage, though, is the critical importance of managing resources. In the game, whoever maximizes the use of their bricks, wood, iron, wheat, and gold wins the game. Out here, the sailor who maximizes the use of the sails, current, fuel, solar power, water, and crew energy will make landfall the safest and fastest.

And just like we learned to play Settlers of Catan, we're learning to play the resource game out here:

- In Catan, the resources needed at the beginning (lots of brick and wood to build roads) aren't necessarily what a player needs later. Out here at the beginning, we needed full water tanks at all times in case the watermaker broke en route (not unheard of on this passage) and we were forced to survive for 30 days off our measly 75 gallons of fresh water. As we get closer to Hiva Oa, the risk is reduced, so our water resource is less critical. Before we crossed the Equator, we depended on the wind to move us. Now we are pretty dependent on the currents and fuel.

- In both the game and passage, it's critical to put the resources to good use. The person who wins the game isn't the person who has the most resource cards left but the person who has turned the resources into settlements. The goal of the passage isn't to make it to Hiva Oa with all our fuel. The fuel should be used if it can get us there faster and safer.

+ In Catan, the settlements start to grow when the player combines several different kinds of resources. Same thing out here. Combining resources can get us further. If we use fuel to run the engine, we try to raise the sails to increase fuel efficiency and run the watermaker off the free power generated by the engine.
+ I remember the first time I lost half my resource cards in Catan. It was a tough lesson to learn: it does not pay to hoard resources. In fact, it can cost you. When we left La Paz, *Ana María* was the heaviest we'd ever seen her, yet we could have stuffed more jerry cans of fuel on the side decks and more food in all the nooks and crannies. It was tempting. We chose instead to travel as light as possible since a heavy boat can't sail in light winds. Our gamble is paying off. We're managing to sail at 4 knots in 5 knots of apparent wind thanks to *Ana María*'s slim figure.
+ My mother-in-law's go-to strategy in Catan is to establish a port. In the game, a port allows the player to trade at a more favorable exchange, enabling them to more efficiently leverage their resources. Our solar panels do the same thing for us. Since they are so efficient, we can run the watermaker off the solar power. Only on the worst day of the ITCZ did they perform so poorly that we were forced to use fuel to top up the batteries.
+ And just like the game, we can strategically use all our resources yet still win or lose by the luck of the draw.
+ (Apparently, we drew the card of doom: 10 days of zero wind forecasted between here and Hiva Oa.)

THE GALLEY

Carrie Hoffman, a friend in St. Louis, asked for some of the recipes I am making on the passage. Here are two favorites when simplicity is the name of the game:

THE BOAT GALLEY COOKBOOK'S CHICKEN TOMATO COUSCOUS

INGREDIENTS

1 cup boiling water

1 cup couscous

1 teaspoon chicken bouillon

1 can diced tomatoes with their juices

1 tablespoon dried tarragon

Salt and pepper to taste

2 servings of cooked chicken—out here I use Wild Planet organic canned chicken, but shredded rotisserie chicken would also work well.

DIRECTIONS

1. Pour boiling water into a bowl with couscous and chicken bouillon. Stir, cover, and let sit 5 minutes. Heat diced tomatoes and their juices in a small saucepan until just boiling. Add tarragon, salt, pepper, and the chicken. Heat until chicken is warm, about 3 minutes. Serve over fluffed couscous.

CHICKPEA MELT FROM THE KITCHN™

We serve the recipe as written at anchor and eat a deconstructed version of it on passage. It's shelf-stable and delicious!

INGREDIENTS

2 tablespoons olive oil
2 garlic cloves, minced
2 tablespoons tomato paste
¼ teaspoon red pepper flakes
1 can chickpeas, drained and rinsed
1 can diced tomatoes with their juices
½ cup water
1 teaspoon kosher salt
1 teaspoon oregano
1 teaspoon basil
½ teaspoon ground pepper
4 thick slices of crusty bread
4 slices of cheese, mozzarella or provolone work well

DIRECTIONS

1. Heat olive oil in a deep skillet over medium heat. Add minced garlic to the oil and cook, stirring constantly, for 2 minutes until fragrant. Add tomato paste and red pepper flakes and cook for 1 minute.
2. Add chickpeas, diced tomatoes with their juices, water, salt, oregano, basil, and ground pepper. Bring to a simmer and cook for 20 minutes or until the sauce has thickened and most of the liquid has evaporated.
3. At anchor, we'd put it on bread, cover it with cheese, and broil it in the oven for 3 minutes. Out here we serve it in large bowls so it can't spill if we get tossed by a wave, sprinkle shredded cheese on top, and eat it with the last of the Bimbo bread we bought in Mexico.

DAY 18

March 9, 2023
Distance sailed: 104 nautical miles
Total distance sailed: 2,150 nautical miles
Distance to Hiva Oa: 530 nautical miles
Winds: E 5-8 knots
Weather: Mostly sunny and hot
Sail plan: Spinnaker and mainsail from first light to sunset then wing-on-wing

Spinnaker flying. Making 5.3 knots direct to Hiva Oa with only 6 knots of apparent wind. No squalls yet to break our progress.

Now *this* is smooth sailing.

THE CHALLENGE

We're just over 500 nautical miles away from landfall, so we are relatively confident we can make it, even if we have to swim and tow the boat behind us. The question now is "When we will make it?"

Forecasts show *zero* wind for the next 10 days, and we don't have quite enough fuel to motor all the way to Hiva Oa, so we have three options:

1. We can relax, bob around with the swell and current, and get there in two weeks.
2. We can break our own rule and start to fly the spinnaker at night to get there in five days. There is a high probability, though, that we get smacked with an unseen 40-knot squall in the middle of the night, rip the only sail that has kept us limping along, and then get to Hiva Oa in three weeks.
3. We can rearrange our watch schedule to maximize the time we can fly the spinnaker. We can raise the spinnaker at the first hint of light on the horizon and keep it up until daylight has disappeared completely. We can do frequent sail adjustments to take advantage of

every puff of wind. We can withstand some sail flogging at night to inch out 3 knots of progress under white sails. With all this effort, we may get there in a week.

Door #3 it is!

DAY 19

March 10, 2023
Distance sailed: 99 nautical miles—our slowest day yet but every mile counts!
Total distance sailed: 2,249 nautical miles
Distance to Hiva Oa: 434 nautical miles
Winds: ESE 5-10 knots
Weather: Partly cloudy
Sail plan: Spinnaker and mainsail from first light to dusk then mainsail, genoa, and staysail at an angle of 70° apparent wind through the night

Dad on his daily check-in: "Here's a quote from your boat's designer I found when reading about your Crealock 34: *'I believe there is a great difference between speed around the buoys and speed on an ocean passage consisting, perhaps, of an undersized emaciated skipper and a mildly mutinous spouse. That's when the boat must take care of the crew.'*

Does the shoe fit?"

The mutiny in the belly of the crew has been quelled since exiting the ITCZ, and the appetite of the captain has been restored since leaving the steep seas of the northeast trade winds behind, but Bill Crealock's quote still rings true.

This is a loooooong passage, and we're starting to experience the cumulative effects of fatigue heaped upon fatigue. We desperately need *Ana María* to cradle us in the safety and comfort of her hull.

Many boats have a specialty, conditions in which they excel. They're designed for those conditions. *Ana María* is a study in compromise. She is neither the heavy, broad, full-keel boat made to withstand storms and heavy seas, nor is she the light, sleek, fin-keel boat that races upwind.

With her compromises, she has performed splendidly in the vast array of conditions we've experienced in the 2,200 nautical miles thus far. She was a sturdy champ in the six days of non-stop heavy trade winds. She was a safe responder to the unexpected gusts of the squalls in the ITCZ. And now in

5 knots of wind, she's nimbly using every puff of every gust to propel us at 5 knots toward Hiva Oa.

Ana María has taken great care of us, just as we've taken care of her. No wonder the Crealock 34 is on every list of Best Bluewater Cruisers.

THE HIGHLIGHT

It's hard to imagine completing this passage without our weather routing apps PredictWind and LuckGrib. These powerhouses have gotten us this far, this fast. Now, I know there are people who will read this who navigated oceans pre-GPS using sextants, and I know in two years it will be unheard of to cross an ocean without real-time forecasts from Starlink. In this moment in sailing history, however, we will appreciate what we've got.

Twice a day, Andrés downloads weather forecasts (GFS and ECMWF models) of varying resolutions using our satellite phone and apps. These apps use our boat's polars, the theoretical speeds at which *Ana María* can sail at various wind angles and strengths, to recommend the fastest and most comfortable route to the destination, much like a sophisticated Google Maps.

These apps, particularly LuckGrib, have been instrumental in helping us find the wind and favorable currents to avoid using the engine.

DAY 20

March 11, 2023
Distance sailed: 132 nautical miles
Total distance sailed: 2,381 nautical miles
Distance to Hiva Oa: 320 nautical miles
Winds: ESE 5-10 knots
Weather: Mostly sunny and hot
Sail plan: Spinnaker and mainsail from first light to dusk then mainsail, genoa, and staysail at an angle of 70° apparent wind through the night

There is little luxury on a 34-foot sailboat crossing an ocean, but there is one. A sublime one: the cockpit shower.

Ana María has a wet head (or bathroom in landlubber speak), meaning, it is technically possible to shower in the head, but by the time you dry the whole head, you're sweaty again. Andrés designed an improved system featuring a summer shower that uses gravity fill from the mast step and has a shower curtain to enclose the spray. We use the shower setup almost every day.

A daily shower is a luxury on a small boat, but the cockpit shower like the one we took today is the ultimate luxury: The warm air. The space to move about. The time to linger. The cool water with enough pressure to imagine I'm having my hair washed in a salon. The sweet raspberry scent of the kids' 3-in-1 shampoo. The gentle breeze to dry me off. The easy clean up. The freedom.

For a brief 10 minutes afterward, I'm no longer a salty sailor. I've been reborn, made new again, whole again, a human again.

DAY 21

March 12, 2023
Distance sailed: 115 nautical miles
Total distance sailed: 2,496 nautical miles
Distance to Hiva Oa: 191 nautical miles
Winds: E 3-5 knots
Weather: Sunny and unbearably hot
Sail plan: Spinnaker and mainsail up from first light to last light then motorsailing with all three white sails

OH CAPTAIN, MY CAPTAIN

I can count on one hand the number of people I would trust to sail me safely across an ocean. Lucky for us, Andrés is one of those very few.

Here's why he is such a fantastic captain:

1. He is so smart. *Ana María* is an amalgamation of many complex systems sailing in an environment of complex systems (wind, swell, current, squalls, etc.). He understands them all and how they all interact.
2. He is strategic. He can foresee and avoid problems as well as seize opportunities. We're reaping the benefits of this strength and avoiding the worst of the swell ("If we jibe tomorrow at 9:00 a.m., then for the entire time we are in the trade winds we will have the swell on our stern instead of our beam.") and making the most of the wind. When you examine our achieved average speed and minimal use of the engine, you'll see the proof is in the pudding.
3. He's got a sailor's intuition. All those afternoons learning to sail in alligator-infested Florida lakes, all those Saturdays sailing a Laser on Lake Washington, all those evenings sailing the wooden boats on Lake Union—all that time invested is now paying major dividends. He instinctively understands how to get the most power and comfort from *Ana María*.

4. He's a skilled problem solver. Our friend Seth once told us, "The most important skill in sailing is being able to quickly figure out what's wrong and how to fix it." Time after time, Andrés demonstrates this skill.
5. He's an economist. Most people are surprised to learn he majored in economics, not computer science, at the University of Florida. He is an economist at heart, always thinking on the margin. Every decision he makes is made with the utility curve in mind. Sure, there may be some folks who cross an ocean using less fuel or who use more fuel to get there faster, but I can't imagine any captain who can maximize the utility of the fuel better than Andrés.
6. He's so handsome. If I have to look at only one person for 21 days, it sure helps that he's good-lookin'.

THE GRATITUDE

Many people have helped get us where we are today. For instance, Captain Phyllis Woolwine taught me to sail. Luke and Emily Jost showed up for dinner one night and ended up helping us mount Paulita, the Monitor windvane, on the back of *Ana María*. My father-in-law dedicated weeks to helping us prepare *Ana María* for an ocean passage.

Then there's Hal, our South African rigger, the most experienced ocean sailor we know. We would not be the bluewater cruisers we are today without him.

Hal was generous toward us, always willing to share his expertise and experience, never leading us astray but always nudging us in the right direction with an "If I were you …"

"If I were you, I would fix that crack in your rudder."

"If I were you, I would replace that pitted shaft before it breaks and punctures your hull and sinks your boat."

"If I were you, I would refurbish that whisker pole so you can run wing-on-wing."

Many times on this trip when the conditions have challenged us, I've found myself asking, "What would Hal do?"

We've felt his spirit of patience, graciousness, and wisdom present with us on this crossing.

DAY 22

March 13, 2023
Distance sailed: 95 nautical miles
Total distance sailed: 2,591 nautical miles
Distance to Hiva Oa: 98 nautical miles
Winds: ESE 5-8 knots
Weather: Sunny and hot
Sail plan: Spinnaker and mainsail up from first light to last light then motorsailing with all three white sails

"You may discover that time spent alone on the vast 'ocean wilderness' is equally magical—some might even say spiritual. In any case, you are in for a grand adventure, which you will not soon forget." –Pacific Puddle Jump Fleet Letter #2

As a person of faith, when I read that, I wondered, "What kind of spiritual experience awaits me in the Pacific?"

Now I can say the most profound experience has been a humbling of my spirit.

With the impending achievement of a colossal goal, I have no accompanying sense of conquest. I don't feel victorious over the wild ocean. No, if anything, I feel simple relief and gratitude that we've been *allowed* safe passage.

I have been humbled by this mighty and expansive and terrifying and authoritative ocean.

I have cowered in fear against the electrified power of the squalls.

I have been amused by the sight of our dinky little masthead light paling in comparison to the brilliance of all the stars in the universe.

I have been amazed by the birds, fish, whales, and dolphins we have seen thriving in an environment that seems so inhospitable to us.

We have come out here and found we have limits, limits much more constraining than those of the natural world surrounding us.

"You have made us finite creatures that we might be held and known.

You have made us finite creatures that we might exult in the infinite wonders of your beauty, your majesty, your love, your power.

We have traveled this day to the bounding sea, O Lord, to the far edge of the habitable land, as to the utter end of our own measure and ability and strength,

To find here reminders of your limitless presence extended immeasurably beyond us."

A Liturgy for Arriving at the Ocean from *Every Moment Holy, Volume 1: New Prayers for Daily Life*

DAY 23

March 14, 2023
Distance sailed: 112 nautical miles
Total distance sailed: 2,703 nautical miles
Distance to Hiva Oa: 17!
Winds: Dead calm
Weather: Partly cloudy and stifling heat
Sail plan: Motorsailing with mainsail and staysail

For the past two days, my mind has been anxiously flipping through "What Ifs."

What if North Korea hacked the GPS while we've been out here and we're not actually close to land at all?

What if our engine gets flooded with salt water and bites the dust?

What if our sails get tired, give up, and rip to shreds?

We're so close, yet it feels like we're never gonna get there. It reminds me of when my pregnant friends get to the point in their pregnancy when they're convinced they won't ever have the baby and they'll be the first woman to be pregnant forever.

It's probably normal to be going stir-crazy. Imagine driving from Miami to Seattle (about the same distance we've just sailed) at only 6 mph without ever being able to pull over and stop. Wouldn't you too be going a little mad?

The light winds and flogging sails haven't helped morale much, but I have come into the cockpit for the last night watch and see we're only 17 nautical miles away from land.

The anxiety melts into excitement as we sail the final miles toward Hiva Oa, the Southern Cross serving as a guidepost to port and Mars its counterpart to starboard.

Toward the end of my shift, the time on my phone abruptly changes from 6:40 a.m. to 3:10 a.m. Marquesan time, the first official sign that we're close. Real close. My heart starts to beat faster, but no land is visible yet. Twenty minutes later, red splotches start to appear on the 8-mile radius of the radar screen—I don't think it's a squall!

Half an hour later, I get my first whiff. Dirt. Earth. It's true what they say: you really can smell land. It's a smell you don't even realize you've missed, a smell you don't even realize you can identify until it once again fills your senses after a long absence.

I watch the radar and my AIS target map but avoid looking at the horizon. I want to wait until Andrés wakes up to actually see land so he can share the moment with me, but I'm more impatient than a kid on Christmas morning. Turning my back to the direction of land is the only way I can contain my excitement and keep a grip on my last ounce of patience.

To buy some time, I shut off the engine and trim the sails. We've lost a knot and a half of speed, but the sails are still gently pulling us toward safe harbor.

Finally, at 14:27 UTC, 4:57 a.m. local time, with the sun rising behind me, I can't wait any longer. "Bud, you're gonna wanna see this."

"Ok, I'm coming," he mumbles from below.

He climbs out into the cockpit, and we turn to look to starboard. The steep cliffs of the eastern point of Hiva Oa stare back at us.

Land ho!

A squeal of excitement bubbles up within me as my arms instinctively shoot up in the universal sign of victory.

We made it.

WE MADE IT!!!

PASSAGE STATS

Weighed anchor in Los Frailes, Baja California Sur, México on 2/20/23
Made landfall in Hiva Oa, Marquesas, French Polynesia on 3/14/23
Total Distance Sailed: 2,703 nautical miles
Passage Duration: 22 days, 4 hours
Average speed: 5.08 knots, significantly faster than the 4-knot average we planned
Engine hours: 56 hours
Fuel used: 17 gallons
Max wind speeds: 40 knot squalls, 32 knots sustained apparent winds
Spinnaker days: 9
Ships seen: 19 (only in the Northern Hemisphere)
Squalls: Dozens, felt like hundreds
Number of times divorce was mentioned: 0
Crew injuries: 0

Items broken on passage: Autopilot compass*, tear in mainsail at first reef, chafed genoa foot, Monitor windvane sacrificial tube*, boat speed instrument, screws in genoa furler*, wind instrument on masthead*, rudder bearings, screws in boom vang*, head exhaust fan, SeaTalk data connection*.

*fixed at sea

NUKU HIVA

Baie de Hakatea
8° 56' 40" S 140° 09' 50" W

Town of Taioha'e
8° 54' 23" S 140° 06' 02" W
8° 54' 37" S 140° 06' 10" W

HIVA OA

Village of Hapatoni
9° 58' 14" S 139° 07' 37" W

TAHUATA

Village of Hanavave
10° 27' 54" S 138° 39' 52" W

Village of Omoa
10° 30' 45" S 138° 41' 03" W

FATU HIVA

MARQUESAS ISLANDS
(FRANCE)

VOLUME 2, ISSUE 6: MEET THE MARQUESANS

April 16, 2023
Baie de Hakatea, Nuku Hiva, Îles Marquises, Polynésie française
8° 56' 40" S 140° 09' 50" W
Winds: SE 25 knots
Weather: 83°F Sunny with squalls

"You're gonna love the Marquesans," our French friend Robert remarked nostalgically before we left La Paz, Mexico.

It was hard to imagine we would sail 2,700 nautical miles just to meet lovely people. I mean, can a group of people actually be *that* nice?

Oh, but then we met them for ourselves.

Village of Omoa on the island of Fatu Hiva
10° 30' 45" S 138° 41' 03" W

"We arrived on Fatu Hiva on our sailboat. A fisherman brought us here to Omoa from Hanavave so we can hike the 14 km road through the island," I try to explain to the Madame at the boulangerie who studies me quizzically, obviously wondering how an American is in her bakery at 6:30 a.m.

Her face brightens, "Oh it's a tough hike but beautiful! You'll need food."

I hold up the baguettes she's just sold me and smile.

"On this side of the mountain, there should still be mangoes on the trees that you can pick and eat, but hold on. I will give you some just in case there aren't many." She disappears through the back door as I leave out the front door to pack the bread into our backpacks. She then reappears in front of the bakery with two grown men following her, each with their shirts cradling a half dozen ripe mangoes freshly plucked from the nearby trees. Our mouths begin to water until we realize we will be carrying them on our backs for the eight miles to Hanavave. Still, we are already imagining ourselves snacking on the juicy fruit as we trek across the island.

I've always heard that "generosity begets generosity." The more generous we are with our gratitude, the more generous she becomes. A few words in Marquesan from the Madame sends the men scurrying to fetch a long stick with a basket on the top. They poke at fruit toward the top of a tree and down come eight mamoncillos. She hands these to us with a smile. Thrilled, we pack some away and munch on a couple right there on the spot.

Delighted with our delight, Madame sends the men to fetch la pièce de résistance, reserved only for the guests who will truly appreciate it. They return with handfuls of gumball-sized fruit; its name Madame only knows in Marquesan. "This is our best fruit. Most of it is sent to Tahiti to be sold for $10 a bag, but *chez moi*, we enjoy them ourselves." Madame teaches us to crack open the hard shell to reveal the most delicious pulp. Imagine the best gummy candy in the world, textured but not chewy, sweet but not sugary. *Délicieux*!

Our friends Carsten and Vinni on *Capri* had heralded this kind of generosity. "You'll walk up to a Marquesan and ask to pick some fruit off their tree. They'll say, 'No, but here, have this whole box of fruit I have already picked.'" Their world-renowned reputation of generosity is well deserved!

Village of Hanavave on the island of Fatu Hiva
10° 27' 54" S 138° 39' 52" W

We've followed the sound of music echoing in the Hanavave valley. It's so loud that I'm surprised it's not bothering someone in the village, but now we understand why: half of the village, or at least all the young adults, are on the soccer field, running and doing drills to the upbeat music pumping from loudspeakers.

We hang back, watching them practice from afar. I ask Andrés for his assessment: "Are they any good?"

"They're not professionals, but they're not bad. They must have played soccer together forever. Look at their coordination. And they know exactly what drill they have to perform when the coach blows the whistle."

"Do you want to go play with them?"

"I can't. I'm wearing sandals."

"Maybe they'll practice another day this week and you can play with them."

Before his introversion can stop me, I take off toward the field. I spot the coach, a middle-aged man with earrings in both ears, covered in traditional tattoos, wearing shorts that barely survived a shark attack, pacing barefoot in the middle of the field, chain-smoking hand-rolled cigarettes as he barks instructions in Marquesan to the guys practicing on one side of the field and to the women warming up on the other side. I wait for the moment when I am least likely to take a soccer ball to the head and jog up to him.

"*Bonjour Monsieur.* My husband plays soccer and would like to know if he can practice with your team this week."

"*À toute à l'heure,*" he sends me off the field with a nod.

I jog back to Andrés who has followed me to the sidelines. "He said to wait, but I think it's a yes!" We hover awkwardly near the bench, not sure exactly what we're waiting for. Coach blows the whistle and all the guys come over to the bench for a water break. Chatting with them, we discover they are the island's soccer team, practicing every day this week for a big inter-island tournament on Saturday in Hiva Oa.

Coach blows the whistle again, and the guys take last swigs of their water before once again taking the field. Coach points directly to Andrés, barks more Marquesan, then points to the defender position on the far side of the field.

"Oh he can't play today," I try to explain in French. "He doesn't have shoes."

"*Pas de souci,*" says one of the players, holding up a pair of rough, smelly cleats. There's no way my OCD husband is going to wear a stranger's smelly cleats.

But his appetite to play must be roaring because he takes them from the player, determines they're more or less his size, puts them on, laces them up, and jogs briskly to his assigned position.

For 45 minutes, Andrés is in his element.

On the grass field flanked by the Pacific Ocean on one end and towering spires of rock on the other, he scrimmages with the team. He's a gracious guest, passing the ball often, fetching it when it goes out of bounds, always trying to be an asset rather than the star ball hog. They're polite players but driven to be at top performance for Saturday. It's the most fun Andrés has had in a while.

By the time Coach blows the last whistle, the team is affectionately calling him "Amigo" and asking him to come back to play tomorrow and every day this week. He joins the end-of-practice huddle, his arms around their shoulders and theirs around his as they recite the Lord's Prayer and Hail Mary in Marquesan, before giving a celebratory "WHOOP!"

We had been told Fatu Hiva is paradise but playing your favorite sport with the locals on the most beautiful field in the world ... well, that's truly heaven.

Village of Hapatoni on the island of Tahuata
9° 58' 14" S 139° 07' 37" W

"Excuse me, do you know Tehina?"

Even for me, an extreme extrovert, asking random strangers about another stranger takes a bit of courage. A cruising guide instructed us to look for "Tehina, who will make you some of the most delicious food you'll ever eat." Imagine if you arrived in a tiny town in a remote area of the U.S. and you just started knocking on doors asking for a housewife to cook you dinner. Strange, right? But there are no restaurants in many of the remote anchorages so hungry cruisers with cash begin knocking on strangers' doors looking for the black market "restaurants" that have popped up in carports on every island.

A chain of four strangers eventually leads us to Tehina's blue house. Still dressed in her Sunday best, she explains that she can make dinner for us tomorrow night, but a friend of hers is already making a traditional lunch for cruisers today at noon. Would we like to join? Sure, why not? Cost is $20 per person. Is it worth it? We have no idea. Guess we'll find out.

At noon we arrive at Rose's carport with four French cruisers. Quite the crowd has gathered, with probably a dozen Marquesan adults and a gaggle of children running about. Unexpectedly, we recognize many of the faces. The artisans we had seen this morning at the village market and the strangers who had led us to Tehina were there, and so were the children who had met us on the kayak at the quay and begged so pleadingly for a ride that Andrés finally relented and spent 20 minutes giving them kayak rides around the bay as they squealed with excitement.

Apparently, we had been invited to the weekly Sunday supper that Rose cooks for her nine children and numerous grandchildren, but today is not just any Sunday. This Sunday is a party celebrating a little boy's 6th birthday. We kick off the party with a gigantic homemade sheet cake with candles and rounds of "Happy Birthday" in French, Marquesan, and Tahitian. The kids squabble over who has to pray for the little boy, then everyone prays the Lord's Prayer and Hail Mary.

With the birthday festivities officially started, we are then led to a buffet table, and oh my goodness, mountains of traditional food overflow the table. We devour the chow mein, *poisson cru* (French Polynesian ceviche), beef stir fry, fried breadfruit, steamed taro, caramelized taro, steamed bananas, bananas braised in coconut milk, goat braised in coconut milk, pork braised in coconut milk, a raw seafood platter, crabs boiled in coconut milk and curry, grilled chicken, pommes frites with a Roquefort sauce, octopus, and birthday cake.

As we feast, we talk to Rose and her children. We learn how to properly suck the juicy meat from the crabs. We learn how Rose's son met his wife in the Australes archipelago. We learn about their woodcarving craft. We learn about the kids' school in the town five miles away.

It's a big risk to sail to French Polynesia. It's a big risk to anchor in rolly bays in front of tiny villages. It's a big risk to ask to eat at a stranger's home, especially when you're eating strange seafood. But for the risk and just $20 each, what a reward!

Town of Taioha'e on the island of Nuku Hiva
8° 54' 23" S 140° 06' 02" W

"OpenStreetMap says there is a barbershop here."

"Here???" Looking around at all the houses, I know that can't be right. A truck is passing slowly so I hail it. Four smiling faces greet me, giving me the courage to ask, *"Bonjour! Est-ce qu'il y a un coiffeur près d'ici?"*

They nod energetically and point to the house across the street. "In *that* house?" I confirm and receive a chorus of *Oui*'s in response.

Cautiously, we walk up the driveway to the carport full of scooters and motorbikes. *"Bonjour,"* I call out questioningly while still quite a few yards away.

A fit man with short hair, shorts, and a tattered Air Tahiti shirt pokes his head out of the house.

"He needs a haircut," I gesture toward Andrés. "Is it possible for you to cut it tomorrow or Saturday?"

"I'll cut it right now."

Relieved that we are indeed in the right place, and he seems to be often asked to cut hair, I explain, "Oh, we are running errands, but we can come back tomorrow or Saturday."

"I'll cut his hair now," he insists, as he pulls out one of the chairs lined up as a makeshift waiting area to the center of the carport and gestures to Andrés to sit down.

Being accustomed to the long waits at Great Clips in the U.S. and a bit shocked at the rapid turn of events, Andrés hands me his backpack and sits down in his plastic patio chair.

The barber returns with a bright pink sarong, which he wraps around Andrés, and a cracked plastic pail children use to build sandcastles at the beach. His pail is full of the tools of his trade: razors, combs, and *fingers crossed* not lice. "He wants it shorter but not as short as yours," I instruct, and the barber gets to work. After only a couple of minutes, I worry I should have given different instructions as the barber nearly shaves off all of Andrés' curls. Oh well, too late now.

With the barber making quick work of Andrés' head, I have only a few minutes to take in our surroundings. This is one of many carports we've randomly found ourselves in since landing in the Marquesas. The barber has a waiting area but no mirror. Not sure if this is better for Andrés' anxiety or worse. Instead, the barber has hanging goat hides from his second career as a prized goat hunter. Equipment and tools for the scooters and motorbikes take up much of the real estate, so he might also be a mechanic. A huge Air Tahiti sign hangs from the side of the house, which, combined with the barber's tattered Air Tahiti shirt, makes me wonder if he has a fourth career as an airline representative. I don't want to distract him from the important task at hand by asking.

Ten minutes and $15 later, the barber gives Andrés a big smile and two thumbs up. It was definitely a different experience than any other haircut he's had before, but Andrés looks sharp and ready for Easter.

Town of Taioha'e on the island of Nuku Hiva
8° 54' 37" S 140° 06' 10" W

We're awake early on Easter morning so we can kayak to shore, change into "nice clothes" on the beach, and walk the half mile to the Église de Notre Dame for Easter Mass. Throngs of Marquesans arrive at the Nuku Hiva cathedral with us. We didn't get the memo, but everyone else did: they're all dressed in sharp, all-white clothing. The women have crowned their heads with beautiful arrangements of pink and red tropical flowers. They greet each other with the Paschal greeting and a French *bisous* (a quick kiss on each cheek).

They have decorated the cathedral for the hopeful occasion. Bouquets of pink, green, and yellow plants line the pews. The various hand-carved wooden figures of Jesus hanging at the altar have all been adorned with garlands of fresh white flowers.

A parishioner graciously hands us the bulletin. It would be helpful, except it's entirely in Marquesan. Though we don't speak Marquesan, the Mass is familiar, especially to Andrés. Where it differs from all other Masses, though, is the music. This is neither the day nor the place for somber music and half-hearted singing. Pews of musicians expertly strumming guitars and ukuleles and beating traditional drums lead the congregation in the most beautiful, harmonious, exuberant singing I have ever heard. The Marquesan voices fill the stone cathedral with joyful singing, which, in turn, fills our hearts with joy.

THE LINGO

"*Bienvenue!*" Over 15 years after living in Toul, France as a Rotary Youth Exchange student, it feels *magnifique* to live once again in a Francophone country. All those hours invested in conjugating verbs in the *imparfait* and flipping through piles of index cards to memorize vocabulary words are once again paying dividends.

A part of my soul, my identity, was birthed in France, the part of my soul that delights in new experiences, the part of me okay with making a fool of myself in an effort to understand and be understood, the part of my soul that is curious and inquisitive. Speaking French again has reawakened that part of me. Speaking French with the Marquesans, who have responded with such warmth, has caused this curiosity, this openness, to blossom like the tropical plants surrounding us.

"Nothing is comparable to the new life that a reflective person experiences when he observes a new country. Though I am still always myself, I believe I have been changed to the very marrow of my bones." - Goethe

THE CHALLENGE

Getting to know the lovely people of these beautiful islands has indeed been the highlight of our month, yet it's also presented the biggest challenges.

In *Talking with Strangers*, Malcolm Gladwell explores the challenges of talking with strangers and warns of the perils of underestimating this challenge. The stories he includes in the book have often come to mind this month as we've tried to navigate tricky situations with our hosts. Though I speak one of their languages—most here speak French, Marquesan, and Tahitian—their society and culture are distinctive. Their cultural norms, their hand gestures and non-verbals, their values, and their etiquette all developed for centuries upon centuries before the arrival of Europeans. As a result, we often find ourselves at a loss when trying to interpret meaning and intention.

Have I done something to so egregiously offend the Fatu Hiva women's soccer team that they refuse to acknowledge my existence at the soccer field? Should we offer to pay for the fruit in Omoa, or will it offend Madame's generosity? Why are those people on shore yelling in our direction ... and why is one of them wearing a turtle costume? Can you believe she not only looked into my wallet but practically reached in and took money out? Paying 60 bucks for a boat ride to Omoa—are we getting ripped off or is that a fair deal? Do these parents suspect we might try to kidnap their children when we relent and take their young kids on kayak trips around the bay?

It's tough to know what to do and how to respond.

But how else do strangers become friends besides talking and spending time together?

So, we sit in their carports and try to get to know them and their culture. We ask questions about their lives when they seem open and respect their privacy when they don't. We listen as they share their opinions on everything from Ukraine ("Putin is evil for slaughtering civilians"), to the effect of global warming on their weather ("It's the fault of the U.S. and China's pollution"), to famous people who have loved the Marquesas ("Jacques Brel is our hero, but Paul Gauguin just got our women drunk, had them take of their clothes, and violated them for the world to see"). We practice imitating the beat they put in between the second and third syllables of their hello: *"Ka oh *pause* ha."*

We give them the benefit of the doubt and hope they grant us the same grace.

THE GALLEY

After spending a year in the Baja desert, we now find ourselves in the Garden of Eden. The islands are covered in fruit trees. Mangoes. Pineapple. Coconuts. Limes. Guava. Gigantic grapefruit. Bananas. We've tasted sweet fruit plucked straight from the tree, and our palates will never be the same.

THE WILDLIFE

"I can't believe it! You are in the Marquesas one day and already you get to see mantas!" Dirk and Silvie, our welcoming committee on *LisonLife*, couldn't believe our luck. "What's the big deal?" we wondered. Manta rays were a near daily sighting in the Sea of Cortez.

Then we saw them.

These mantas weren't the spry but small mantas we're accustomed to seeing. Mantas here are mammoth, with a wingspan of 12 feet. While anchored in Fatu Hiva, the mantas provided the dinnertime entertainment, swimming graceful circles around *Ana María*, barely skimming the surface of the water as the sun set over the anchorage.

THE ENTERTAINMENT

We arrived at the tall, volcanically-formed Marquesas Islands at the beginning of the rainy season. After 22 days at sea, our legs have loved taking on the challenging hikes to waterfalls with miles of trekking up hills, across streams, through swarms of no-see-ums, underneath acres of fruit trees, listening to the exotic birds sing to one another.

With all the effort to arrive at the basin, cliffs towering high above us, fresh water cascading down 1,500 feet to an inviting pool before forming a river that will babble its way down to the sea, what was the reward? Well besides the view, which has always been worth the climb, we enjoy the treat of a home-cooked meal of fried breadfruit, marinated and grilled tuna, and steamed bananas at one of the villager's homes.

THE HORIZON

Tomorrow, we start a 5-day sail to the Tuamotu Archipelago. We hear we're about to enter a totally different world.

Fair winds and following seas,

Katherine

P.S. During our passage to the Tuamotu, the Captain's Log tracks *Ana María's* position and her condition and provides a vital point of contact for our families stateside. You'll be able to follow our progress by reading Andrés' daily update.

THE CAPTAIN'S LOG: PASSAGE FROM THE MARQUESAS TO THE TUAMOTU

MARQUESAS ISLANDS

● Day 1
10° 11' 02" S 140° 52' 25" W

● Day 2
12° 15' 20" S 142° 08' 29" W

FRENCH POLYNESIA

(FRANCE)

● Day 3
15° 15' 42" S 143° 14' 01" W

TUAMOTU ARCHIPELAGO

DAY 1

April 18, 2023
10° 11' 02" S 140° 52' 25" W
Distance traveled in 24 hours: 146 nautical miles
Fuel remaining: 45 gallons

And we're off to a new archipelago. More specifically, the "Dangerous Archipelago," as it has been known to mariners because of the high number of boats lost to reefs due to difficult navigation. With GPS, radar, and the latest charts, the situation should be somewhat less dire, but the navigation will definitely be more demanding than the Marquesas.

So far, we have been sailing upwind on a close reach, about 60° off the wind, for the past 24 hours with pretty consistent 15- to 25-knot winds. Paulita, the Monitor windvane, is doing all the steering. We had two large squalls last night attack right after shift change, so we opted to head down to a broad reach as they had more than 30 knots of wind in them. Our velocity made good (VMG) is pretty good, albeit about 10° north of our next waypoint. We could sail on the rhumb line if we sailed close-hauled, about 40° off the wind, but that is a pretty miserable point of sail against the mighty trade winds for any length of time. I am betting on a wind shift later today that should allow us to reach our next waypoint without the need for any major sail changes. – Andrés

DAY 2

April 19, 2023
12° 15' 20" S 142° 08' 29" W
Distance traveled in 24 hours: 132 nautical miles
Fuel remaining: 45 gallons

Another day reaching toward the Tuamotu! As predicted, the wind has shifted ever so slightly toward the east, allowing us to meet our waypoint without touching the sails. Paulita is now automatically steering a more southerly course. Not too much drama aboard so far. We did have a few more squalls last night, which gave us a bit too much wind, then a bit too little wind, then a bit of just the right amount of wind in the wrong direction. We've barely touched the sails since we hoisted them in Nuku Hiva. Sailing with a second-reefed mainsail, genoa, and staysail. –Andrés

DAY 3

April 20, 2023
15° 15' 42" S 143° 14' 01" W
Distance traveled in 24 hours: 138 nautical miles
Fuel remaining: 45 gallons

The Marquesas and their lushness are now far behind. We have about 100 nautical miles left before we reach Makemo, the atoll we have decided to attempt to enter after lots of debate. We are now wing-on-wing surfing down waves, although the wind rarely exceeds 20 knots. No major squalls last night so that was nice. Co-Captain is sick and will rest today as much as possible. Our thermos lid cracked from excessive pressure. Maybe the valve got clogged? It's a pity as we use it every day for cooking, but I am also content to state that it has been our gravest gear failure in this passage so far. – Andrés

MARQUESAS ISLANDS

FRENCH POLYNESIA
(FRANCE)

Passe Tapuhiria, Makemo Atoll,
Tuamotu, Polynésie française
16° 26' 03" S 143° 58' 05" W

Pouheva Village
16° 37' 20" S 143° 34' 02" W

Makemo
Southeast Anchorage
16° 39' 18" S 143° 23' 30" W

MAKEMO

TUAMOTU ARCHIPELAGO

VOLUME 2, ISSUE 7: THE DANGEROUS ARCHIPELAGO

April 21, 2023
Passe Tapuhiria, Makemo Atoll, Tuamotu, Polynésie française
16° 26' 03" S 143° 58' 05" W
Winds: SE 12 knots
Weather: 75°F Sunny

The sun is barely announcing its presence to port. Finally, after three hours of hovering in the pitch black outside the pass entrance to the atoll, we have just enough light to see.

The guesstimator tool developed by fellow cruisers using tide charts and recent weather conditions estimates that slack tide, the only safe-ish time to go through the pass, was an hour ago. There will likely be current now, but hopefully, we can see the markers on the dangerous reefs lurking on either side of the pass.

I head to the bow and tether in, trying to ignore the roar of the waves breaking against the reefs on both sides of us. I'm up here to look out for the three red channel markers to port and two green to starboard that are supposed to guide us through safe water into the atoll. Thankfully, the current is coming from the same direction as the wind, so no standing waves await to pummel us as we try for the pass.

Andrés is back at the helm, with one eye on the surroundings and one on the chart plotter and radar.

"I see swirling water for the next quarter mile. It's probably due to strong current," I call back in warning. This pass can have as much as 6 knots of current pushing you out of or into the atoll.

"Oh yeah, there are almost 3 knots of current against us. I have the engine at full throttle, and we're only making 1.8 knots forward progress," he calls back.

My stomach twists in knots for the five minutes we're getting pushed around by the strong current. Just like the feeling of car tires sliding uncontrolled on ice, *Ana María*'s stern is thrust side to side before Andrés powers through the last of the reefs, relieving us of the current's influence.

One obstacle down, many more to go.

Once we've made it through the pass, I climb up the mast to tackle the next obstacle in the atoll: navigating around the thousands of coral heads or "bommies" that climb from the sea bottom 80 feet below and lurk right below the surface of the water.

We're in Makemo, which, like most atolls in the Tuamotu, is uncharted. We have no official map showing us where all the dangers are hiding. In the absence of official charts, we've spent hours cobbling one together, recording the coordinates of cruiser-reported bommies and bommies visible on satellite images and infrared charts. We have what we think is a safe 48-nautical-mile route to the southeast end of the atoll.

Running into a bommie would total our boat, so we're not content to blindly follow the route. Hence my trip up the mast.

I climb up each of the mast steps originally installed for a man with legs a good 6 inches longer than mine, pulling my safety line along as Andrés pulls the slack out of the main halyard attached to me. Finally, I reach the spreaders and settle my weight in my bosun's chair, ready for a couple hours of eyeball navigation.

Everyone said, with the right conditions, it would be easy to spot the bommies. I had my doubts, but yeah, from all the way up here and the sun high and slightly at my back, the minefield lights up. Scattered among the dark blue deep water of the lagoon are huge brown splotches, their edges tinged with neon blue.

"I see a big bommie about a quarter mile to starboard at 1:30," I relay to Andrés via walkie-talkie.

"Bommie to starboard, yes, it's .3 miles away. We identified it in the satellite images. The next one should be to port, about .7 miles away," comes his reply.

For hours, we perform this call and response. "Bommie to starboard, a thousand feet at 2 o'clock." "Roger that. There's a bommie to port, but it's quite far off the track." "I can see a bommie straight ahead at maybe .5 miles." "Yes, I am about to make a course change, and I plan to leave that bommie to port."

All our pre-work and route planning are paying off. It's such a smooth process, I wonder why I am even up here.

Then I spot a bommie to starboard. It's small, but a small bommie can still tear the keel off *Ana María*. It's less than 700 feet away, and I can't believe we routed ourselves this close. "Is the bommie to starboard at 1:30 on the chart?"

"Uh, lemme look. ... Negative. We do not have a bommie charted."

"It definitely exists," I call down as I watch us pass it uncomfortably close.

"Good catch. I'll mark it down, so we know to give it a wider berth when we leave the atoll."

By the time we reach our anchorage, I've spotted three bommies close to our route that the satellite images hadn't picked up. Those three close calls definitely merited the uncomfortable hours hoisted up the mast.

Now that we're at our anchorage, I climb the 25 feet down to the deck, change into a swimsuit, and grab my flippers, mask, and snorkel. Into the water I go. Miniature versions of the bommies we've just avoided are scattered throughout the sandy bottom. They can't wait to wrap themselves with our anchor chain, eating away at the galvanized links.

I swim around the area where Andrés wants to anchor, looking for bommies taller than our keel. At 5'5", I know if I can touch the coral head with my head touching the surface of the water then it's too close for comfort for our 4'1" keel.

"This one over here is 6 feet," I yell to Andrés on the boat.

"Okay. It's outside our swinging room but I'll mark your spot, so we know to watch for that one."

Confident in my survey, I swim back to the anchor spot, pick the sandiest patch, then poke my head out of the water to instruct Andrés to "drop the anchor here." Eyes back below the surface, I watch our anchor and chain drop into the sand. It takes a minute to settle, and *Ana María* drifts back as Andrés lets out enough chain to allow the anchor to catch. Our Rocna anchor is designed to set at the angle created when we have 3 to 1 scope, or 3 feet of anchor chain out per 1 foot of water depth. He lets out 30 feet of chain given the 10 feet of water below us.

The angle of the chain looks good, and the anchor is settled on the bottom, but it's not set *into* the sand. Poking my head back up out of the water, I suggest,

"Give the engine 10 seconds of reverse idle." I watch the effect underwater: the sharp point of our Rocna digs all the way into the sand, burying itself completely. "It's set! I can only see the roll bar of the anchor."

We put out 70 feet of chain to get 7 to 1 scope so that the anchor holds in the forecasted storm this week, but we don't want all that chain to wrap around the shallow coral heads. For one, our chain destroys the precious coral. And two, a wrap around the coral could reduce our scope to 1 to 1. With any wind and that little scope, the coral could yank the chain, our bow cleat, and anchor windlass right out of the deck. To prevent this, we tie buoys to the chain. The buoyancy keeps the chain off the coral but will sink in heavy winds, giving us adequate scope for the coming blow.

Content with the set anchor, the distance from the bommie, and the chain floating high, all we have to do now is wait for this forecasted anticyclone to show up.

Later that night, someone shines a flashlight into our portlights, waking me up.

Oh. No, that's just lightning. A lot of lightning. A lot of close lightning.

I look at the clock. It's 5:00 a.m. We made it through the night. It wasn't that bad. Yesterday's forecasts showed the wind would peak at 30 knots at about midnight. Turns out, it wasn't even strong enough to wake me up. I must've slept straight through it.

We thought we might leave the atoll today, but the GFS model shows this weird blob of unstable weather just south of us. Both the GFS and ECMWF models forecast some crazy rain: 27mm or an inch per hour. The color scale on the models doesn't even go that high. It seems prudent to stay here in case that blob moves north to us. Plus, it's never fun to sail in hurricane-strength rain.

By 7:00 a.m., the wind has started to climb again. We're seeing 30 knots. Not a big deal as we clearly survived those winds last night, but the direction scares us. With every gust, it seems the wind is clocking more and more to the south, not southeasterly as predicted. We have no wind protection from the south, and there is half a mile for the fetch to build from the reef south of us.

By 9:00 a.m., it's clear that the blob has found us. Winds are constantly 30 knots, with gusts pushing 40 knots. It's a comfort knowing that I saw the anchor dug all the way into the sand. With each gust, though, we are inching closer to that 6-foot bommie I spotted.

The 40-knot gusts create 5-foot standing waves that crash into our bow every 3 seconds. It's raining so hard that we're worried the scupper drains on the decks won't be able to keep up with the torrential downpour.

The sheets of rain make it difficult to make out the bommie behind us, but our anchor alarm app indicates we're 15 feet in front of it. If the anchor pops in one of these gusts, and we drag back at all, our rudder will go BOOM against that bommie.

We pull out our cruising guides and weather references: "If forecasts show strange weather, get protection from the south. The strongest winds will come from the south. Every year an average of three boats are lost when caught off guard by southerly winds."

Are we going to be one of this year's unfortunate three?

Looking out the portlights, we can see one ... or is that two? ... of the neighboring boats dragging anchor. Unfortunately, we can do nothing to help.

There's a brief lull in the rain, so Andrés braves the elements to check on the anchor chain and bow roller. The snubber on the anchor is taut as a tightrope, but with the bommie behind us, we can't let out more chain to take off the strain. He fixes the chafe guard, checks the deck, and climbs back into the cabin just in time for us to clock our highest wind ever.

47 knots! That's 55 mph!

Ana María bucks violently against the wind and the seas it brings.

We seem to hold our breath for the next hour, eyes darting between the conditions outside the portlights and the anchor alarm app.

Finally, with great relief, we observe the gusts drop to 30 knots, and the wind shifts back to the southeast. Each hour gives us more distance from that bommie and more protection from the nasty waves.

By 3:00 p.m., the blob has dissipated, the black clouds have given way to sunny skies, and the lagoon water is once again flat and bright blue.

We've weathered the storm. Our beloved Rocna anchor held. We're all okay.

THE LINGO

Honestly, I had no idea what an atoll was before we set sail for French Polynesia. I mean, what makes an atoll different from an island?

Then I found a diagram explaining the formation of an atoll in our *RCC Pilotage: Pacific Crossing Guide* and it all made sense.

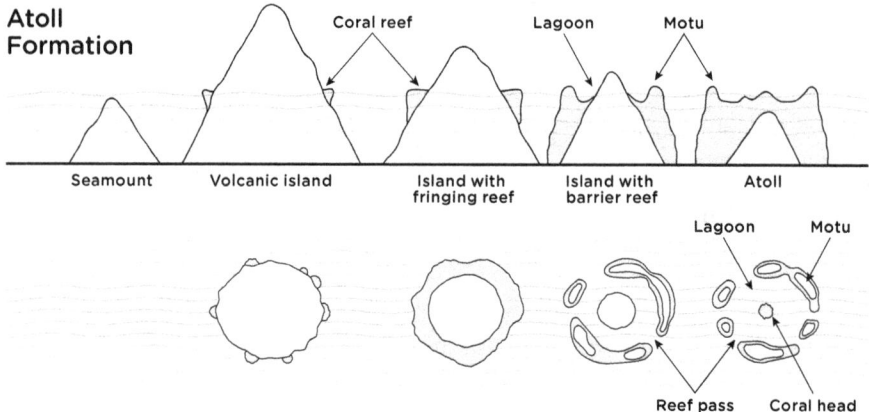

An atoll begins as a seamount. The seamount erupts and creates a volcanic island (like the Marquesas). A reef grows along the entire perimeter of the island (like Tahiti and Bora Bora). Over time, the volcanic island sinks, but the reef remains. This circular reef becomes an atoll (like the Tuamotu) with a lagoon in the middle.

Some sides of the atoll are reefs barely awash in the surf. Other sides have land formations or motu with palm trees. Currents and swell can carve gaps in the atoll. Boats use these gaps or passes to enter the lagoon in the center of the atoll and get protection from ocean swell.

THE WILDLIFE

We're snorkeling from *Ana María* to the coral beach of the motu. Visibility is so fantastic that I'm still 50 feet away when I get my first glimpse. That's no 3-foot fish.

I motion underwater to Andrés, pointing. Clearly, he was expecting something different because even through his goggles I see his eyes go wide when he sees it—a shark!

"These are only blacktip reef sharks. These are not the great white sharks you went cage diving with in South Africa," I try to remind myself to stamp down the panic. Sure enough, the shark seems completely uninterested in our presence.

Once at the motu, we discover a shark "nursery." Dozens of baby sharks about 6 inches long swim in the warm shallow water. They're almost cute. The troublesome foot-long teenage sharks are a bit too curious for us, swimming straight for our ankles, so we give them their space, not wanting to alert Mama Shark.

THE ENTERTAINMENT

Here in Makemo we've had one of the most incredible experiences of our lives. Right before the tide turned to start pushing water from the ocean into the lagoon, we climbed into our neighbors' dinghy and together we exited the lagoon through a pass in the motu. Just outside the exit, we tied ourselves to the dinghy so we wouldn't accidentally get swept out to sea and then hopped in the water. The flood current pushed us ever so gently back into the lagoon. They call this "drift pass snorkeling." If timed right with the current, it is the coolest "lazy river" in the world.

The coral reef extends 30 yards from the motu before the shelf drops straight into the abyss of the pass. We snorkeled along the shelf, watching the thousands of fish, hundreds of sharks, and the shy turtle as they darted in and out of the caves created in the coral. In a strange way, it evokes images of the cliff dwellings of the American Southwest, but with much more hustle and bustle. After an hour of the best snorkeling of my life, the flood current spit us out of the pass back into the lagoon. Amazing!

THE GALLEY

What do you get when you cross a food desert with a desert island?

Yep, you guessed it: a food desert island, aka the Tuamotu. The motu on the atolls aren't fertile enough to produce much more than coconuts, so besides fish and maybe some chicken, the only food available to the eight hundred residents of Makemo arrives on a supply ship from Tahiti every three weeks or so. This means you can only buy very limited amounts of frozen meat and fresh produce in the tiny village of Pouheva. If you come toward the end of the three-week cycle, good luck finding anything on the shelves but the most basic dry goods. Luckily, we've been able to time our visits to arrive in the village the day or two after the supply ship, thus finding it no problem to stock up and eat well.

THE CHALLENGE

Dangerous passes + dangerous navigation + dangerous anchoring + dangerous winds from the south = Atolls with a well-earned reputation as "the dangerous archipelago."

As we leave the atoll, a 40-knot squall catches us completely by surprise, drenching us and nearly ripping our sails, giving us one last kick in the pants before we can escape.

After three weeks weathering the dangers of the atoll, I confess: all three of us are a bit "rode hard and put away wet."

THE HIGHLIGHT

As in many ventures, exploring the Tuamotu is a study in high risk, high reward.

In exchange for the dangers, we were rewarded with a secluded paradise. Except for the storm, the anchorages are the smoothest we've ever experienced. It's more peaceful and stable than being in a marina. The lagoon water is so clear that we could see our anchor 50 feet below. We kayaked through water so blue, it surely inspired the color of Gatorade's Glacier Freeze. We hiked along the motu to watch the gigantic 20-foot swell from the Southern Ocean crash against the southwestern reefs. We enjoyed some of the best snorkeling in the world.

High risk? Yes, but definitely high reward.

THE HORIZON

We'll spend a couple weeks in Tahiti and Bora Bora doing boat projects, seeking medical attention for the stomach bug that keeps pestering me, and hosting Andrés' parents.

Fair winds and following seas,

Katherine

THE CAPTAIN'S LOG: PASSAGE FROM MAKEMO TO TAHITI

FRENCH POLYNESIA
(FRANCE)

MAKEMO

Day 1
17° 02' 22" S 144° 34' 44" W

Day 2
17° 11' 19" S 145° 21' 00" W

TAHITI

Day 3
17° 41' 27" S 147° 45' 35" W

Day 4
17° 43' 53" S 149° 19' 45" W

DAY 1

May 14, 2023
17° 02' 22" S 144° 34' 44" W
Distance traveled in past 24 hours: 81 nautical miles
Fuel remaining: 30 gallons

After a bit of nice upwind sailing on a close reach while exiting the Tuamotu and dodging atolls, the wind, as expected, completely died on us, leaving us to motor. The forecast for the next few days paints a bleak picture with very little wind. On top of that, big choppy seas are coming from the south, making the ride extremely uncomfortable.

Why in the world would we choose this weather window to move on to the Society Islands?!? Good question! Three things: First, Katherine has been suffering on and off from a stomach bug that started in the Marquesas. Since she hasn't recovered 100 percent, we decided she needs professional medical care to figure out what is going on. The only place in French Polynesia to get detailed exams done is in Tahiti. Second, we have a pile of miscellaneous boat work that needs to be done before we keep moving west. Tahiti is the only place we can knock off most of those items. We have one week to do it all. Last, my parents will be visiting us in a week, so we need to make sure we're actually there to be with them! 'Tis the classic sailing on a schedule that is so often frowned upon by sailors, but I have three good excuses, so that should make me innocent in sailing court.

The immediate problem now is the lack of wind. We need some wind as these lumpy seas are not letting us motor at our usual speed. Without wind, we might be forced to drift or run out of fuel, and that would not be good for my mental health. Plus, it would subtract one precious day we've allotted to medical tests and boat tasks. But the ocean is the ocean, and it has the final word on when we get there. – Andrés

DAY 2

May 15, 2023
17° 11' 19" S 145° 21' 00" W
Distance traveled in 24 hours: 95 nautical miles
Miles sailed: 0.5 nautical miles
Fuel remaining: 21 gallons

We've been listening to the hard-working iron genny humming almost non-stop for the past 36 hours. We had a brief spell of 5- to 7-knot winds, so we rushed to set up the spinnaker to sail nicely at 3.5 knots—for about 10 minutes, that is. The wind changed direction completely, then said goodbye to us. It's crazy and depressing for us to realize we're putting more hours on the engine on this trip than our entire Pacific crossing from Mexico. That's sailing on a timeline for you! We're going to add to our list of boat projects in Tahiti an oil and fuel filter change since we will likely add as many engine hours as a typical weekend sailboat gets in one year.

Do I sound frustrated? Yup. I don't like to motor, and, in my defense, the heat it generates makes the cabin almost unbearable during the day (something that was actually a plus in the Pacific Northwest), and the noise makes it harder to sleep at night. But I am grateful that we have a reliable engine for times like these—knock on wood.

On the plus side, we made a brief stop in Anaa, a beautiful atoll almost no yachtie stops at since it has no navigable pass. It was really true that the clouds above the atoll were emerald green and could be seen from 50 nautical miles away—that was really cool! – Andrés

DAY 3

May 16, 2023
17° 41' 27" S 147° 45' 35" W
Distance traveled in 24 hours: 101 nautical miles
Fuel remaining: 10 gallons

Another 24 hours of motoring. We've had zero wind, except for a couple of hours when we were able to motorsail. We are trying to make it to Tahiti by sunset today, but given the limited fuel remaining, we can't throttle up the engine to ensure an arrival before dark. We can only hope for a little wind to motorsail a bit and for the diesel fumes to keep powering the engine. Maybe a sea breeze near Tahiti? Anything helps! – Andrés

SAFELY IN TAHITI

May 17, 2023
Baie Phaëton, Tahiti, Îles de la Société
17° 43' 53" S 149° 19' 45" W
Fuel remaining: 4 gallons

We arrived safely in Tahiti last night around 8:30 p.m. local time. Navigating the pass and the often broken or nonexistent navigation aids proved to be quite a nerve-racking experience. We thought about heaving-to outside the pass, but there was no wind and, to our delight, there was a 1-knot current carrying us east, away from Tahiti. (!) So we decided to put all of our navigation skills to use, go through the pass, and navigate the narrow 5-mile channel, flanked by invisible reefs on both sides, into the anchorage—fun times! In the end, though, we were really happy to be in a flat anchorage with a cool zephyr and get eight hours of solid sleep. – Andrés

FRENCH POLYNESIA
(FRANCE)

● Bora Bora, Îles Sous-le-vent
16° 29' 19" S 151° 45' 41" W

Moorea, Îles du Vent
17° 29' 07" S 149° 50' 36" W

Papa'ete, Tahiti, Îles du Vent
17° 32' 14" S 149° 33' 59" W

TAHITI

VOLUME 2, ISSUE 8: PANIC IN PAPEETE

June 7, 2023
Papa'ete, Tahiti, Îles du Vent, Polynésie française
17° 32' 14" S 149° 33' 59" W
Winds: SE 18 knots
Weather: 75°F Mostly sunny

We're walking through the winding streets in Papeete as evening falls. It's been one of those perfect international travel days.

This morning, Andrés and I drove with Andrés' parents for an hour along the northern coast of Tahiti, watching the world-famous surfing waves crash against the reefs. We found a municipal parking garage where we could safely and reasonably leave the car all day. We then took exhilarating transport—a ferry that sped at 30 knots!—to the island of Moorea. Once we arrived, we easily found a cab to take us to the Hilton Moorea, where we lounged in the resort all day with my best friend and her sister who were there on vacation. We said goodbye to my friends, then Andrés, his parents, and I took the fast ferry back to Tahiti, where we devoured fresh seafood for dinner at the food trucks in Vai'ete Square.

What more could we want?

We were already dreaming of our beds waiting for us an hour away in the town of Taravao when we turned the corner and ...

We see the rolling gate.

The closed and locked rolling gate!

Our car is trapped behind that gate. That gate with no phone number. No name. No emergency contact or even company listed.

It takes the four of us only a moment to realize the seriousness of the situation. We're stuck in a strange, foreign city at night without access to our way back to Taravao. A pit forms in the bottom of my stomach. I'm the host. I'm the one who found the parking garage. Now I have to figure out how to get my in-laws back safely to the Airbnb.

How much do you think an hour-long taxi ride costs at night in Tahiti?

Whatever it is, I know it's worth more than my pride.

Almost immediately, I take off running down the street, desperately searching for any sign with a name or phone number.

The shells on the necklaces handed to me by the valet at the Hilton resort jangle loudly like sleigh bells, announcing my presence as an idiot tourist to all those lingering on the street.

Suddenly, I remember seeing an official city office on the backside of the town hall building above the garage, so I pivot and run like a mad woman.

The offices I remembered seeing earlier come into view. More gates. MORE GATES! All doors have massive gates dashing any hope of help.

Finally, one gate is open. There's no sign on the door to indicate what's behind it, but I think I see a faint light behind the opaque window.

I bang and bang and bang and bang on the door.

It's futile I know.

What are the chances anyone is behind it?

What are the chances any angel behind the door is going to say anything but, "I'm so sorry, but I can't help you. You have to wait until the garage opens tomorrow morning at 8:00 a.m."?

Already I am developing a plan to get a taxi, pay the exorbitant sum, and take the first bus back to Papeete in the morning to fetch the car.

My father-in-law appears behind me. He sees what I missed in the panic—a buzzer. If my banging didn't rouse any movement, what good would the buzzer do? We ring it three times in due diligence.

Defeated, we turn to walk away.

Then, lo and behold, we hear the door open behind us.

A 7-foot-tall man in a police uniform with a nightstick on his hip opens the door. (Okay, okay, he wasn't 7 feet, but he was at least 6'8"!) I instinctively take a step back before falling onto my knees to beg in French. "*Bon soir, Monsieur.* We're tourists here and parked in the garage around the corner. We had no idea the garage closed. We checked for signs but never saw any, we promise! Our car is trapped in there. Is there any way you can help us?"

The gentle giant puts his hands up to calm me before reaching for his radio. "Yo, I need the keys to the garage. And can you hurry? A pretty lady is waiting." Turning back to me, *"Pas de problème,* Madame. I'll meet you in five minutes at the garage gate."

THERE IS A GOD!!!

The four of us scurry back to the gate, not wanting to keep him waiting a moment, and already talking through how we will pay quickly and get the heck out of here.

Sure enough, three minutes later, he arrives with a key and lifts the heavy gate with his pinky.

We run to the payment kiosk, scan our ticket, and insert our credit card. "Card not read." Another scan, a different card. "Card not read." Another scan, a quick prayer, a different card. "Card not read" then "Machine broken."

Are you kidding me???

The relief of finding the policeman was short lived. I take off running (again!) toward the kiosk at the far end of the garage. Cash in hand, I scan the ticket. In goes the bill, out it comes again. Argh! In goes the bill, out it comes again. I use a corner of the machine to smooth out the crinkles in the bill and try again. Success!

The tires of the rental car squeal as Andrés drives Jason-Bourne-style to pick me up before we race back to the exit. Monsieur Policeman is patiently waiting but stops us as Andrés is about to pull onto the street.

"You might want to turn on your headlights." Instead of giving us a ticket, this man receives our gushing gratitude with a smile and waves us goodnight.

As we drive the hour back to Taravao, we all keep smiling and sighing. The deep sighs of people who know they're ever closer to comfortable beds in an Airbnb instead of sleeping on the dirty sidewalks of a foreign city until a garage gate opens.

Even in civilization, adventure seems to chase after us.

THE HIGHLIGHT

Moorea, Îles du Vent, Polynésie française
17° 29' 07" S 149° 50' 36" W

In college, my best friend was voted "Most Likely to Sneak into the DoubleTree Hotel on North Glenstone to Use the Hot Tub and Eat the Free Cookies." Her skills have been invaluable as we've traveled together but maybe never more so than this past month. She was able to sneak Andrés, his parents, and me in as guests to the Hilton Moorea where she was staying with her sister. We napped in lounge chairs on the beach. We snorkeled together in the crystal-clear water. We splashed in the pool. We sipped on locally-distilled pineapple rum. A delightful and luxurious break from cruising life!

THE WILDLIFE

At night in Tahiti, the ground comes alive with tupas, a type of land crab. These suckers are gigantic but quite tasty when you find them on a local menu.

THE LINGO

The sights, sounds, topography, and people have all changed as we've sailed from the Marquesas to the Tuamotu and through the Societies. One thing that's remained constant: the smell of burning coconut husks.

It's a challenge to export many of the specialties of French Polynesia. Mangoes and bananas here may be the best in the world, but they are too fragile and ripen too quickly to make export economical. Coconuts abound, however, and French Polynesia has found a market: your pantry.

Copra is the dried meat of the coconut. The Polynesians harvest it even on the tiniest islands. They crack open the husks, which they burn every night on the beach, dry the coconut in specially built shelters, and ship the copra to Tahiti. The oil is extracted from the copra and shipped all over the world as an ingredient in consumer product goods. As an abundant resource requiring little capital to produce and as a shelf-stable export with a healthy market, it's a key staple of the economy here.

THE GALLEY

Everyone warned us that food in French Polynesia would be three times the prices we were paying in Mexico. Since we're not working right now, we live on a paltry budget. We weren't sure how we would afford to buy food, but then we learned about food subsidies.

Most food, except fruit, some poultry, and pork, is imported, so it's expensive. To keep the local population fed, the government subsidizes some food items: canned corn and peas, coconut milk, pasta, pasta sauce from San Francisco, grass-fed steaks from Uruguay (still trying to figure that one out), UHT milk from New Zealand, and the staple of the French Polynesian diet: baguettes. Baguettes are sold for about $0.70 USD. Judging by the people who visit the store each morning and walk out with 10 in hand, we're pretty sure many people here are surviving off these baguettes.

We've been able to keep our food spending stable by building our meals around the various food items with the subsidized red price tag on the grocery shelves. One perk? French toast is cheaper than cereal, so our breakfasts have been pretty luxurious.

THE HORIZON

Bora Bora, Îles Sous-le-vent, Polynésie française
16° 29' 19" S 151° 45' 41" W

I'm finally healthy thanks to the heavy-duty antibiotics prescribed by the Tahitian doctor and the day Andrés and I spent flushing and bleaching our water tanks. Turns out, we had filled our tanks with contaminated water in an isolated village in the Marquesas—oops! We won't do that again! After three weeks full of trips to the hardware store and the fully stocked Carrefour grocery store in Tahiti, *Ana María* is fixed up and stocked up, ready to sail once again to remote islands. We then sailed to Bora Bora to spend the last week of our 90-day visas hiking and snorkeling the island's world-famous topography.

Now, the Gendarmerie is chasing us out of French Polynesia due to our expiring visas, so we're leaving Bora Bora to sail west. Where in the west? Well, we have no idea. Between the heavy trade winds, the incoming front from the Southern Ocean, and the ever-changing immigration rules in the next set of islands, we're setting off and we'll land where we land. Stay tuned!

In short, if French Polynesia is on your bucket list, it's time to cross it off. We give our experience here a 10 out of 10. Highly recommend!

Fair winds and following seas,

Katherine

MARQUESAS
ISLANDS

Anchorage Island,
Suwarrow, Cook Islands
13° 14' 59" S 163° 06' 29" W

COOK
ISLANDS

South Pacific Ocean,
170 nautical miles east of
Suwarrow, Cook Islands
13° 18' 54" S 160° 10' 17" W

TAHITI

FRENCH
POLYNESIA
(FRANCE)

NEW
ZEALAND

SOUTH
PACIFIC
OCEAN

VOLUME 2, ISSUE 9: AN ISLAND (ALMOST) TO ONESELF

June 21, 2023
South Pacific Ocean, 170 nautical miles east of Suwarrow, Cook Islands
13° 18' 54" S 160° 10' 17" W
Winds: E 15 knots
Weather: 88°F Sunny and sweltering

I am listening to leadership podcast episodes in which Carey Nieuwhof and Craig Groeschel discuss the criticality of planning:

"Every night, I block my next day and schedule my priorities according to my energy levels."

"Oh, I would take that even one step further: I block out my whole week in advance, ensuring I write my book on Monday and Tuesday and have most of my meetings on Wednesdays."

"If you look at my calendar, you can say, 'Carey, what are you doing in March of 2023?' I can look ahead *two years* because it's the same every week."

And yet here *I* sit in *Ana María*'s cockpit, sailing in the middle of the Pacific Ocean, sailing west without even knowing our next destination.

Will we be allowed to make landfall in the tiny atoll of Suwarrow in 36 hours? Will we detour to American Samoa so we can eat at Pizza Hut and hike in the national park? Or will we try to skirt the fine line between the weather front from the Southern Ocean and the dreadful South Pacific Convergence Zone to continue for six more days straight to Tonga?

The difference in mindset is striking. Many people back home are proactively planning their days, weeks, months, and even years while we are making and remaking plans every six hours when a new forecast becomes available.

What a different life we lead!

Many days I long for the predictability of life ashore, the luxury of looking forward to something because it's likely to happen if it's planned right.

Many days I tire from decision fatigue. We plan and make decisions and replan and overturn our decisions and get new information and scrap the plan altogether for a new route. Over and over and over we do this.

Today I listen to experts talk about the critical skill and discipline of proactive planning. At the same time, I try to get excited for, yet not attached to, any of our three current possible destinations.

"When will we be able to return to the best practices and luxuries of planning and following through with a plan?" I wonder.

But then I think of this new skill we have, this new strength we can exercise as a team: We have become incredibly nimble.

On land, we would be going crazy if, at some point in the next 2 to 10 days, we could be in one of three very different countries.

We're out here, though, and calmly handling the unknowns and accompanying anxieties.

Does it sometimes feel futile to make plans when we are completely confident they will drastically change? Absolutely.

Does it feel totally unproductive to fill out a 15-page Advanced Notification of Arrival form for a country we only have a 33 percent chance of actually visiting? Absolutely.

Can we survive out here in the South Pacific without making plans of some kind? Absolutely not.

Maybe on land, when I spent all that time planning, I was doing it for a false sense of control. You don't have to be an adult very long before you realize our grip on control can disintegrate faster than we can imagine.

Cruising on a tiny sailboat simply magnifies the truth that, while we have agency in our lives, we don't always ... or ever? ... have control. Something can always change. Something unexpected can always catch us off guard. Something can always derail our best-laid plans.

And cruising on a tiny sailboat has taught us that's okay.

Even if we gain something from all our planning, we also lose something.

Being nimble has brought some unexpected delights to our life:

It's brought us *contentment*. It was tough to miss out on most of the Tuamotu due to storms and health issues, but we learned to be thankful for the time we were given in Makemo.

It's birthed in us *optimism*. Even if our plan doesn't work out, we've learned that something else will.

It's allowed us to take advantage of *unexpected opportunities* to enjoy that which we didn't even know was possible: opportunities like eating the Marquesan feast at Rose's, pass snorkeling in Makemo, and bow-and-stern anchoring in the crystal-clear water of Ua Pou.

Am I gonna throw out my calendar when we step back onto land?

Unlikely, but I hope Andrés and I continue to find ways to build, exercise, and flex our nimble muscles in whatever life we have.

THE CHALLENGE

We are sailing in the South Pacific Convergence Zone (SPCZ), the area where the southeast trade winds battle for dominance over the fronts spinning toward the northeast from the Southern Ocean. It's El Niño now (or very shortly will be) so the fronts are winning.

The squalls in the SPCZ are less isolated incidents and more like never-ending conveyor belts of lightning and pelting rain. As we get whacked with squall after squall, my mind floats to the famous *I Love Lucy* scene when Lucy and Ethel try to work the chocolate factory assembly line and quickly get overwhelmed. As I watch squall after squall develop right on top of us, I feel like them, except, instead of eating sweets to keep up, I am gulping down rainwater.

The winds here are fluky, not easily or reliably forecasted, hence our inability to set our sights on a specific destination.

THE HIGHLIGHT

Anchorage Island, Suwarrow, Cook Islands
13° 14' 59" S 163° 06' 29" W

In the end, we were allowed to land in Suwarrow, and thanks to daily snorkel adventures, lovely hikes, delightful company, and a deep-seated sense of peace, it was a highlight of our cruising life!

Suwarrow is a tiny atoll in the northern Cook Islands, about 200 miles from the nearest inhabited island, with a population of ...

Sooty Tern birds: Millions
Red-throated frigatebirds: Thousands
Sharks (blacktip, gray, tiger, nurse): Hundreds
Coconut crabs: I'm too scared of 'em to count 'em
Humans: 0 permanent residents and 2 park rangers from June to November

Ana María was the sixth boat to call on Suwarrow this year, and we thoroughly enjoyed this new corner of paradise with sailboats #4 and #5.

THE ENTERTAINMENT

"I chose to live in the Pacific islands because life there moves at the sort of pace which you feel God must have had in mind originally when He made the sun to keep us warm and provided the fruits of the earth for the taking ..." –Tom Neale

If you've ever heard of Suwarrow, it's likely thanks to Tom Neale who famously lived alone on the atoll for many years in the 50's, 60's, and 70's.

His memoir *An Island to Oneself* recounts his struggles to establish a life on the isolated atoll and the fulfillment he found in Suwarrow. All the cruisers devoured the book during our stay, amazed at how little has changed on the island since he lived here.

"This story is like Tom Sawyer for grownups!" remarked Andrés. And it's true! If you need a light adventure read this summer, we highly recommend this book. It's begging to be read aloud. If you like to read aloud like we do, give your Netflix a vacation this week and find yourself transported to Suwarrow.

THE WILDLIFE

We were just finishing a great snorkel with Ian and Ann on *Afrikii* and Brian and Sue on *SeaRose* at the southern reef in the Suwarrow pass. Visibility was great, and the reef was teeming with activity. We were climbing into the dinghies when Sue shouted "Manta!"

Our exhaustion was immediately replaced with adrenaline as we ducked back under the water and swam as fast as we could toward Sue. Sure enough! Right next to her was a 12-foot-wide manta! In fact, a rare manta, with jet black velvety skin on both the back *and* the stomach.

She swam gracefully, barely flicking her wings yet gliding like Aladdin's magic carpet through the water. She was gracious, allowing us to swim within feet of her for several minutes as she swam toward the pass.

Magical!

THE GALLEY

Even though it's winter here in the Southern Hemisphere, we are close to the Equator, so it's unbearably hot during the day. There is no way we're turning on the oven to cook. Instead, we've increased our grilling. Besides feasting on grilled tuna and barracuda freshly caught and generously shared by *Afrikii* and *SeaRose*, we tried our hand at baking on the grill: oatmeal cookies for a finger food potluck and homemade hamburger buns for black bean burgers.

THE LINGO

Every boat cruising for any length of time has a Signature Story. As our small group of fellow cruisers sat on the beach under the vast starry sky, I asked our new friends on *Afrikii* and *SeaRose* as well as the park rangers, Harry and Taina, to share theirs.

Ian and Ann on *Afrikii* told of transferring diesel and medical supplies to a dismasted boat in the middle of the Pacific.

Brian and Sue on *SeaRose* shared about losing their last sailboat in a tsunami in Malaysia.

We recounted the knockdown and leg break at Mendocino.

Taina surprised us with her story: "I am 58 years old, and I told my kids I wanted an adventure! So, I signed up to come to Suwarrow, but there was a mix-up in my transportation. I couldn't get on the same cargo ship as Harry. Instead, I traveled the 550 miles from Rarotonga on the *Marumaru Atua*, a traditional Polynesian voyaging canoe. It was only 22 meters long and there were 18 of us onboard. No privacy at all! They told me it would take two days so I didn't think it would be that bad. Wrong! It took more than five days, and they wouldn't even let me smoke!"

We all listened with rapt attention as Harry finished off the evening with his story of spending three days at sea in a life raft after the ship taking him, 20 fellow passengers, and a deck full of butane and gasoline to the Manihiki atoll caught fire then exploded! They were eventually rescued, all unscathed, by a cargo ship.

What riveting campfire stories!

THE HORIZON

After a delightful week in Suwarrow, we are inching our way toward American Samoa, the only permanently inhabited U.S. territory in the Southern Hemisphere. As a longtime territory in a strategic location, we expect to observe a strong U.S. military presence, but we're not expecting to find much in the way of American culture. Unlike Puerto Rico and other U.S. territories, the 45,000 residents of American Samoa are not U.S. citizens at birth. Many of the residents have fought against this status, declining the protection and rights granted by the U.S. Constitution in favor of their traditional culture, chiefdom, and property laws.

Though we'll still be 5,000 miles from the mainland U.S., American Samoa represents the Promised Land for American cruisers in the South Pacific, a land flowing with Budweiser and Heinz ketchup. Stores are stocked with familiar American brands and products, like 2-ply toilet paper, which are impossible to come by or prohibitively expensive on other South Pacific islands. We're on the hunt for canned chicken, a Midwest Can diesel jug, a propane refill, and a McDonald's Big Mac.

Fair winds and following seas,

Katherine

THE CAPTAIN'S LOG: PASSAGE FROM SUWARROW TO PAGO PAGO

MARQUESAS
ISLANDS

SAMOA

COOK
ISLANDS

TAHITI

Day 1   13° 38' 02" S 164° 34' 11" W
Day 2   13° 47' 35" S 165° 19' 56" W
Day 3   13° 56' 12" S 166° 55' 02" W
Day 4   14° 16' 42" S 169° 26' 35" W
Day 5   14° 16' 24" S 170° 41' 41" W

FRENCH
POLYNESIA
(FRANCE)

NEW
ZEALAND

SOUTH
PACIFIC
OCEAN

DAY 1

June 22, 2023
13° 38' 02" S 164° 34' 11" W
Distance traveled in 24 hours: 90 nautical miles
Fuel remaining: 32 gallons

We've had a slow and frustrating start toward American Samoa. We already broke our iPad charging cable and our bow light got obliterated by the spinnaker tack line. Plus, lots of squalls to keep us on our toes! – Andrés

DAY 2

June 23, 2023
13° 47' 35" S 165° 19' 56" W
Distance traveled in 24 hours: 92 nautical miles
Fuel remaining: 28 gallons

Winds are nowhere to be found. We managed to eke out some (slooow) miles under sail yesterday by poling out our spinnaker with the whisker pole.

I feel it is appropriate to take this moment to apologize for the negative tone of my post yesterday. As I was writing it, I witnessed, with my own eyes, the spinnaker tack line break free and start violently whipping around the bow, indiscriminately destroying anything around it with full force. Before I could pull the spinnaker's sock down and kill the beast, it ripped out our bow light with such violence I'm glad no children were aboard to see it. Naturally, that put me in a bad mood.

No more disasters have happened at sea since then, but the lack of wind has us going very slowly, which is quite frustrating. We need to save what precious little fuel we carry onboard, which means we must motor slowly and spinnaker whenever possible. – Andrés

DAY 3

June 24, 2023
13° 56' 12" S 166° 55' 02" W
Distance traveled in 24 hours: 92 nautical miles
Fuel remaining: 21 gallons

Same old, same old. No wind, lots of motoring. Bonus: Our galley foot pump broke! Thankfully, we were able to rebuild it so we can keep drinking water. We'll see how long the rebuild lasts.

We are slowly making our way toward our destination. At least the seas have been quite calm so not a lot of rolling. We'll be overdue for yet another oil and fuel filter change upon arriving at our destination. Sigh. Well, things could be a whole lot worse out here! – Andrés

DAY 4

June 25, 2023
14° 16' 42" S 169° 26' 35" W
Distance traveled in 24 hours: 97 nautical miles
Fuel remaining: 11 gallons

I forget what the world is like without the constant purring of a diesel engine. We are less than 100 nautical miles away from American Samoa, where we will have to stop to refuel.

Not much has changed since the previous day. We have started to spot islands belonging to American Samoa, but we must move on to Tutuila Island, where we will be able to refuel and obtain provisions. – Andrés

SAFELY IN AMERICAN SAMOA

June 27, 2023
Pago Pago, American Samoa
14° 16' 24" S 170° 41' 41" W

After tons of officialdom, we are safely anchored and checked into American Samoa, where the fresh smell of canned tuna from the local Starkist factory fills the air.

It is a beautiful island, although the harbor is quite industrial and pleasure boats are an afterthought.

We will reprovision here before moving westward. – Andrés

VOLUME 3

SAMOA

1   South Pacific Ocean,
    48 nautical miles southwest
    of Pago Pago, American Samoa
    14° 52' 37" S 171° 15' 01" W

2   South Pacific Ocean,
    172 nautical miles southwest
    of Pago Pago, American Samoa
    16° 37' 08" S 172° 23' 55" W

3   South Pacific Ocean,
    256 nautical miles southwest
    of Pago Pago, American Samoa
    17° 41' 35" S 173° 20' 13" W

4   Port Maurelle, Kapa Island,
    Vava'u, Kingdom of Tonga
    18° 42' 01" S 174° 01' 48" W

*SOUTH
PACIFIC
OCEAN*

NEW
ZEALAND

VOLUME 3, ISSUE 1: WOULD YOU RATHER...?

July 3, 2023
South Pacific Ocean, 48 nautical miles southwest of Pago Pago, American Samoa
14° 52' 37" S 171° 15' 01" W
Winds: S 15 knots
Weather: 70°F Partly cloudy

We're in the middle of night one of a three-night passage from Pago Pago in American Samoa to Neiafu in Tonga.

"Waaaah!!! Waaaah!!!"

The loud 1:00 a.m. alarm rudely disturbs the deep sleep I managed to slip into during my six-hour nap.

Tempting as it is to hit the snooze button, Andrés has spent the past six hours in the cockpit keeping watch. He'll be ready to go to sleep. I try to shake the cobwebs from my brain, gather the motivation to lift myself up and over the lee cloth we've set up to keep us from flying out of bed in the rough seas, and I step ...

... into a pool of water.

Poof! All cobwebs have instantly disappeared and have been replaced with images from a video of our favorite YouTube couple, Beau and Brandy. Before we left on our own sail, we were traumatized when we watched the YouTube video where Beau and Brandy's boat nearly sank a hundred miles off the coast of Grenada.

The second my own toes touch water I remember Brandy waking up to find salt water filling their boat. The unrelenting bashing against the waves had cracked their hull, allowing gallons and gallons of water to fill the boat. By the time they noticed, water had come up to the floorboards and was rising fast. They couldn't keep up with the leak despite constant use of the bilge pumps and a mini-bucket brigade. Miraculously, a fisherman heard their mayday call and saved them with enough underwater epoxy to fix the leak.

Needless to say, I'm glad at this moment we brought our own emergency stash of underwater epoxy, but I really hope we don't need to use it tonight.

Andrés' face brightens as I switch on our red night-vision light. Already he can taste the sweet sleep he knows awaits him in the warm and dry sea berth.

I dash his hopes for a good night's rest with a simple, "We have water all over the floor."

His face crestfallen, he climbs into the cabin to examine the problem.

We stare into the puddles of water on the floor, both our minds pondering.

"Would you rather have a saltwater leak or a freshwater leak?"

The first means your boat is at risk of sinking. The second means you're at risk of losing all your drinking water.

Our watermaker has been working great, so our preference tonight is clear. We're crossing our fingers for a freshwater leak.

There's only one way to find out.

Andrés cups his hand, lifting the mystery water up to his lips, and tastes it.

"Fresh water."

Phew! Our emergency supply of underwater epoxy will survive to see another day in storage.

Pulling sopping wet cushions aside, we trace the water to the previously full freshwater tank on our starboard stern. Without the cushions, we can actually hear the likely cause of the leak. Each wave slams *Ana María*, rolling the boat, and sending the 35 gallons in the tank sloshing against the lid like a sledgehammer. Hours of the persistent slamming of the water against the lid have loosened the screws. Andrés is able to screw most of them back in by hand, a decent stopgap for the night.

Hourly checks during each of our watches show a dry tank lid lip. Thank goodness. This temporary fix might even hold until we get to Tonga.

South Pacific Ocean, 172 nautical miles southwest of Pago Pago, American Samoa
16° 37' 08" S 172° 23' 55" W

Night 2 of 3: Once again, I'm up at 1:00 a.m. to relieve Andrés from his watch duties. Tonight, though, it's his news that ramps up the stress level onboard.

"The wind has shifted. Right now, we are headed west to Fiji. We don't have the wind angle to sail to Tonga."

"Was this forecasted?" I ask, knowing he downloaded updated forecasts while I slept.

"No. The strength of the wind is right, but it's coming too much from the south. We'll never make Tonga."

"Okay, so what are our options?"

"Well, *would you rather* sail to Fiji and skip Tonga altogether, turn around to sail to the Niuatoputapu Islands, or turn around and sail all the way to Western Samoa? The Niuatoputapu Islands are 80 miles behind us, but the entry will be a challenge and we might get stuck there for a whole week. Western Samoa would be nice, but we will lose the 250 miles of progress we just made. And who knows if there will be a better weather window to make this passage? We may end up in the same position as we are now."

Having just woken up, my brain isn't functioning yet. Having just spent six hours on watch, I know Andrés' brain is not functioning either.

"When do we need to make the decision?" I ask.

He does some calculations: "If we decide to turn to Niuatoputapu, we need to do so in the next three hours; otherwise, we'll arrive in a dangerous pass at nighttime."

"Let's wait three hours to make the call. You go get some rest, and I'll watch our course like a hawk. This wind isn't forecasted, so maybe it's a fluke. If our course hasn't improved in three hours, I'll wake you up. Three hours of sleep isn't as good as six, but you'll make a better decision after some sleep than you will now."

Andrés quickly falls asleep while I obsessively track any changes in our course. Just like we don't keep our eyes on the speedometer every moment we drive a car, I normally check our course only every 10 or 15 minutes. It's too fatiguing to monitor it every second for six hours, but tonight, my eyes are glued to our course over ground.

By hour one, our course has improved 5°. By hour two, another 15°. By hour three, we're back on track.

When Andrés sleepily checks in after six hours of rest, I smile and let him know: "We're headed straight to Neiafu, Tonga." His smile matches my own.

South Pacific Ocean, 256 nautical miles southwest of Pago Pago, American Samoa
17° 41' 35" S 173° 20' 13" W

We're finally in the home stretch. Only one night to go before we hopefully reach Neiafu, Tonga in the morning.

The night's not going to be an easy one.

Recognizing how fatiguing it is to be on watch in the cockpit, we've reduced our watches from six hours to four hours each.

We're sailing on a close reach, 60° off the 27-knot winds, which means we are heeling sideways. Instead of surfing the waves as we do in downwind sailing, we are T-boning each wave. *Ana María* shudders at the impact. The water displaced in the crash pours overboard, often right onto my head. If we head downwind to right the boat and reduce the splash, we'll sail right past Tonga.

Once again Dave Gable's joke comes to mind: "Want the experience of sailing but don't own a boat? All you have to do is stand under an ice-cold shower in front of an industrial fan and rip up hundred-dollar bills."

Would you rather sail upwind against 25-knot winds and 10-foot seas all night long or stand in an ice-cold shower in front of an industrial fan while you rip up hundred-dollar bills?

Right now, there's not much of a difference between the joke and my reality. Except in the joke, I could turn off the shower and the industrial fan. Out here, our only option is to stay the course.

Tonight, there is no enjoyment. No relishing the night sky. No becoming engrossed in an audiobook. Instead, we hold on, keep a careful watch, and count down the miles until Tonga.

Mid-watch, I see a 30-knot gust register on the instruments. Boats get dismasted on passages like these.

"Lord, please help our mast stay on," I mutter over and over under my breath. I suck on Jolly Ranchers to keep my sugar high, listen to Garrison Keillor and Paula Poundstone tell lightbulb jokes from the *Prairie Home Companion Pretty Good Joke Show*, and try to endure.

Lo and behold, around 4:00 a.m. the sea state begins to settle. The winds haven't subsided, so I stand up to check our position on the iPad charts.

Land ho! The Vava'u island group I can faintly see ahead of us is breaking up the ocean swell. Neiafu is only a couple hours away.

Andrés wakes up so we can hoist a yellow "Q" quarantine flag to signal, per maritime law, our request to clear into Tonga. Normally this feels like a bureaucratic chore, but today raising the yellow flag feels like an act of triumph. We thank God we survived the passage: No broken bones! No broken rig! No broken hull!

THE LINGO

Would you rather have an upwind sail or a downwind sail?

Most of the sailing we've done in the South Pacific has been with the wind at our backs. The downwind sailing hasn't always been stress-free, but for the most part, it's been pleasant.

The passage from American Samoa to Tonga has been entirely upwind sailing, aka sailing to windward, aka "beating" or "bashing."

It's "bashing" that truly resonates when the waves continually hammer the hull, intent on stopping progress. The wind does everything it can to push you away from its direction. It blows you off course, causing "leeway." It's your job to trim the sails to create enough pressure differential to pull the boat forward.

On this passage, we understand the old saying, "A gentleman never sails to windward."

THE HIGHLIGHT

The best part of the tough passage to Tonga was spotting the rowboat *Maiwar* with our binoculars.

Would you rather sail across the Pacific Ocean or row across it?

When we were in American Samoa, we had the great privilege of meeting Tom Robinson, a 24-year-old who is crossing the Pacific on his 24-foot rowboat *Maiwar*. He set off alone from Lima, Peru, and rowed for over 160 days to the island of Penrhyn in the Cook Islands. The small village on Penrhyn hosted him for the four-month cyclone season before he set off for American Samoa.

If you think we're crazy for crossing the Pacific on a 34-foot sailboat, he is two levels crazier than we are! We have an engine and sails. Couples like Lin and Larry Pardey have crossed oceans without an engine, which we think is crazy, but Tom is crossing with neither an engine nor sails. As crazy as it sounds, we found him to be very down-to-earth, more normal than you might imagine.

He left American Samoa a couple days before us, so it was a delight to run across his rowboat in the open ocean. He is headed straight for Brisbane, and we wish him the best of luck with this crazy weather.

THE WILDLIFE

Would you rather have a booby bird on your masthead, solar panels, or radar?

We picked up a hitchhiker for most of our passage to Tonga. A booby bird circling the masthead gets an immediate aggressive response. We can't afford a broken wind instrument up there. A booby landing on the solar panels gets an immediate aggressive response. We can't afford him pooping on the solar cells, reducing their energy output. A booby landing on our radar ... well, we're okay with that. The radar offers a safe perch, conveniently aiming any poop overboard.

Our passenger left often to fish but always returned. Sometimes he forgot his position and tried for the solar panels. A quick flick of the lines in his direction and he resumed his position on his permitted campsite.

THE CHALLENGE

Port Maurelle, Kapa Island, Vava'u, Kingdom of Tonga
18° 42' 01" S 174° 01' 48" W

Would you rather replace the pumps on your engine on a remote island in the Pacific or cross your fingers and hope they survive until you can get to a Yanmar dealer in New Zealand?

The raw water pump that brings salt water from the sea to cool our diesel engine bit the dust. As we were diagnosing that problem, we saw a tiny coolant leak around the freshwater pump that pumps the coolant throughout the engine.

Remember when we thought it was difficult to get the furling blocks in Mexico pre-passage? Oh, how naïve we were then. Getting parts in Tonga is infinitely more challenging, more expensive, and more time-consuming.

Incredibly our friends on *Noason* have two of our same engine models on their catamaran. They graciously gave us a spare water pump and freshwater pump. We changed out the raw water pump immediately, and we're crossing our fingers the freshwater pump will hold until New Zealand.

THE GALLEY

For five months, we've been surrounded by palm trees and coconuts. And yet it took five months and the guidance of our friends Parker and Jess on *Noason* for us to finally taste the sweet fruit from the wild.

Jess picked out coconuts during our hike on Vaka'Eitu. Parker buried a sharp stick deep on the beach to husk them. He taught Andrés to find the seam of the nut and use a machete to whack them at a 90° angle to the seam. WHACK! WHACK! WHACK with the machete and fresh coconut water was spilling into his hands. We passed around the coconut like a flask, each taking a swig, then ate the coconut right out of the shell (much to the horror of our dentists I'm sure).

Would you rather spend 5 seconds opening a can of coconut water or spend 30 minutes opening up a coconut you found in the wild?

One sip of fresh coconut water and you'll know the answer for sure.

THE ENTERTAINMENT

"Make new friends but keep the old. One is silver and the other's gold." When my Girl Scout leader taught us this song in second grade, it struck me as an odd song. For whatever reason, it's stuck with me all these years later.

Cruisers are constantly on the move, meeting new people as they go from place to place. This can often feel like a bizarre mix of the first day at college and Groundhog Day. Instead of asking and answering, "Where are you from? What's your major? Which dorm did you get assigned to?" every new encounter includes "Where are you from? How long have you been sailing? Where are you headed next? What's your final destination?"

Many, if not most, of these encounters never get beyond the initial questions because you never see the people again. But sometimes, our community feels less like "every day is the first day of college" and more like the community on the Oregon Trail. The distances we're all covering are enormous, but our world is quite small, the trail quite common. We're always surprised but never shocked to meet cruisers in the tiniest remote anchorages 4,000 nautical miles away from where we last saw them.

We were surprised then, but not shocked, when the crewing couple on *Noason* found us in French Polynesia. "We met you in Puerto Peñasco last summer, right?"

After reconnecting with both the crewing couple and the owner couple aboard *Noason* in Makemo, we've become friends, real friends. As friends, we've hiked the national park in American Samoa, celebrated successful passages with pizza nights and Chinese dumplings, macheted our way through the Tongan trails, troubleshooted engines, dominated trivia night at the Kraken, snorkeled, played Mexican Train dominoes on the rainy days, and lounged on pool floats in the lagoons on the sunny days.

This week after we waved goodbye and wished them fair winds and following seas on their sail to Fiji, Andrés whispered, "The hardest part of cruising is saying goodbye to friends."

Would you rather make new friends or keep the old?

We're eager to meet the new round of cruisers who've just arrived in Tonga, but we're pretty sad to see *Noason* sail off into the sunset.

THE HORIZON

Would you rather keep moving, trying to make it to Cape Town, South Africa before November, or would you slow down to explore the 45 plus protected anchorages in Vava'u before meandering south to New Zealand?

We have friends who've elected the first, but we are firmly in the second camp. We hope to spend at least five weeks exploring this Tongan archipelago and experiencing the Tongan culture.

Fair winds and following seas,

VAVA'U

Lape Island, Vava'u
18° 43' 24" S 174° 06' 01" W

HA'APAI

KINGDOM OF TONGA

*SOUTH
PACIFIC
OCEAN*

TONGATAPU

VOLUME 3, ISSUE 2: SWIMMING WITH WHALES

August 23, 2023
Vaka'Eitu, Vava'u, Kingdom of Tonga
18° 43' 24" S 174° 06' 01" W
Winds: SE 21 knots
Weather: 72°F Mostly sunny

In the spring of '96, I was sitting in the passenger seat of the car as my dad ran errands on a beautiful day in the Ozarks. We were chatting about our upcoming summer vacation to California.

"I want to swim with the dolphins at SeaWorld. I'll sell my Barbie collection to make the money to do it."

This was before we had Internet at home, so I have no idea how I knew at eight years old that you could pay to swim with dolphins, but I vividly remember setting the goal and figuring out what I'd have to do to reach it. A couple weeks later, after our garage sale, I had zero Barbies left and $125 in hand.

That summer in San Diego, I donned a wetsuit for the first time in my life, walked to the edge of a pool, jumped in, and swam with dolphins. It was awesome!

You bet when I found out that I could legally swim with humpback whales in Tonga (with a licensed operator), it filled the top spot on my Tongan bucket list.

This morning, with adrenaline and nerves filling my tummy, we went on a bulky aluminum boat with our guides Kirstie and Kylie to search for a whale.

We hadn't been searching long when, to our starboard side, a 50-foot female breaks through the water, turns like an expert high jumper, and flops back into the sea.

We all squeal, shouting, "Good morning to you, too!"

Next to the big whale, we see a little spout. It's a mama and her calf! What luck!

We follow at a safe distance as they come to the surface every four minutes so Baby can breathe. Each time they come up, they're another hundred yards farther away.

Turning west, they enter the open channel and Baby starts to show off. His breaches aren't as high as his mama's, but they are at once adorable and impressive. He breaches again and again, copying the majestic moves of his mother.

"Why do they breach?" I ask Kirstie.

"Several reasons. They have barnacles they're trying to get off. Sometimes they breach just for fun, but they are also training to swim to Antarctica. Once they reach the higher latitudes, the 'Roaring Forties,' the mist from the seas covers the surface, so they have to breach to get a good clear breath."

We track behind them and follow their every move as they breach, and Mama slaps her 15-foot pectoral fin on the surface. If they'd just stay put for a little while, we could all jump into the water and play with them. They're moving too far and too fast. We can't figure out why they won't stay still long enough for us to join them.

All our attention is fixed on our starboard side, watching the surface of the water for any sight of the Mama and Baby, when "WHOOOOOOOOOSHH!" a 45-foot male surfaces a hundred feet from the boat.

Mystery solved. Mama is in heat and getting harassed by an eager suitor. Like that annoying guy in a bar who just can't take a hint, he's keeping Mama and Baby on the move.

We thank them for a spectacular show and head off in search of another whale.

Kirstie is expertly navigating her whale-watching boat through the channel east of Hunga: one bare foot on the captain's seat, one bare foot turning the wheel to and fro, head out of the hatch above, eyes trained on the young male whale swimming ahead.

He isn't coming up as frequently as the mama and baby, but he is more stationary. This might be our chance to swim with him.

"Get ready! When I say go, follow Kylie into the water and swim as fast as you can toward the whale."

We see him come up for the first breath, the second breath, the third breath. We wait with bated breath as he comes up for a final fourth one. With this breath he dives down, flicks his tail, and like a footprint in the forest, gives us a clue as to where he dove.

Kirstie gives the signal and points toward the tail print. We slip into the water one by one and swim toward his last known position. We can't see him, but we can hear him singing. Long, deep melodies punctuated by the sounds of the brass section in an orchestra clearing their spit valves.

We swim around for eight minutes, searching frantically for any spots of white in the deep water below.

Kirstie spots him as he comes back up for breath and she pulls us all back in the boat. "Must be a young male because he knows some of the song, but not all of the song," she explains. We follow him to his next location, wait for the four breaths and the tail flick before back in the water we go.

He sings and sings as we swim and swim, but each time he comes up, he's 300 meters away. He's putting on a great concert, but he swims too fast for us, so we peel off in search of another playmate.

In the past hour, as we've searched and searched, we've come up with a list of better names for the day than "whale swim."

Wave Watching.

Whale Chasing.

Hide and Go Seek with the Whales.

Finally, our friend Sue spots a blow behind us. Maybe third time's the charm? Maybe we'll finally get to swim with a whale? Kirstie points out the tail print, and once again we slide off the back of the boat.

We swim a hundred feet and suddenly ... there's a reef. No, that's not a reef, that's a tail!

A tail! A tail! I can see a tail!

Under the water, I catch the eyes of our guide Kylie and give her an ungraceful fist pump before turning my full attention to the whale.

We still our bodies, floating easily in the salt water, and we watch her.

And we watch her.

And we watch her.

She sits at the bottom for 20 full minutes. Is she dead? The baby was surfacing every 3 to 4 minutes, the singer every 8 minutes.

She is stone-still for a long time.

But then her arms start to move. A little wiggle. Then another.

Then she gets bigger and bigger. Her enormous size, once disguised by the distance, is coming into its full glory.

I realize, "Oh, I'm right in her flight path. I better get out of the way."

Andrés must feel the same as he suddenly swims closer to me, grabs my arm, and gently pulls back from the whale who is coming to swim right beside us. We see the moment when she seemingly becomes aware of our presence, deviating abruptly to miss us.

We swim as fast as we can to keep up with her as she takes one breath. Another breath. We're swimming as fast as our flippers can kick, but with the third breath, she pulls away, quickly out of sight.

I've never been hunting, but I suddenly understand the allure. After searching all day, I'm high on adrenaline with one glimpse of this magnificent creature.

Next time she spouts even closer to shore, in shallower waters. We're back in the water and spot her almost immediately. Her white belly, like a waving flag, announces her presence.

What is she doing? Yoga? She is below us, nose down, with her back arched to lift her tail behind her head, the most amazing headstand I've ever seen.

Her yoga pose gives us a great view of her speckled tummy and baleen plates. She holds the pose for several magical minutes before returning to her resting pose with her back to us as we float above.

Once again, we watch for 10 minutes before she heads back to the surface for a breath. She must know she has an audience. As she comes close to us, she slows to half-speed and allows us to get a long look at her entire front side while she's suspended in the water.

First breath. Second breath. Third breath. Fourth breath and down she goes.

Our spotter indicates the tail print isn't that far from where we are, so instead of jumping back in the boat, we all take off swimming in her direction.

We're swimming at her tail, expecting her to dive deep and behave exactly as she has the past two times, so we're completely caught off guard when, with our eyes trained on her, another whale charges at us at lightning speed.

It takes a second to realize that we are looking at two whales. A male has found the female, and in an incredible moment, we watch as they swim nose to tail, tail to nose in one slow circle, another slow circle, and yet another slow circle.

It's like watching couples figure skating in the Olympics. The couples move so gracefully yet so powerfully, so close and in tune with each other's every move. These whales, spinning and turning and flipping and twirling in perfect sync, give us a gold medal performance.

We've just watched a whale courtship.

We have no chance to catch up to them as they swim off to ... *ahem* ...

Well, let's just say, if you want to watch these whales for yourselves, there'll be plenty of baby whales in Vava'u in about 11 months.

THE WILDLIFE

Hundreds of whales travel from the Southern Ocean to Tonga each July–October to mate and give birth in these warm protected waters. They're so ubiquitous here, they're like deer in the backyards of Missouri. We've seen loud groups of males "thwopping" and "whopping" as they carouse the islands like a bachelor party in Vegas. We've listened through our hull to the whales call to each other throughout the night. Nearly every time we move anchorages, we see a mama and calf pair. The calf's daily diet consists of 26 gallons (100 liters) of double cream milk, allowing it to gain 154 lbs (70 kg) each day.

THE ENTERTAINMENT

There are over 60 boats scattered among more than 40 anchorages in the Vava'u island group. Cell signal is sparse and Internet unreliable. We all rely on our VHF radios to communicate with each other and with the businesses around here. Thanks to repeaters installed throughout the archipelago, we can hear and speak to anyone on channel 26 anywhere in Vava'u.

Our radios stay on channel 26 all day, every day, and it provides not only valuable information but also great entertainment. Channel 26 is a mix between a neighborhood group text and the town hall scenes in *Gilmore Girls*. The morning Cruisers' Information Net at 8:30 a.m., our version of the *Today Show*, fills us in on the news, weather, special events, and the availability of produce at the market. Each day we listen to a familiar cast of characters, like Brian ("DJQ") who missed his calling as a Coast Guard Radio Operator, Greg

("Cafe Tropicana") who fills propane tanks for cruisers, and the ever-evolving cruising boat fleet as they chatter among themselves.

Our favorite episode so far:

"All stations. All stations. All stations. This is Vava'u radio. It has come to my attention that some female cruisers are naked near the Neiafu wharf. We'd like to remind you it is *illegal* to be nude here. Anyone caught in the nude is subject to huge fines and jail time. Please respect the laws and customs of our country. This is Vava'u radio standing by on channels 26 and 16." You bet Andrés ran out to the cockpit real fast to survey the situation for himself.

THE GALLEY

"We're going to have a beach bonfire, and the Catalan couple on *Glam* is going to make a paella on the fire with the lobster and squid we caught today. Would you like to come?" They didn't have to ask us twice! We jumped straight into our kayak and headed for the beach. *Glam* cooked up the most delicious paella we've ever tasted in one of the most primitive kitchens we've ever seen.

THE CHALLENGE

It's rained 75 percent of the time we've been in Tonga. We hear it's related to El Niño, the position of the South Pacific Convergence Zone, the jet stream, the size of the hole in the ozone layer over Antarctica, or the long-lasting effect of the volcanic eruption here in 2022. Maybe it's a combination of it all. Whatever the cause, when Tonga's bad, it's miserable. On the other hand, when Tonga's good, it's great! So, on the days when it's not raining, we're paddling around like madmen who've escaped from the loony bin, knowing we could at any moment be shackled back into straitjackets. We swim and snorkel and hike and kayak from sun-up to sun-down. Gotta make hay while the sun is shinin'.

THE HIGHLIGHT

The islands here are made up of limestone, so there are caves along the shores. Swimming in Swallow's Cave and Mariner's Cave is considered a must-do while here. We hesitantly paddled our somewhat fragile inflatable kayak through the 30-foot entrance to Swallow's Cave. Once through the small entrance, the cave opens up to an area as big and high as any high school cafeteria. No wonder they used to lower food down through the holes in the ceiling and hold special feasts in the expansive space.

Mariner's Cave is a bit more intimidating since you must dive underwater to enter the cave. I've been practicing holding my breath and swimming as fast as I can, but I still wasn't sure I could make it. We paddled 3 1/2 miles to the cave, found it, held our breaths, and swam into darkness. To our relief, it wasn't as scary as we were expecting. To our surprise, we could see mist fill the cave when the swell entered. Our popping ears told us the air pressure in the cave was changing with each new wave. While really cool, that's probably the extent of any cave diving we'll ever do.

THE LINGO

You've probably heard the term "farm-to-table" to describe certain modern urban restaurants that claim to source ingredients from local farms. Here in Vava'u, there are no conventional supermarkets, so we source our produce through what Andrés calls "garden-to-galley."

Or more accurately ...

garden to skiff (most produce arrives from gardens on the outer islands via small boats) ...

to market (the outdoor plaza next to the wharf) ...

to backpack (our huge water-proof bags) ...

to kayak (our only way to get to and from shore) ...

to tube socks (to protect the produce from bruising) ...

to net bags (hanging above our salon table) ...

to galley.

THE HORIZON

We'll spend the final months of the cruising season in the Ha'apai Islands south of Vava'u then look for a weather window to cross to New Zealand.

Fair winds and following seas,

Katherine

VAVA'U

Lape Island, Vava'u
18° 42' 56" S 174° 05' 01" W

KINGDOM OF TONGA

HA'APAI

'Uiha, Ha'apai
19° 54' 14" S 174° 24' 54" W

SOUTH PACIFIC OCEAN

TONGATAPU

VOLUME 3, ISSUE 3: THE TONGAN FEAST

September 13, 2023
Lape Island, Vava'u, Kingdom of Tonga
18° 42' 56" S 174° 05' 01" W
Winds: SE 25 knots
Weather: 75°F Mostly sunny with the occasional trade winds squall

"*Palangis* are coming! *Palangis* are coming!"

We hear the gleeful warning calls of the little Tongan children waiting on the small concrete wharf as we paddle our kayak to Lape Island. The school-aged kids disappear up the path as we beach the kayak, but we catch glimpses of their faces poking out from behind trees to study us foreigners.

Cordio, today's host, shuffles quickly down the sidewalk to greet us with a bright smile and warm handshakes. "You came! I didn't think you would remember, but when I heard the children, I knew, I just *knew* it would be you."

We met Cordio a month ago when he and his toothless brother-in-law stopped by *Ana María* on their skiff. He invited us then to return to Lape Island for a Mass and authentic Tongan feast to celebrate the Assumption of Mary, the island's patron saint.

We've shown up today with no small amount of trepidation. Are the festivities still planned for today? What's this going to be like? What time should we have come? Are we wearing the right clothes? Are the brownies we baked from our last Betty Crocker mix the right thing for us to bring? Will there be enough food? Will this take all day? Will Cordio remember inviting us? Will he even remember us?

Yet we've shown up, drawn here by the memories of Cordio's friendliness and a curious appetite for the advertised Tongan feast.

Cordio is one of four permanent residents on the small island of Lape. Cordio, 76, and his brother-in-law care for Cordio's wife, 74, and a 95-year-old aunt. Last week, a Methodist minister was assigned to live on Lape to pastor the brother-in-law and aunt. The minister arrived with his wife, five kids, an assistant, and a schoolteacher, effectively tripling the population of the island.

Our host has dressed up for the celebration in typical Tongan church fashion: an ironed white dress shirt, maroon necktie, and tie clip that would make any American Midwestern church-going grandfather proud, paired with a sky-blue traditional lava lava (an ankle-length wrap skirt worn by men here), a woven tapa wrapped around his waist, and flip flops. Tongan American fusion fashion at its finest!

Cordio's English is excellent. He lived in American Samoa in his twenties where he taught the Tongan expatriate community in Pago Pago. There he met his wife, a native of Lape Island, and they had three children who all joined the U.S. military and moved to the States. On our first meeting, he regaled us with funny stories of his visits to them in Alaska, North Carolina, and Arizona, all with drastically different climates and cultures compared to Tonga.

His mild manner and friendliness probably aren't that unique among the Tongans here, but his English allows us to fully experience it. He is a man of faith, and he carefully explains his beliefs, inviting us to share with him the aspects of his life he considers the most precious.

After depositing the covered 9" x 13" pan full of American brownies with the women folk who are preparing for the feast in the kitchen, Cordio invites us to sit in the yard with the men at the folding table covered with a bedsheet. We aren't sitting very long when the Methodist minister's assistant gingerly walks out from behind the house carrying a baby bathtub full of brown murky water. It takes me a second to wipe off the weirded-out look on my face when the teacher sets down a ladle and a stack of dried coconut shell halves.

Whatever this brown water is, we're about to drink it.

Unbeknownst to us, we've been invited to participate in a "kava circle." I've read about the ceremony, but never did I imagine a circumstance in which we'd actually take part in one. Normally I, as a woman, wouldn't be invited to join, but Cordio is making a cultural exception for me as a *palangi*.

The Methodist minister picks up the ladle, stirs the cloudy emulsion with one sweep, two sweeps, three sweeps, then ladles out a cup into a coconut shell and hands it with a grin to Andrés. Andrés and I communicate telepathically as he hesitantly accepts it. "Should we drink this? We have no idea where this water came from. We could get very sick, but we really can't refuse ... " He lifts the cup to me, and I know he is saying "Cheers!" in his head before he tips the kava back into his mouth. The minister repeats the same motions, and I have a kava-filled coconut in my palm in short order. Crossing my fingers to ward off food poisoning, I taste the kava for myself. The liquid tastes bitter and makes our tongues and lips tingle.

The men take turns sipping the kava and throwing the leftover residue over their shoulders. We stop at one cupful, not wanting to be drunk or high or whatever effect this is supposed to cause, but the rest of the men have several rounds. With each round, they become chattier in their Tongan and their stances relax into their folding chairs.

"It's time to open the oven. Would you like to watch?" The schoolteacher stands and invites us to the other side of the yard where smoke is coming from the ground.

Finally, the moment we've been waiting for: the feast!

We follow the teacher over to the *'umu*, the underground oven, in which the feast has been roasting over a fire since early this morning. We stand next to it, fascinated with this huge culinary device. We stare at the novel *'umu* while the Tongan children stare at us *palangis,* a novelty to them.

The minister's assistant uses a shovel to clear off the mound of dirt covering the oven. The minister's oldest boy steps up to help the assistant pull back the two bed sheets protecting the oven from any stray dirt. Once again picking up the shovel, the assistant uses it to brush off the enormous tree branches serving as insulation. With a great heave of the shovel, the assistant pitches away the corrugated tin roof serving as an oven lid, allowing the heavenly smell of roasted pork and smoke to fill our noses.

A few more branches are thrust away to reveal the feast: two pigs parceled up and surrounded by veggies steamed in foil and palm fronds. The teacher, assistant, and oldest boy lift the chicken wire full of food up and onto the tin roof. The teacher packs the food into palm-frond baskets woven this morning while the assistant lifts out logs sitting directly on the coals at the bottom. Turns out, these aren't logs, but *kahokaho ufi*, 3-foot-long, 8-inch-wide tubers that taste like slow-roasted sweet potatoes.

Our mouths begin to water.

The Catholic priest who lives in Neiafu, an hour's boat ride away, must either have excellent timing or he smelled the oven being opened because he shows up right as they finish unpacking the ʻumu. We rejoin him and the other men at the kava circle. He doesn't look like a priest in his rumpled American Eagle collared shirt and cargo shorts, but you can tell he is good-humored and respected by the easy way all the men converse with him and laugh at his jokes. When he's drunk enough kava and smoked enough hand-rolled cigarettes, he stands and moves to the porch. That's our signal: it's time for Mass.

One by one, the 16 of us make our way to the porch, slip off our shoes, and sit cross-legged on the floor. The porch has been transformed since we last saw it. At one end, a white ironed bedsheet hangs from ceiling to floor. An altar has been constructed using a small folding table, no higher than 2 feet off the ground, and covered with another bedsheet. The altar is adorned by two small candles and a tiny crucifix set upon a mason jar covered in aluminum foil.

We're sitting on a beautiful hand-woven tapa mat. In Tonga, tapa mats are woven from tree bark that is first dried then pounded flat. Large pieces of tapa, often as big as 30 square yards, are given to young couples at weddings and grieving families at funerals.

The priest has slipped on a white embroidered robe. Cordio keeps trying to put on his oversized suit jacket, but we can tell even in their Tongan that the group is teasing him, so he smiles and leaves it folded on the porch railing behind him. The priest pulls out his "Mass-in-a-box" briefcase. He pours grape juice into an exquisite brass chalice and spikes it with clear liquor from a flask. He takes the wafers from a small Tupperware and lays them on the brass plate. He opens his big black book, and Mass officially begins.

He welcomes everyone in Tongan and welcomes us, as special guests, in English. Then everyone around us begins to sing. They have no hymnals, no sheet music in front of them to read, yet they sing in perfect harmony. It's as if each Tongan is born already knowing the songs as well as his or her part to sing. Cordio and his wife both read passages from the Tongan translation of the Bible. Amazingly, it's only been a few decades that Mass here has been in Tongan and not Latin. The priest, as a hospitable gesture to us, reads in English of the angel Gabriel visiting Mary from the Gospel of Luke. He steps out from behind the altar so he and Cordio can serve the elements.

As I watch Andrés take a sip from the beautiful brass chalice, I realize these humble people in their humble clothes on this humble porch have invited us to enter a sacred space.

The Mass has been full of reverence, but once it finishes, the priest rather unceremoniously takes off his robes, clearly preferring his cargo shorts to his priestly uniform. We take the opportunity to greet everyone and thank the priest for his considerate inclusion of us throughout the Mass.

Cordio, knowing the strong winds won't allow us to stay in the anchorage for long, comes up to us, our covered 9" x 13" pan in hand, to escort us back to the beach. "Thank you for the cake. The children will love it. We have put some food in here for you." We snap a picture and make promises to keep in touch somehow. He waves from the wharf as we paddle back to *Ana María*.

Our stomachs grumble the whole way, and it takes all our willpower to leave the mystery-filled pan covered on our trip home. Once in the cockpit, we open the pan to find a big hunk of roasted pig leg and a chunk of *kahokaho ufi*. We devour the crispy skin and juicy meat right from the bone, as well as the sweet flesh of the *kahokaho ufi*, grateful for today's once-in-a-lifetime experience.

Cordio showed us the best that Tongan life has to offer: the best food, the best faith, the best community, the best hospitality.

THE GALLEY

Kava (piper methysticum or "intoxicating pepper") is a plant endemic to and enjoyed in islands across the South Pacific. Once the plant is five years old, it is harvested. The roots are dried and then pulverized against coral or a rock, before being blended into water. The emulsified mix is drunk in Kava circles during celebrations and often before and after a religious ceremony. The bitter drink has been popular for centuries thanks to it acting as a sedative without impairing cognitive function.

THE LINGO

Here in Tonga, as white foreigners, we are *palangis*. Tonga is the only country in the South Pacific that was never ruled by a colonial European power, so the presence of *palangis* is less ubiquitous than, say, French Polynesia. We *palangis* are a small minority despite the seasonal wave of tourists from New Zealand and Australia. Since this is the first year the country's borders have been open since Covid and the 2022 volcanic eruption and tsunami, we are the first *palangis* some of the children have ever seen.

When we leave our bubble of fellow cruisers, it can feel quite uncomfortable, especially when the children yell *"Palangis! Palangis!"* at us from the playgrounds as if we were lepers getting too close to the village. Men see us, talk to each other in Tongan, muttering something about *"palangis,"* then laugh and laugh. We get the distinct sense that there are systems, traditions, customs, and power structures that we not only don't participate in but also don't come close to understanding.

If traveling is about broadening your horizon, for us both literally and figuratively, then living as a *palangi* is a fantastic experience. To live as a minority, not just imagine it, builds our empathy for those around the world who live every day as a minority. We cannot hide our minority status since, with our skin color, clothes, and language, we stick out like sore thumbs. We can't even fall back on the "security blankets" Americans typically take for granted when they travel internationally: there is no U.S. embassy to run to in Tonga if something goes wrong and, while we have money to spend here, there isn't a lot to buy. So, we live as minorities, at the mercy of those in power, and hope one day we can be as kind to minorities as the Tongans have been to us.

THE HIGHLIGHT

'Uiha, Ha'apai, Kingdom of Tonga
19° 54' 14" S 174° 24' 54" W

We left the protected waters of the Vava'u Islands for the less protected islands of the Ha'apai in search of long white sand beaches. Man, have we found them! We love circumnavigating these islands without ever having to slip on shoes. Ha'apai has the best beaches we've encountered anywhere.

THE ENTERTAINMENT

Neither Andrés nor I were familiar with the story of John F. Kennedy's heroics in the South Pacific during World War 2, so when we stumbled across a story from a 1944 edition of *The New Yorker*, we climbed into the cockpit so Andrés could read the story aloud, complete with an excellent JFK accent! We were captivated by how much we related to even the first sentence: "Our men in the South Pacific fight nature, when they are pitted against her, with a greater fierceness than they could ever expend on a human enemy."

Though the Solomon Islands are a thousand miles from here, the story could have easily taken place in the reefs and channels surrounding the Ha'apai Islands. As we read, we feel in our bodies the strain against the wind and waves in a two-person canoe, the painful steps over the sharp coral, and the immense fortitude it must have taken John F. Kennedy to swim to an island five miles away while carrying an injured comrade.

What a story! What a hero!

THE WILDLIFE

We've discovered the horror of flying carpenter ants, or, shall I say, the horror of flying carpenter ants has discovered us! In researching them, we learned that they play a vital role in the forest ecosystems by helping to decompose dead trees, but we have established a "no mercy" policy aboard *Ana María*.

THE CHALLENGE

We are struggling to live fully in the present during these final weeks and months of sailing. A big transition to landlubber life and all that entails is waiting just around the bend. It's easy for our minds to drift to the comforts and conveniences of the next season, e.g. a dishwasher and washing machine, or to the mountain of boat work we must do in New Zealand. But we don't want to waste this precious time by living for the future. After reading William Bridges' classic *Transitions*, I am doubling down on my mental and psychological discipline to not rush the ending so we can complete this adventure well.

THE HORIZON

For the past month, we've been studying the weather daily in order to understand the weather patterns in the South Pacific and identify a good weather window to sail from Tonga to New Zealand. We'll leave when the weather window opens up. The 1,000-plus-nautical-mile sail will take us at least 10 days, more if the conditions permit a layover in Minerva Reef.

Fair winds and following seas, my friends,

VAVA'U

KINGDOM OF TONGA

HA'APAI

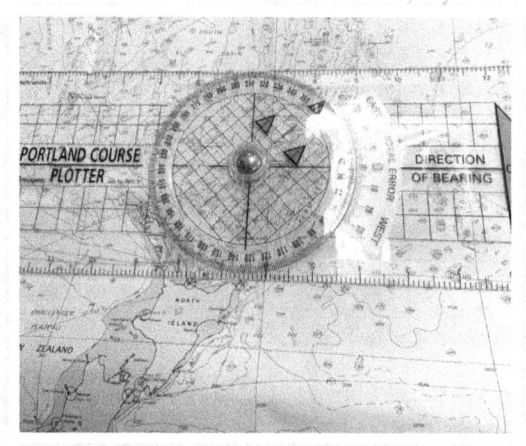

SOUTH PACIFIC OCEAN

Nuku'alofa, Tongatapu
21° 08' 15" S 175° 10' 06" W

TONGATAPU

A QUICK UPDATE

October 11, 2023
Nuku'alofa, Tongatapu, Kingdom of Tonga
21° 08' 15" S 175° 10' 06" W
Winds: S 10 knots
Weather: 70°F Mostly sunny

Is this what it's like to wait for the arrival of a baby?
My sister asked this week what life lessons we've learned while sailing. We've learned so many. One lesson I thought we would have mastered by now is how to wait well. Lord knows we've had ample opportunity to practice.

Yet here we are, struggling to wait well while still anchored in front of the Tongan capital, Nuku'alofa, a whole two weeks after we arrived to catch a weather window. This morning, I caught Andrés singing his own rendition of "Hotel California": "Welcome to the hotel Nuku'alofa. You can check out any time you like, but you can never leave."

I've never had a baby, but I imagine the final weeks of pregnancy feel a bit like this.

We're prepared to leave any day now but know we could be waiting an entire month. We've loaded *Ana María* with fuel and food for the passage. We study the forecasts three times a day, tweak the weather routing, looking for signs that today is the day we should leave. We experience the sailor's version of Braxton Hicks contractions as weather windows open and close again, getting us hyped up before throwing us into despair. Instead of reading *What to Expect When You're Expecting,* Andrés has read dozens of blog posts from other sailors' passages, and we've both studied John Martin's guidance about which high-pressure systems to take and which to let pass.

We're excited about arriving in New Zealand, but we know the intense interactions of the trade winds, the tropical depressions, and the fronts from the Tasman Sea may hand us the most challenging sail we've had yet. Intimidated by the challenge ahead of us and weary of waiting, we wonder what it takes to apply for Tongan Permanent Residence.

As much as we're struggling, we know the value of waiting well. We know patience is rewarded. A couple months ago we rushed to leave Suwarrow, worried about overstaying our Cook Islands visas and too impatient to let the winds fill in behind us. We ended up motoring the whole four days to American Samoa. Our veteran cruiser friends, Brian and Sue on *SeaRose*, waited four more days in Suwarrow and sailed the entire leg to Samoa. We remind ourselves that "fortune favors the brave," but the seas favor the patient!

Alas, *finally* it looks like our time has come. A weather window has appeared, and a stable high-pressure system is propping it open for us to depart.

We'll set sail for Minerva Reef with its submerged reefs that offer swell protection in the middle of the ocean. We may hang out in Minerva for a couple of days to let a low-pressure system move across New Zealand, or we may make a mad dash for New Zealand's northeast shore. It'll all depend on the actual weather we encounter.

Fair winds and following seas,

Katherine